TABLE OF CONTENTS

Top 20 Test Taking Tips

1. Carefully follow all the test registration procedures
2. Know the test directions, duration, topics, question types, how many questions
3. Setup a flexible study schedule at least 3-4 weeks before test day
4. Study during the time of day you are most alert, relaxed, and stress free
5. Maximize your learning style; visual learner use visual study aids, auditory learner use auditory study aids
6. Focus on your weakest knowledge base
7. Find a study partner to review with and help clarify questions
8. Practice, practice, practice
9. Get a good night's sleep; don't try to cram the night before the test
10. Eat a well balanced meal
11. Know the exact physical location of the testing site; drive the route to the site prior to test day
12. Bring a set of ear plugs; the testing center could be noisy
13. Wear comfortable, loose fitting, layered clothing to the testing center; prepare for it to be either cold or hot during the test
14. Bring at least 2 current forms of ID to the testing center
15. Arrive to the test early; be prepared to wait and be patient
16. Eliminate the obviously wrong answer choices, then guess the first remaining choice
17. Pace yourself; don't rush, but keep working and move on if you get stuck
18. Maintain a positive attitude even if the test is going poorly
19. Keep your first answer unless you are positive it is wrong
20. Check your work, don't make a careless mistake

Human Development, Divers[illegible]r in the Environment

Social-psychological area of community

There are several versions of the social-psychological [illegible] belief that people of a community are bound together by an [illegible] feel connected based on goals they share, needs, values and activities that makeup the feeling of community. Another is the belief that there is a personal-psychological community within each individual. This is the view from one person that reflects what the community is like. Children and lower-class individuals tend to view community as having narrow boundaries than the middle and upper class adults do. Another view is the cultural-anthropological view of community, which looks at community as a form of social living that is defined by attitudes, norms, customs, and behaviors of those living in the community.

Freud's Psychosexual Stages of Development

Sigmund Freud's Psychosexual Stages of Development are summarized below:

- Oral stage: birth to 1.5 yrs, gratification through mouth/upper digestive tract
- Anal Stage: 1.5-3 yrs, child gains control over anal sphincter, bowel movements
- Phallic Stage: 3-5 yrs, gratification in genital zone and is sought without concern for others. Major task is resolution of oedipal complex and leads to development of superego. This begins about age 4 and the child's phallic striving is directed toward opposite-sex parent and in competition with same-sex parent. Out of fear and love, the child renounces his desire for opposite sex parent and represses his or her sexual desires. Child then identifies with same-sex parent, internalizes their values, etc., which leads to development of superego and ability to experience guilt.
- Latency stage: 6-10 yrs, sublimation of oedipal stage, expression of sexual/aggressive drives in socially acceptable forms
- Genital stage: 10 yrs-adulthood, acceptance of one's genitalia, concern for others' well-being

Adult personality types

Adult personality types according to Sigmund Freud are:

- Oral Personality: Infantile, demanding, dependent behavior; preoccupation with oral gratification.
- Anal Personality: Stinginess, excessive focus on accumulating and collecting. Rigidity in routines and forms, suspiciousness, legalistic thinking.
- Phallic Personality: Selfish sexual exploitation of others, without regard to their needs or concerns.

Defense mechanisms

Defense mechanisms are an unconscious process in which the ego attempts to expel anxiety-provoking sexual and aggressive impulses from consciousness. Defense mechanisms are attempts to protect the self from painful anxiety and are used universally. In themselves they are not an indication of pathology, but rather an indication of disturbance when their cost outweighs their protective value.

The following are terms as they pertain to Anna Freud's defense mechanisms:

- Compensation - Protection against feelings of inferiority and inadequacy stemming from real or imagined personal defects or weaknesses
- Conversion - Somatic changes conveyed in symbolic body language; psychic pain is felt in a part of the body
- Denial - Avoidance of awareness of some painful aspect of reality
- Displacement - Investing repressed feelings in a substitute object
- Association - Altruism; acquiring gratification through connection with and helping another person who is satisfying the same instincts
- Identification - Manner by which one becomes like another person in one or more respects. Is a more elaborate process than introjection.
- Introjection - Absorbing an idea or image so that it becomes part of oneself.
- Inversion (turning against the self) - Object of aggressive drive is changed from another to the self, especially in depression and masochism.
- Isolation of Affect - Separation of ideas from the feelings originally associated with them. Remaining idea is deprived of motivational force; action is impeded and guilt avoided.
- Intellectualization - Psychological binding of instinctual drives in intellectual activities, for example the adolescent's preoccupation with philosophy and religion
- Projection - Ascribing a painful idea or impulse to the external world.
- Rationalization - Effort to give a logical explanation for painful unconscious material to avoid guilt and shame.
- Reaction Formation - Replacing in conscious awareness a painful idea or feeling with its opposite.
- Regression - Withdrawal to an earlier phase of psychosexual development.
- Repression - The act of obliterating material from conscious awareness. Is capable of mastering powerful impulses.
- Reversal - Type of reaction formation aimed at protection from painful thoughts/feelings
- Splitting - Seeing external objects as either all good or all bad. Feelings may rapidly shift from one category to the other.
- Sublimation - Redirecting energies of instinctual drives to generally positive goals that are more acceptable to the ego and superego.
- Substitution - Trading of affect for another, i.e., rage masking fear
- Undoing - Ritualistically performing the opposite of an act one has recently carried out in order to cancel out or balance the evil that may have been present in the act
- Identification with the Aggressor - A child's introjection of some characteristic of an anxiety evoking object and assimilation of an anxiety experience just lived through. In this, the child can transform from the threatened person into the one making the threat.

Erikson's Psychosocial Stages of Development

Epigenetic Principle
The individual develops after passing through eight well-defined stages, each of which demonstrates a unique combination of needs and vulnerabilities. Each developmental stage has its focus on some aspect of growth and culminates in an encounter or crisis. The outcome of the encounter or crisis leads to the development of an important human quality. The impact of the broader environment, society, and its culture on the child's development are taken into consideration.

Eight stages of development
- Trust vs. Mistrust
  - Birth to 1.5 yrs
  - Infants develop a sense of trust in self and in others.
  - Psychological dangers include a strong mistrust that later develops and is revealed as withdrawal when the individual is at odds with self and others.

- Autonomy vs. Shame and Doubt
  - 1.5 to 3 yrs—same ages as Freud's Anal Stage
  - In this phase, rapid growth in muscular maturation, verbalization, and the ability to coordinate highly conflicting action patterns is characterized by tendencies of holding on and letting go.
  - The child begins experiencing an autonomous will, which contributes to the process of identity building and development of the courage to be an independent individual.
  - Psychological dangers include immature obsessiveness and procrastination, ritualistic repetitions to gain power, self-insistent stubbornness, compulsive meek compliance or self-restraint, and the fear of a loss of self-control.

- Initiative vs. Guilt
  - 3-6 years (same ages as Freud's Phallic Stage)
  - Incursion into space by mobility, into the unknown by curiosity, and into others by physical attack and aggressive voice.
  - This stage frees the child's initiative and sense of purpose for adult tasks.
  - Psychological dangers include hysterical denial or self-restriction, which impede an individual from actualizing inner capacities.

- Industry vs. Inferiority
  - 6-11 yrs (same as Freud's Latency Stage)
  - Need of child is to make things well, to be a worker, and a potential provider.
  - Developmental task is mastery over physical objects, self, social transaction, ideas, and concepts.
  - School and peer groups are necessary for gaining and testing mastery.
  - Psychological dangers include a sense of inferiority, incompetence, self-restraint, and conformity.

- Identity vs. Identity Diffusion
  - Adolescence (same age range as Freud's Genital Stage)
  - Crucial task is to create an identity, reintegration of various components of self into a whole person—a process of ego synthesis.
  - Peer group is greatly important in providing support, values, a primary reference group, and an arena in which to experiment with various roles.
  - Psychological dangers include extreme identity confusion, feelings of estrangement, excessive conformity or rebelliousness, and idealism (a denial of reality, neurotic conflict, or delinquency).

- Intimacy vs. Isolation
  - Early adulthood
  - Task is to enter relationships with others in an involved, reciprocal manner.
  - Failure to achieve intimacy can lead to highly stereotyped interpersonal relationships and distancing. Can also lead to a willingness to renounce, isolate, and destroy others whose presence seems dangerous.

- Generativity vs. Stagnation
  - Adulthood
  - Key task is to develop concern for establishing and guiding the next generation, and the capacity for caring, nurturing, and concern for others.
  - Psychological danger is stagnation. Stagnation includes caring primarily for oneself, an artificial intimacy with others, and self-indulgence.

- Integrity vs. Despair
  - Later adulthood
  - Task is the acceptance of one's life, achievements, and significant relationships as satisfactory and acceptable.
  - Psychological danger is despair. Despair is expressed in having the sense that time is too short to start another life or to test alternative roads to integrity.
  - Despair is accompanied by self-criticism, regret, and fear of impending death.

Piaget's theory

Action and Operation, Activity in Development, and Adaptation
- Action is overt behavior. Operation is a particular type of action; may be internalized thought.
- Activity in Development: Child is not a passive subject, but an active contributor to the construction of his or her personality and universe. The child acts on his or her environment, modifies it, and is an active participant in the construction of reality.
- Adaptation: Includes accommodation and assimilation. Accommodation entails adapting to the characteristics of the object. Assimilation is the incorporation of external reality into the existing mental organization.

Sensory-Motor Stage
- Birth-2 yrs
- Infant cannot evoke representations of persons or objects when they are absent—symbolic function.
- Infant interacts with his or her surroundings and can focus on objects other than self. Infant learns to predict events (door opening signals that someone will appear). Learns that objects continue to exist when out of sight. Learns a beginning sense of causality.

- Pre-Operational Stage—2-7 yrs
  - Developing of symbolic thought draws from sensory-motor thinking. Conceptual ability not yet developed.

- Concrete Operational Stage—7-11 yrs
  - Child gains capacity to order and relate experience to an organized whole. Child can now explore several possible solutions to a problem without adopting one, as he or she is able to return to his or her original outlook.

- Formal Operational Stage—11-adolescence
  - Child/youth can visualize events and concepts beyond the present and is able to form theories.
  - A systematic approach to problems replaces cognitive random behavior.
  - Child/youth acquires objectivity and awareness of relative relationships, the ability to reason by hypothesis, and the relate past, present, and future.

Learning Theory and Behavior Modification

[handwritten: Conditioned Stimuli = manipulated stimuli]

- Pavlov
Pavlov learned to link experimentally manipulated stimuli (or conditioned stimuli) to existing natural, unconditioned stimuli that elicited a fixed, unconditioned response. Pavlov accomplished this by introducing the conditioned response just prior to the natural, unconditioned stimulus. Just before giving a dog food (an autonomic stimulus for salivation), Pavlov sounded a bell. The bell then became the stimulus for salivation, even in the absence of food being given. Many conditioned responses can be created through continuing reinforcement.

- B.F. Skinner
[handwritten in left margin: learn behavior through Reward or Punishment]
Empty Organism Concept—an infant has the capacity for action built into his or her physical makeup. Also has reflexes and motivation that will set this capacity in random motion. The Law of Effect governs development. Behavior of children is shaped largely by adults. Behaviors that result in satisfying consequences are likely to be repeated under similar circumstances. Halting or discontinuing behavior is accomplished by denying satisfying rewards or through punishment. Schedules of Reinforcement—rather than reinforcing every instance of a correct response, one can reinforce a fixed percentage of correct responses, or space reinforcements according some interval of time. Intermittent reinforcement will reinforce the desired behavior.
- Skinner was an operant theorist.

- 9 -

Operant Behavior and Respondent Behavior

Operant Behavior is controlled by consequences of that behavior. Actions preceding or following the behavior need to be changed. Respondent Behavior is behavior which is brought out by a specific stimulus. The individual must be desensitized to the stimuli, for example, in the case of phobias.

Flooding and Systematic Desensitization

Flooding is a form of desensitization by exposure to anxiety producing stimulus at full intensity for prolonged period of time. Is used by behaviorist in treating patients who suffer from anxiety. Systematic Desensitization is similar to flooding, except much more gradual. Patient is progressively led through images, pictures, and/or events of the anxiety producing situation and is encouraged to discuss and cope with the affect.

Theory of Cultural Relativism

Values, beliefs, models of behavior, and understandings of the nature of the universe must be understood within the cultural framework in which they appear. The outlines and limitations of normality and deviance are determined by the dominant culture. Ethnic/minority behavioral norms and expressions of emotional needs may be defined as abnormal in that they differ from those of the larger, dominant culture. If understood through a unique cultural context behaviors/attitudes may be perceived differently. It is important for a worker to know whether a client from a particular ethnic group who displays unorthodox behavior is also deviant within his or her own culture, as well as in his or her self-assessment.

Children in poverty

The following are some basic facts/statistics dealing with children in poverty in the U.S.:
- Almost one in four children under age six lives in poverty.
- Minority children under age six are much more likely than White children of the same age.
- Many of these children in poverty are homeless or are in the child welfare system.
- Fewer than one-third of all poor children below age six live solely on welfare.
- More than half of children in poverty have at least one working parent.
- Children of single mothers are more likely to live in poverty.
- Poor children have increased risk of health impairment.

Some additional disabilities that children in the child welfare system face in this country are as follows:
- Children in foster care often go through frequent relocations due to rejection by foster families, changes in the family situation, returning to biological families and later returns to foster care, agency procedures, and decisions of the court. Additionally, many foster children experience sexual and physical abuse within the foster care system.
- Due to frequent changes in their situation, children in foster care may change schools multiple times, which can have an adverse impact on their academic achievement.

- *10* -

Copyright © Mometrix Media. You have been licensed one copy of this document for personal use only. Any other reproduction or redistribution is strictly prohibited. All rights reserved.

- Many youth "age out" of the foster care system at age 18; this can abruptly end the relationships with foster families and other supportive structures.
- Compared with children raised with their own families, children who have been through the foster care system have a higher incidence of behavioral problems, increased substance abuse, and greater probability of entering the criminal justice system.

Kohlberg's Theory of Moral Development

Lawrence Kohlberg's Theory of Moral Development is summarized below:
- Build on Piaget's moral development research in which he argues that children's experiences shape their understanding of moral concepts (i.e. justice, rights, equality, human welfare) and that moral development is a process that takes an extended period.
- Kohlberg distinguishes six stages of moral reasoning, each of which reveals a dramatic change in the moral perspective of the individual.
- Moral development is linear (no stage can be skipped) and takes place throughout the life span.
- Progress between stages is contingent upon the availability of a role model offering a model of the principles of the next higher level.

Stage 1
- Stage one is the pre-conventional or primitive level. The individual perspective frames moral judgments, which are concrete.
- The framework of Stage 1 stresses rule following, because breaking rules may lead to punishment.
- Reasoning of Stage 1 is ego-centric and is not concerned with others.

Stage 2
- Stage 2 emphasizes moral reciprocity. It has its focus on the pragmatic, instrumental value of an action.
- Individuals at this stage observe moral standards because it is in their interest, but they are able to justify retaliation as a form of justice.
- Behavior in this stage is focused on following rules only when it is in the person's immediate interest.
- Stage 2 has a mutual contractual nature, which makes rule-following instrumental and based on externalities. There is, however, an understanding of conventional morality.

Stage 3
- Individuals in Stage 3 define morality in reference to what is expected by those with whom they have close relationships.
- Emphasis of this stage is on stereotypic roles (good mother, father, sister).
- Virtue is achieved through maintaining trusting and loyal relationships.

- Stage 4
  - This stage shifts from basically narrow local norms and role expectations to a larger social system perspective. Social responsibilities and observance of laws are key aspects of social responsibility.
  - Individuals reflect higher levels of abstraction in understanding laws' significance.
  - Individuals at Stage 4 have a sophisticated understanding of the law and only violate laws when they conflict with social duties.
  - Observance of the law is seen as necessary to maintain the protections that the legal system provides to all.

- Stage 5
  - Stage 5 is characterized as the post-conventional level.
  - Ethical reasoning is shaped on the basis of general principles and is understood in accordance with underlying rules and norms.
  - Stage 5 rejects uniform application of rules and norms.
  - The level of moral judgment is rooted in the ethical fairness principles from which moral laws are created.
  - The person at this level critically evaluates laws and judges whether or not they conform to principles of basic fairness.
  - This level values human life and human welfare are primary principles of existence.

Carol Gilligan's Morality of Care

Carol Gilligan's Morality of Care is summarized below:
- Is the feminist response to Kohlberg's moral development theory. Kohlberg's theory based on research on males. Gilligan purports that a morality of care reflects women's experience more accurately than one emphasizing justice and rights.
- Women's morality reflects caring, responsibility, and nonviolence; morality of justice and rights emphasizes equality.
- Another perspective is that these two moralities give two distinct charges—to not treat others unfairly (justice/rights) and not to turn away from someone in need (care). Care stresses interconnectedness and nurturing. Emphasizing justice stems from individualism.
- Differences in moral perspectives are explained by aspects of attachment. Masculine—requires individuation and separation from the parent which leads to awareness of power differences and concern over inequity. Feminine—continuing attachment to parent, less awareness of inequalities, not primarily focused on fairness.

World view

World view is an integral concept in assessment of clients' experience. This can be defined as a way that individuals perceive their relationship to nature, institutions, and other people and objects. This comprises a psychological orientation to life as seen in how individuals think, behave, make decisions, and understand phenomena. It provides crucial information in the assessment of mental health status, assisting in assessment and diagnosis, and in designing treatment programs.

Cultural competence

Cultural competence for the individual practitioner is the capability to function with cultural differences. It includes:
- Awareness and acceptance of differences.
- Awareness of one's own cultural values.
- Understanding the dynamics of difference.
- Development of cultural knowledge.
- Ability to adapt practice skills to fit the cultural context of the client's structure, values, and service.

It is an ongoing process that requires continuing education, awareness, management of transference/countertransference, and continuous skill development.

Cultural competence for the institution is the practice skills, attitudes, policies, and structures that are united in a system, in an agency, or among professionals and allow that system, agency, or group of professionals to work with cultural differences.
It includes:
- Values diversity—diverse staff, policies that acknowledge and respect differences, and regular initiation of cultural self-assessment.
- Institutionalization—the organization has integrated diversity into its structure, policies, and operations.

A social worker can do the following to acquire more knowledge in order to become more culturally competent:
- Read applicable practice or scientific professional literature.
- Become familiar with the literature of the relevant group(s).
- Identify and consult with cultural brokers.

Communication

Interpersonal communication is shaped by both culture and context. According to Hall's Theory of Communication, High Context communication styles are used in Asian, Latino, Black, and Native American cultures in the U.S. In this style, there is a strong reliance on contextual cues and a flexible sense of time. This style is intuitive, and in it social roles shape interactions, communication is more personal and affective, and oral agreements are binding. According to Hall's theory, low context communication styles are used more in Northern European, white groups in the U.S. These styles tend to be formal and have complex codes. They tend to show a disregard for contextual codes and a reliance on verbal communication. In these styles there is an inflexible sense of time. They are highly procedural, relationships are functionally based, and linear logic is used. The clinician should be aware of the potential for cross-cultural misunderstanding and that all cultures exhibit great diversity within themselves.

A worker use language and communication to become more culturally competent by doing the following:
- Learn to speak the target language.
- Use interpreters appropriately.
- Participate in cultural events of the group(s).
- Form friendships with members of different cultural groups than one's own.

- Acquire cultural and historical information about cultural groups.
- Learn about the institutional barriers that limit access to cultural and economic resources for vulnerable groups.
- Gain an understanding of the socio-political system in the U.S. and the implications for majority and minority groups.

Limitations

Some cultural differences may be damaging or unacceptable. The worker needs to have a balanced approach to assess cultural norms within the context of American practices, norms, and laws. There are illegal and unacceptable cultural practices, such as:
- Child labor
- Honor killings
- Private/family vengeance
- Slavery
- Infanticide
- Female circumcision
- Clitorectomies
- Infibulations
- Wife or servant beating
- Bigamy
- Child marriage
- Denial of medical care
- Abandonment of malformed or defective children
- Extreme discipline of children

Characteristics of culturally competent social worker

The following are some characteristics of the culturally competent social worker:
- With regard for individuality and confidentiality, he or she approaches clients in a respectful, warm, accepting, interested manner.
- He or she understands that opinions and experiences of both worker and client are affected by stereotypes and previous experience.
- Is able to acknowledge his or her own socialization to beliefs, attitudes, biases, and prejudices that may affect the working relationship.
- Displays awareness of cross-cultural factors that may affect the relationship.
- Able to communicate that cultural differences and their expressions are legitimate
- Is open to help from the client in learning about client's background.
- Informed about life conditions fostered by poverty, racism, and disenfranchisement.
- Is aware that client's cultural background may be peripheral to the client's situation and not central to it.

Stages of development in organizations

The stages of development of cultural competency in organizations are as follows:
- Cultural destructiveness (devaluing different cultures and viewing them as inferior)
- Cultural incapacity (aware of need, feels incapable of providing services—immobility)
- Cultural blindness ("colorblind," lack of recognition between cultural groups, denial of oppression and institutional racism)

- Cultural pre-competency (starting to recognize needs of different groups, seeking to recruit diverse staff and include appropriate training)
- Cultural competency (addresses diversity issues with staff and clients; staff is trained and confident with a range of differences)
- Cultural proficiency (Ideal; ability to incorporate and respond to new cultural groups)

Measures of cultural competence
The measures of cultural competence are:
- Recognizing effects of cultural differences on the helping process.
- Fully acknowledging one's own culture and its impact on one's thought and action.
- Comprehending the dynamics of power differences in social work practice.
- Comprehending the meaning of a client's behavior in its cultural context.
- Knowing when, where, and how to obtain necessary cultural information.

Barriers to cross-cultural practice
Some barriers to cross-cultural practice are:
- Cultural encapsulation (ethnocentrism, color-blindness, false universals)
- Language barriers (verbal, non-verbal, body language, dialect)
- Class-bound values (re: treatment, service delivery, power dynamics)
- Culture-bound values

Immigration issues

The following are some stresses associated with immigration:
- Gaining entry into and understanding a foreign culture.
- Difficulties with language acquisition.
- Immigrants who are educated often cannot find equivalent employment.
- Distance from family, friends, and familiar surroundings.

Some clinical issues associated with immigration are the following:
- Symptoms related to stress such as depression, social isolation, etc.
- Reason for emigrating from home country (i.e. refugee?)
- How immigrants use social services is greatly impacted by language and world view.

Assessment
The areas that a worker should consider when assessing an immigrant client's needs are as follows:
- Why and how did client immigrate?
- What social supports does the client have? (community/relatives)
- Client's education/literacy in language of origin and in English.
- Economic and housing resources (including number of people in home, availability of utilities)
- Employment history, ability to find/obtain work.
- Client's ability to find and use institutional/governmental supports.

- Health status/resources (pre and post-immigration)
- Social networks (pre- and post-immigration)
- Life control—degree to which he or she experiences personal power and the ability to make choices

Bias in clinical work

Health and mental health services express the ideology of the culture at large (dominant culture). This may cause harm to clients or reinforce cultural stereotypes.
Examples of this—
- Minorities and women often receive more severe diagnoses and some diagnoses are associated with gender.
- African-Americans are at greater risk for involuntary commitment.
- Gays and lesbians are sometimes treated with ethically questionable techniques in attempts to reorient their sexuality.

Working with gays and lesbians

The following are problematic treatment models for practice with gays and lesbians:
- The moral model for treatment is religiously oriented and views homosexuality as sinful.
- The medical model in some forms views homosexuality as a mental illness.
- Reparative or conversion psychotherapy focuses on changing a person's sexual orientation to heterosexual. Traditional mental health disciplines view this type of treatment as unethical and as having no empirical base.

Practice issues that a worker may have to deal with when working with clients who may be gay, lesbian, bisexual, or transgender are:
- Stigmatization and violence
- Internalized homophobia
- Coming out
- AIDS
- Limited civil rights
- Orientation vs. preference (biology vs. choice)

Working with older adults

Ageism is an attitude toward the capabilities and experiences of old age which leads to devaluation and disenfranchisement. The following are some stereotypes of the elderly:
- Asexual
- Rigid
- Impaired psychological functioning
- Incapable of change

Some strategic practice issues to be considered when working with older adults are:
- Role reversal (worker often younger than client)
- Physiological changes
- Variation in physical and mental decline

- Clients often have experienced multiple losses
- Clients are often involuntary
- Respect/formality can be important to client
- Differences in generational perceptions: socialization around problems, values, mores; and attitudes toward receiving help, charity, counseling
- Two categories of older adults: young-old (60-80), old-old or frail-old (80+)

The following are some clinical considerations the worker should make in practice with older adults:

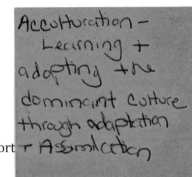

- Shorter interviews, possibly more frequent
- Varied questioning styles
- Worker is more active, directive, and demonstrative
- Home visits may be preferred to office visits
- Consider roles and attitudes of relatives and caretakers
- Awareness of possibility for abuse or exploitation
- Access to social services or other publicly funded programs
- Possible hearing impairment and need to make responses short
- louder, and slower
- Reminiscence is an important style of communication

Important terms

Acculturation — The process of learning and adopting the dominant culture through adaptation and assimilation.

Actual Social Identity — Characteristics the person actually demonstrates

Culture — Integrated patterns of human behaviors that include thought; communication, actions; customs; beliefs; values; and institutions of a racial, ethnic, religious, or social group.

Discrimination — Discrimination is the act of expressing prejudice with immediate and serious social and economic consequences.

Diversity — This refers to social groups that are not easily subsumed in the larger culture. These groups differ by socioeconomic status, gender, sexual orientation, age, and differential ability.

Ethnic Identity — A sense of belonging to an identifiable group and having historical continuity, in addition to a sense of common customs and mores transmitted over generations.

Ethnicity — This is a group classification in which members share a unique social and cultural heritage that is passed on from one generation to the next. Is not the same as race, though the two terms are used interchangeably at times

Normalization — Treating the stigmatized person as if he or she does not have a stigma

Normification — An attempt of the stigmatized person to present him or herself as an ordinary person.

Oppressed Minorities — In the US, Black, Hispanic, Asian-Pacific, and Native Americans are most clearly set apart from other disadvantaged groups by their powerful racial, ethnic, and political consciousness. This consciousness increases self-appreciation and is experienced as racial/ethnic pride. The individuals who belong to these groups are influenced by issues uniquely associated with group membership.

Oppressed minority — A group differentiated from others in society because of physical or cultural characteristics. The group receives unequal treatment and views itself as an object of collective discrimination.

Prejudice — Prejudice is bias or judgment based on value judgment, personal history, inferences about others, and application of normative judgments.

Privilege — Advantages or benefits that the dominant group has. These have been given unintentionally, unconsciously, and automatically.

Race — This concept first appeared in the English language just 300 years ago. There is no biological significance to race, but it has great social and political significance. Race can be defined as a subgroup that possesses a definite combination of physical characteristics of a genetic origin.

Racism — Generalizations, institutionalization, and assignment of values to real or imaginary differences between individuals to justify privilege, aggression, or violence. Societal patterns that have the cumulative effect of inflicting oppressive or other negative conditions against identifiable groups based on race or ethnicity. Is pervasive, ubiquitous, and institutionalized.

Social Identity — The dominant culture establishes criteria for categorizing individuals and the normal and ordinary characteristics believed to be natural and ordinary for members of the society.

Stereotyping — Amplified distorted belief about an ethnic, gender, or other group in order to justify discriminatory conduct.

Stigma — A characteristic that makes an individual different from the group and is perceived to be an intensely discreditable trait.

Virtual Social Identity — The attributes ascribed to persons based on appearances, dialect, social setting, and material features.

Clinical practice

Social work
Clinical practice in social work seeks to improve the internalized negative effects of environmental factors including stress from health, vocational, family, and interpersonal problems. The social worker tries to help individuals, couples, and families to change feelings, attitudes, and coping behaviors that hinder optimal social functioning. Clinical practice is conducted in both agencies and private practice. Clinical practice is differentiated from other practice by its goal of helping individuals change, facilitating personal adjustment, treating emotional disorders and mental illness, or enhancing intrapsychic or interpersonal functioning. Like all social work practice, assessment is psychosocial, focused on the person-in-environment, and has the goal of enhancing social functioning.

Theoretical approaches used to approach social work practice with clients are as follows:
- The Psychosocial approach focuses on intrapsychic and interpersonal change.
- The Problem Solving approach seeks to solve distinct problems, based on psychosocial and functional approaches.
- The Behavior Modification approach seeks symptom reduction of problem behaviors, learning alternative positive behaviors.
- Cognitive Therapy focuses on symptom reduction of negative thoughts, distorted thinking, and dysfunctional beliefs.

Assumptions and knowledge base
The following are the assumptions and knowledge base necessary for clinical practice:
- Individual behavior, growth, and development are brought about by a complex interaction of psychological and environmental factors.
- Theories of personality development
- Systems Theory
- Clinical Diagnosis (DSM-5)
- Significant influences are socio-cultural factors including ethnicity, immigration status, occupation, race, gender, sexual orientation, and socioeconomic class.

Assessment process
The assessment process in clinical practice is a follows:
- Determine the presenting problem
- Determine if there is a match between the problem and available services.
- Ongoing data collection and reassessment to enhance understanding of client's problems (see item below).
- Make a clinical diagnosis.

- Sources of data other than client include interviews with family members; home visits; contacts with teachers, clergy, doctors, social agencies, and friends.
- Clinical diagnosis—a product of the worker's understanding of the client's problems based on the data collected. It categorizes the client's functioning. Also includes relevant medical illnesses or physical conditions and their influence on client's emotional life/functioning.

<u>Contracting or goal setting</u>
The contract is compatible with various models of social work practice and is not limited to an initial working agreement, but is part of the total treatment process. The contract is helpful in facilitating the client's action in problem solving, maintaining focus, and continuing in therapy. The contract is an explicit agreement between the client and the worker concerning target problems, goals, and strategies of social work intervention and distinguishing the roles and tasks of the client and the worker. The contract includes mutual agreement, differentiated participation, reciprocal accountability, explicitness, realistic agreement, and flexibility.

Positive therapeutic relationship

<u>Worker characteristics</u>
The characteristics of the worker necessary to establish a positive therapeutic relationship are non-possessive warmth and concern, genuineness, appropriate empathy, nonjudgmental acceptance, optimism regarding prospects for change, objectivity, professional competence, ability to communicate with client, and self-awareness. Self-disclosure used only purposefully and for client's benefit.

 <u>Client needs</u>
The needs of the client necessary to establish a positive therapeutic relationship are:
- Hope and courage to undertake change process
- Motivation to change
- Trust in worker's interest and skill
- To be dealt with as an individual and not a case, personality type, or category
- To express self
- To make one's own choices
- To change at one's own pace

Interpretation

Worker offers the psychodynamic meaning of the client's thoughts, feelings, and fantasies, particularly about the origins of problem behaviors. Interpretation seeks to improve the client's insight and working through difficult material by deepening and expanding the client's awareness. Interpretation may entail the following:
- Exposing repressed (unconscious) or suppressed (conscious) information.
- Making connections between the present and the past to help the client see present distortions more clearly.
- Integrating information from different sources, so that the client can gain a more realistic perspective.
- Interpretation should be used with clients who are not emotionally fragile.

Resistance

In the psychodynamic understanding, resistance is an unconscious defense against painful or repressed material. Resistance can be conveyed through silence, evasiveness, balking at worker's suggestions, or by wanting to end treatment prematurely. The worker ought to recognize and understand resistance as a chance to learn more about the client and work more deeply with the client to help him or her face resistance and use it effectively.

Transference and countertransference

Transference is the client's unconscious redirection of feelings for another person toward the worker in an attempt to resolve conflicts attached with that relationship or relationships. The worker should help the client understand transference, how it relates to relationships in his or her past, and how it may be contributing to present difficulties in relationships. Countertransference is the worker's unconscious redirection of feelings for another person or relationship toward the client. The worker should understand his or her own countertransference reactions, be aware of their presence and consequences, and use supervision or therapy to gain greater understanding of them and not impose them on the client.

Termination stage

Termination offers an opportunity to rework previously unfinished issues. Frequently, earlier symptoms of the presenting problem resurface at this time. The worker should not necessarily use this reemergence as a reason to continue treatment, but the worker/client should work during the termination period to strengthen earlier gains. Termination offers an opportunity for growth in dealing with loss and endings. The worker should acknowledge, verbalize, and manage feelings about endings (such as anger, abandonment, sadness, etc.). Termination can be an opportunity to reassess the meaning of previous losses in the client's life. Termination provides a chance to evaluate treatment and the treatment relationship. What goals were met or unmet? What was effective or ineffective? Which client resources outside of treatment may continue after termination?

The following factors will affect how the client approaches termination in clinical practice:
- The degree of the client's participation in the treatment process.
- The degree of the client's success and satisfaction.
- Earlier losses the client may have experienced.
- Mastery of the separation-individuation stage of development in early life.
- The reason treatment is ending. If worker is leaving or if ending is seen as against client's wishes or as a rejection, termination may be more intense.
- The timing of termination—is it occurring at a difficult or favorable moment in the client's life?
- Is termination part of a plan to transfer client's work to a new worker? If so, worker and client should use this time to put together ideas about focus and goals for next treatment relationship.

The worker's role in the termination process in clinical practice is as follows:

- Plan sufficient time for termination. In long-term treatment this would be four to eight sessions.
- Inform the client if the work is ending prematurely.
- Be aware of worker's own countertransference attitudes and behaviors about termination.
- Continue to be sensitive, observant, empathic, and responsive to the client's response to termination.
- Encourage client's dealing with the experience of termination. Confront client's inappropriate, dysfunctional coping with the experience.
- Promote the client's believe in his or her ability to care for self and direct his or her own life.
- Present the possibility for future contact at times of difficulty. Go over the client's resources (internal and environmental) that client can draw on before making decision to reenter treatment.

Role in clinical assessment process

The worker's role is to ask questions and ask for elaboration and description, observe client's behavior/affect, and organize data to create a meaningful psychosocial or diagnostic assessment.

Challenges of contracting with clients

It can be difficult to contract with involuntary clients who do not acknowledge/recognize problems, who see the worker as unhelpful, or who are severely disturbed or who have intellectual disability. The worker should acknowledge openly the difficulty for both client/worker in mandated treatment and negotiate a contract within those realities.

Assessment in crisis intervention

The following describes the assessment process in the Crisis Intervention approach:

- Exploring the stress producing event/situation, the individual's response to it, and responses to past crises.
- Characteristic signs, phases, patterns of adaptation and maladaptation to crisis (i.e. PTSD)
- Because of need for quick action, highly focused assessment that emphasizes current state of functioning, internal and environmental supports and deficits.

Treatment planning for behavioral modification

Treatment planning in the Behavioral Modification practice approach is as follows:

1. Prioritize problems. Identify maintaining conditions for selected problems.
2. Engage client in establishing goals for change.
3. Establish baseline data re: frequency of behavior.
4. Develop written or oral contract.

Cognitive therapy

Assessment process

The assessment process in the Cognitive Therapy practice approach is described below:

- List the client's cognitive distortions (e.g., catastrophizing, minimizing, negative predictions, mind-reading, overgeneralization, personalization).
- List the client's negative automatic thoughts and dysfunctional beliefs.

Treatment planning

The treatment planning process in the Cognitive Therapy approach to practice is as follows:

1. Establish baseline data measuring client's negative automatic thoughts, distortions, and dysfunctional beliefs. How often do these thoughts occur and under what circumstances?
2. Create target goals for change and alternative ways of thinking.
3. Agree to contract for goals, homework, and time frame of treatment.

Task-centered practice

Assessment

The process of assessment in the Task-Centered practice approach is as follows:

1. Examination and clarification of problems are primary. The problem must be one that concerns the client and is amenable to treatment.
2. The worker and client create a rationale for resolution of the problem and note potential treatment benefits.

Treatment planning

The treatment planning process in the Task-Centered approach to practice is explained below:

1. A contract must state agreement on what will be worked on, the worker's and client's willingness to engage in the work, and the limits of the treatment (time, etc.). The contract can be formal, oral, or written; it is dynamic and can be renegotiated.
2. Both worker and client agree on a specific definition of the problem/s to be worked on and the changes sought in the process. Expressed in both behavioral and measurable terms.

 ## Systems theory

Assessment

Problems do not belong to the individual, but instead belong to the interaction of the behaviors or social conditions that create disequilibrium. (instability)

Treatment planning

Treatment planning in the Systems Theory approach is described below:

1. Establishing specific goals, their practicability, and their priority.
2. Target systems for intervention are identified in collaboration with the client.
3. Specific contract is developed with the client and/or other systems that may be involved in change.

Family systems theory

The assessment and treatment planning in the Family Systems theory approach to practice are explained below:
- Assessment:
  - o Acknowledgement of dysfunction in the family system.
  - o Family hierarchy: Who is in charge? Who has responsibility? Who has authority? Who has power?
  - o Evaluation of boundaries (around subsystems, between family and larger environment)—are they permeable or impermeable? Flexible or rigid?
  - o How does the symptom function in the family system?
- Treatment planning:
  - o Worker creates a mutually satisfactory contract with the family to establish service boundaries.
  - o Bowenian family therapy's goal is differentiation of the individual from the strong influence of the family.

Narrative therapy

Assessment
The following describes assessment in the Narrative therapy practice approach:
- Mapping how the problem influences the client's life and relationships—how does the problem affect the client(s)?
- Mapping the influence of the person/family in the life of the problem—Clients start to see themselves as authors or co-authors of their own stories.

This therapy builds on strengths and abilities of families and individuals rather than seeking weaknesses and deficits.

Treatment planning
Treatment planning in the Narrative therapy practice approach is described below:
- Together worker and client establish clear goals for their work.
- Worker and client divide out and work on small, specific, limited goals.
- The approach avoids a medical (disease) model that seeks explanations for problems or ascribes pathology to the family system.

Working with children

Assessment
Assessment seeks to understand the child's inner feelings and conflicts, the parent-child interaction, the family dynamics and interactions, and practical difficulties and environmental problems. Assessment will be sensitive to multi-problem families and will be culturally competent.

<u>Treatment planning</u>
The following describes treatment planning when working with children:
- Build on strengths, focus on areas where functioning is problematic (individual difficulties, family dysfunction, environmentally-generated crises).
- Support adaptive behavior
- Set realistic goals and emphasize the issues that directly affect the care of the child.
- Clarify the projected length of time of treatment; ongoing reevaluation.
- Build relationship through management of concrete problems.

Physical and sexual abuse

Physical abuse is extreme physical discipline that exceeds normative community standards. Physical indicators of physical abuse may include bruises or broken bones on an infant without an adequate explanation or that occur in unusual places; lacerations; fractures; burns in odd patterns; head injuries; internal injuries; open sores; and untreated wounds or illnesses. There may be behavioral indicators as well. The child may be overly compliant, passive, and undemanding; overly aggressive, demanding, and hostile; role reversal behavior, extremely dependent behavior re: parental, emotional, physical needs; and developmental delays. Sexual abuse is inappropriate sexual contact, molestation, rape

Child neglect

Child neglect is the failure of a child's parent or caretaker, who has the resources, to provide minimally adequate health care, nutrition, shelter, education, supervision, affection, or attention. Also, insufficient encouragement to attend school with consistency, exploitation by forcing to work too hard or long, or explore to unwholesome or demoralizing circumstances. Indicators of child neglect include abandonment, absence of sufficient adult supervision, inadequate clothing, poor hygiene, lack of sufficient medical/dental care, inadequate education, inadequate supervision, inadequate shelter; consistent failure, unwillingness, or inability to correct these indicators.

Treatment planning for maltreated/traumatized children

Treatment planning in social work practice with maltreated/traumatized children is as follows:
- Principal goal is protecting child from further harm and halting any further abuse, neglect, or sexual exploitation immediately and conclusively. This may require temporary or permanent removal of an offending caretaker or household member, or removal of the child from the home to a safe place.
- Secondary goal is creating conditions that insure that abuse or neglect does not recur after supervision/treatment is terminated. May include prosecution/incarceration of offending party. May include evaluation of non-offending parent's long-term capacity and motivation to protect the child.
- Official agency can and will use legal authority to insure compliance with agency directives when necessary. Worker should be aware that possibility of child's removal may be primary concern of parent and may lead to panic, dissembling, or flight.
- Treatment's goal is to help parents learn parenting/relational skills that can change parental behavior and child's responses

- 25 -

Trauma-Bases social work

Assessment
The assessment for Trauma-Based social work practice is as follows:
- Assessment for PTSD: evaluate the nature of the trauma; the strengths and limitations that pre-date the trauma; the impact of trauma on the client's emotional life, self-esteem, and functioning; if client remains at risk and need for self-protective measures.
- Assessment for domestic violence: evaluate if client is still at risk and if practical protective measures are required. Legal reporting not required for adult-adult domestic violence, however, if children are at risk as witnesses or victims the worker must make a report to child protective services.

Treatment planning
For PTSD, treatments available include:
- Psychodynamic therapy
- Dialectical Behavioral Therapy (DBT)—teaches skills to cope with intense feelings, reduce symptoms of PTSD, and enhance respect for self and quality of life
- EMDR (Eye Movement Desensitization and Reprocessing)
- Group Therapy (support or DBT)

[handwritten note: Help client be self-aware + understand the influence of the past on present behavior]

[handwritten note: Also known as insight-oriented therapy. Focuses on unconscious processes as they manifested in a person's present behavior.]

DSM-5

The DSM-5 is a manual which provides a common language and standard criteria for the classification of mental disorders. It is also a classification system with periodic revisions. It includes comprehensive descriptions of the symptoms and manifestations of mental disorders and associated information such as prevalence. It does not discuss causation (etiology). The DSM offers specific criteria for clinicians to diagnose disorders.
The DSM also takes cultural context, cultural belief systems, and cultural differences between client/worker into account and includes Culture-Bound Syndromes.
The DSM also presents a Defensive Functioning Scale, which assesses the client's defenses or coping patterns at time of the evaluation and just preceding it.

Major DSM-5 classifications
Neurodevelopmental disorders
Schizophrenia spectrum and other psychotic disorders
Bipolar and related disorders
Depressive disorders
Anxiety disorders
Obsessive-compulsive and related disorders
Trauma- and stressor-related disorders
Dissociative disorders
Somatic symptom and related disorders
Feeding and eatingdDisorders
Elimination disorders
Sleep-wake disorders
Sexual dysfunctions
Gender dysphoria

Disruptive, impulse-control, and conduct disorders
Substance-related and addictive disorders
Neurocognitive disorders
Personality disorders
Paraphilic disorders
Other mental disorders
Medication-induced movement disorders
Other conditions that may be a focus of clinical attention

Neurodevelopmental disorders

The classifications of neurodevelopmental disorders are:
Intellectual disability
Communication disorders
Autism spectrum disorder
Motor disorders
Attention-deficit/hyperactivity disorder
Specific learning disorder

Intellectual disability

Intellectual disabilities are neurodevelopmental disorders that include a cognitive capacity deficit and an adaptive functioning deficit. The onset of an intellectual disability must be during the developmental years. The severity of the disability ranges are mild, moderate, severe, and profound. The severity is determined by the client's adaptive functioning level, rather that the client's cognitive capacity. The DSM-5 has changed the wording of "intellectual disability" to intellectual disability to align more closely with other medical, educational, and advocacy groups.

Communication disorders
The DSM-5 includes the category communication disorders. The subcategories include language disorder, speech sound disorder, chldhood-onset fluency disorder (stuttering), and social communications disorder. With the change from DSM-IV to DSM-5, many conditions that previously fell under pervasive developmental disorders will now meet the criteria for communication disorders. Because autism spectrum disorder has a social and communication deficits as part of its defining characteristics, it is important to note that communication disorders should not be diagnosed when there are repetitive behaviors or narrowed interests or activities.

Autism spectrum disorder
Autism spectrum disorder (ASD) has two components in its diagnosis: delays or abnormal functioning in social interaction/language for social communication and restricted repetitive behaviors, interests, and activities. Both of these pieces will be present in the ASD diagnosis. Severity levels are: Level 1 (requires support), Level 2 (requiring substantial support), and Level 3 (requiring very substantial support).
Of note, ASD now encompasses four disorders that were previously separate under DSM-IV autistic disorder, Asperger's disorder, childhood integrative disorder, and pervasive]- No longer developmental disorder. Patients with ASD associated with other known conditions, environmental factors should have the diagnosis written- autism spectrum disorder associated with (name of condition, such as Rett Syndrome).

- 27 -

Attention-deficit/hyperactivity disorder (ADHD)
Characterized by two symptom domains, inattentiveness and or/hyperactivity and impulsivity. Requires symptoms persisting for at least six months, and symptoms not motivated by anger or wish to displease or spite others.

Inattentiveness symptoms (must have 6 for diagnosis for children)
Forgetful in everyday activity • Easily distracted (often) • Makes careless mistakes and doesn't give attention to detail • Difficulty focusing attention • Does not appear to listen, even when directly spoken to • Starts tasks but does not follow through • Frequently loses essential items • Finds organizing difficult • Avoids activities that require prolonged mental exertion

Impulsivity/Hyperactivity (must have 6 for diagnosis for children)
Frequently gets out of chair • Runs/climbs at inappropriate times   • Frequently talks more than peers • Often moves hands and feet, or shifts position in seat • Frequently interrupts others • Frequently has difficulty waiting on turn • Frequently unable to enjoy leisure activities silently • Frequently "on the go" and seen by others as restless • Often finishes other's sentences before they can

Treatment is by medication and/or behavior modification.

Typical drugs used for attention disorders are:
- Amphetamine-like:
  o Ritalin (short acting)
  o Long-Acting Ritalin
  o Concerta
  o Adderall (short acting)
  o Adderall XR (long acting)

These relieve symptoms quickly and individuals can take them on selected days or part-days if desired. Potential for abuse, can suppress appetite and cause weight loss, can cause edgy feelings like too much caffeine. Can cause increased pulse rate.

- Non-Amphetamine like:
  o Strattera - Is less appetite suppressing; weight loss is less of a problem. Takes 2-4 weeks to be effective and must be taken every day. Must be monitored for rarely occurring liver problem. Cannot be abused.

Motor disorders
Motor disorders are a type of neurodevelopmental disorder. Motor disorders can be classified as developmental coordination disorders, stereotypic movement disorders, and tic disorders.

Tic disorders are further classified as Tourette's disorder, persistent motor or vocal tic disorder and provisional tic disorder.
Tic disorders are characterized by rapid, recurrent, stereotyped motor movements or vocalizations. Those with Tourette's disorder typically have multiple motor tics and one or

more vocal tics. Those with chronic motor or vocal tic disorder have either motor or vocal tics.

Schizophrenia spectrum and other psychotic disorders

The schizophrenia spectrum and other psychotic disorders classification includes:
- delusional disorder
- brief psychotic disorder
- schizophreniform disorder
- schizophrenia
- schizoaffective disorder
- substance/medication-induced psychotic disorder
- psychotic disorder due to another medical condition
- catatonia

Psychotic disorders are characterized by psychotic symptoms during an active phase (delusions, hallucinations, disorganized speech, thought disorder) and/or negative symptoms such as flat affect, alogia, or avolition. Psychotic disorders are also characterized by decline from a previous level of functioning in work, social relations, and/or self care. There must be a continuous illness for at least six months with at least one month of an active phase of psychotic symptoms. Onset is typically in adolescence or young adulthood. Shared psychotic disorder is a delusion held with another person in a close relationship.

One delusion for at least one month

Delusional disorders
These disorders are typified by the presence of a persistent delusion. Delusion may be persecutory type, jealous type, erotomanic type (that someone is in love with delusional person), somatic type (that one has physical defect or disease), grandiose type, or mixed.
Delusional Disorder:
Criteria A: The client experiences at least one delusion for at least one month or longer.
Criteria B: The client does not meet criteria for schizophrenia.
Criteria C: Functioning is not significantly impaired, and behavior except dealing specifically with delusion is not bizarre.
Criteria D: Any manic or depressive episodes are brief.
Criteria E: The symptoms cannot be attributed to another medical condition or a substance. It should be specified if the delusions are bizarre. Severity is rated by the quantitative assessment measure "Clinician-Rated Dimensions of Psychosis Symptom Severity".

Schizophrenia
Criteria A: The client must have at least 2 of the following symptoms: _At least two of the following... a months_
- Hallucinations (known as a core positive symptom)
- Delusions (known as a core positive symptom)
- Disorganized speech (known as a core positive symptom)
- Severely disorganized or catatonic behavior
- Negative Symptoms (such as avolition or diminished expression)

For diagnosis the client must have at least one of the 3 core positive symptoms listed above.
Criteria B: Client's level of functioning is significantly below level prior to onset.
Criteria C: If the patient has not had successful treatment there are continual signs of schizophrenia for more than six months
Criteria D: Depressive disorder, bipolar disorder, and schizoaffective disorder have been ruled out.

- 29 -

Criteria E: The symptoms cannot be attributed to another medical condition or a substance.
Criteria F: If the patient has had a communication disorder or Autism since childhood, a diagnosis of schizophrenia is only made it the patient has hallucinations or delusions.

Treatment

Treatment of schizophrenic and other psychotic disorders include:

- Antipsychotic medication. This must be consistently administered and monitored for response and side effects.
- Individual psychotherapy. Supportive, little anxiety inducement, seeks to contain psychotic symptoms, focuses on realistic goals to maintain highest level of functioning. Goal is to aid coping and self-acceptance.
- Family therapy. Education and support for family members.
- Group therapy. To help develop social skills, to begin or sustain relationships. Should be practical and supportive.
- Milieu Therapy. Hospital/institutional treatment entailing therapeutic combination of staff, program, social structure, respite, and expectations of reasonable behavior.
- Social Network Intervention/Case Management. Help with housing, income, social support, educational/vocational opportunities, and medical care.
- Self-Help Groups. Support and education for client and family members.

Psychopharmacological drugs are used for schizophrenia and psychotic symptoms:

- Old antipsychotics
  - Haldol (Haloperidol)
  - Thorazine (Chlorpromazine)
  - Mellaril (Thioridazine)
  - Stelazine (Trifluoperazine)
  - Prolixin (Fluphenazine)
  - Navane (Thiothixene)
  - Clozaril (Clozapine)
- Newer or atypical antipsychotics
  - Clozaril
  - Risperdal
  - Seroquel
  - Olanzapine (Zyprexa)
  - Abilify

A major drawback and potential side effect for the older antipsychotics (which are effective) is Tardive Dyskinesia. TD is irreversible and causes involuntary movements of the face, tongue, mouth, or jaw. Other possible side effects for the older antipsychotics include Parkinson-like tremor or muscle rigidity; these are reversible and can be counteracted with Cogentin. Among the newer antipsychotics, Clozaril requires frequent blood testing due to the risk of agranulocytosis, a blood disorder that decreases white blood cells and increases the risk of infection. Though some atypical antipsychotics have much less risk of TD, they are very expensive and can cause weight gain, affect blood sugar, and affect the lipid profile.

— Schizoaffective disorder
Criteria A: The client must have at least 2 of the following symptoms:
- Hallucinations (known as a core positive symptom)
- Delusions (known as a core positive symptom)
- Disorganized speech (known as a core positive symptom)
- Severely disorganized or catatonic behavior
- Negative Symptoms (such as avolition or diminished expression)

[handwritten: - Hallucinations or delusions for two weeks. - manic or depressive mood (sympt)]

For diagnosis the client must have at least one of the 3 core positive symptoms listed above. The client will experience the above symptoms during a continuous period of illness during which there will also be a significant manic or depressive mood episode.

Criteria B: Client experiences hallucinations or delusions for at least two weeks during illness that do not occur during a significant depressive or manic mood episode.
Criteria C: The client experiences significant depressive or manic mood symptoms for most of the time of the illness.
Criteria D: The symptoms cannot be attributed to another medical condition or a substance.

— Schizophreniform disorder
Criteria A: The client must have at least 2 of the following symptoms: *[handwritten: -1 month]*
- Hallucinations (known as a core positive symptom)
- Delusions (known as a core positive symptom)
- Disorganized speech (known as a core positive symptom)
- Severely disorganized or catatonic behavior
- Negative Symptoms (such as avolition or diminished expression)

For diagnosis the client must have at least one of the 3 core positive symptoms listed above.
Critera B: an illness of at least one month but less than six months duration
Criteria C: Depressive disorder, bipolar disorder, and schizoaffective disorder have been ruled out.
Criteria D: The symptoms cannot be attributed to another medical condition or a substance.

— Brief psychotic disorder
A brief psychotic disorder is a delusion that has sudden onset and lasts less than one month. Brief psychotic disorder is a classification of the schizophrenia spectrum and other psychotic disorders.
Criteria A: At least one of the follow symptoms: Delusions, hallucinations, disorganized speech, or catatonic behavior.
Criteria B: The symptoms last more than one day but less than one month. The client does eventually return to baseline functioning.
Criteria C: The disorder cannot be attributed to another psychotic or depressive disorder.

[handwritten: · List more then One day. but less than One Month]

Mood disorder

Mood disorders are characterized by persistent abnormal mood, which can be either depressed or euphoric. Symptoms may be somatic, affective, cognitive, and/or behavioral. Mood disorders cause psychological distress and impaired role functioning.

[handwritten: Euphoric = happy, elated.]

Treatment for mood ~~disorders include:~~

Bipolar I
· One manic episode
· Lasting most of the day + last 1 week.

Bipolar II
· One or more major depressive episodes
· One or more hypomanic episode
· Last for 4 days (excitement → energy)

- Antidepressa~~nts~~ ~~for~~ ~~major depressive disorder and dysthy~~mia. Anti-psychotics if accompanied ~~by psychotic features. Mood stabilizers if bip~~olar I, bipolar II, or cyclothymia. ~~Consistent monitoring of symptoms for~~ effectiveness and side effects requi~~red.~~
- Interperson~~al/psychotherapy.~~
- Behavioral th~~erapy~~
- Cognitive the~~rapy~~
- Group psych~~otherapy~~
- Self-help gro~~ups~~

Bipolar I Disorder
Criteria A: The client must meet the criteria (listed below) for at least one manic episode. The manic episode is usually either proceeded or followed by an episode of major depression or hypomania.
Criteria B: The episode cannot be explained by schizophrenia spectrum and other psychotic disorders criteria.
Manic Episode Criteria:
Criteria A: An episode of significantly elevated, demon~~strative~~ significant goal-directed behaviors, activities, and an i~~ncrease in the amount of energy the~~ patient normally has. These symptoms are present for ~~most of the day and last at 1~~ week.
Criteria B: During the period described in criteria A, th~~e patient will experience 3 of the~~ following symptoms (if the client presents with only a~~n irritable mood 4 of the following~~ symptoms need to be present for diagnosis: • less nee~~d for sleep • excessive talking •~~ inflated self-esteem • easily distracted • flight of idea~~s • engages in activities that have~~ negative consequences • engages in either goal direc~~ted activity or purposeless activity~~
Criteria C: The episode causes significant impairment ~~socially or functionally.~~
Criteria D: The symptoms cannot be attributed to a su~~bstance.~~

Hypomanic Symptoms
· Mood is highed
· Less need for sleep
· Excessive talking
· Easily distracted

Bipolar II Disorder
Criteria A: The client has had one or more major dep~~ressive episodes and one or more~~ hypomanic episodes. Criteria B: The client has never ~~experienced a manic episode. Criteria~~ C: The episode doesn't meet criteria for schizophrenia spectrum or other psychotic disorder. Criteria D: The depressive episodes or alterations between the two moods cause significant impairment socially or functionally.
Hypomania Criteria: – Elevated or irritable mood.
Criteria A: An episode of significantly elevated, demonstrative, or irritable mood. There is significant goal-directed behaviors, activities, and an increase in the amount of energy the patient normally has. These symptoms are present for most of the day and last at *4 days*.
Criteria B: During the period described in criteria A, the patient will experience 3 of the following symptoms (if the client presents with only an irritable mood 4 of the following symptoms need to be present for diagnosis: • less need for sleep • excessive talking • inflated self-esteem • easily distracted • flight of ideas • engages in activities that have negative consequences • engages in either goal directed activity or purposeless activity
Criteria C: The episode causes a change in the functioning of the individual. Criteria D: The episode causes changes noticable by others. Criteria E: The episode does not cause social impairments. Criteria F: The symptoms cannot be attributed to a substance.

- 32 -

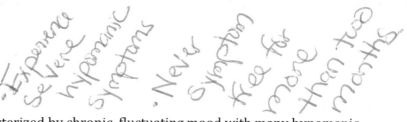
Experience severe hypomanic symptoms. *Never symptom free for more than two months.*

Cyclothymic disorder

Cyclothymic disorder is characterized by chronic, fluctuating mood with many hypomanic and depressive symptoms, however, not as severe as either bipolar I or bipolar II.

Criteria A: The client experiences a considerable number of hypomania symptoms without meeting all the criteria for hypomanic epsidodes and depressive symptoms that do not meet the criteria for major depressive episode for two years or more (can be for one year or more in <18 y/o).

Criteria B: During the above time period, the client exhibits the symptoms more than half of the time and the client is never symptom free more than two months at a time.

Criteria C: The client has not met the criteria for manic, hypomanic, or major depressive episodes.

Criteria D: The episode doesn't meet criteria for schizophrenia spectrum or other psychotic disorder.

Criteria E: The symptoms cannot be attributed to a substance.

Criteria F: The episodes cause significant impairment socially or functionally.

Persistent depressive disorder (dysthymia)

Criteria A: For at least two years the client experiences for most of a day, more days than they don't experience it, a depressed mood.

Criteria B: The client experiences 2 or more of the following when depressed: low self-esteem, decreased appetite or overeating, a feeling of hopelessness, fatigue, difficulty concentrating, insomnia or hypersomnia.

Criteria C: During the episode the client has not had relief from symptoms for longer than 2 months at once.

Criteria D: The client may have met the criteria for a major depressive disorder.

Criteria E: The client does not meet criteria for cyclothymic disorder, manic episode or hypomanic episode.

Criteria F: The episode does not meet the criteria for schizophrenia spectrum or other psychotic disorder.

Criteria G: The symptoms cannot be attributed to a substance.

Criteria H: The symptoms cause distress or impairment socially or functionally.

Mood Disorder Treatments

Bipolar treatment

Bipolar disorder is treated with mood stabilizers:

- Lithium
- Tegretol
- Depakote
- Lamictal

Mood stabilizers can cause weight gain. Regular blood work is necessary to monitor for therapeutic drug levels and for potential side effects. Lithium can cause kidney or thyroid problems, and Tegretol and Depakote can cause problems with liver function.

<u>Unipolar depression treatment</u>
SSRIs (Selective Serotonin Reuptake Inhibitors):
- Prozac
- Zoloft
- Paxil
- Luvox
- Celexa
- Lexapro

Atypical Antidepressants:
- Effexor
- Wellbutrin
- Cymbalta

Tricyclic Antidepressants
- Imipramine
- Amitriptyline
- Elavil

MAO Inhibitors
- Nardil
- Parnate
- Marplan

SSRIs have fewer side effects than other antidepressants and one cannot overdose on SSRIs alone. SSRIs take several weeks to be effective, are expensive, can cause a loss of libido, and can lose effectiveness after years of usage. In a few individuals, SSRIs can cause agitation, suicidal ideation, or manic symptoms (in which case prescriber should discontinue). Of the Atypical Antidepressants, Wellbutrin does not cause libido loss and is sometimes prescribed in combination with an SSRI to counter sexual side effects or to increase the positive antidepressant effect of the SSRI. Cymbalta is recommended for depression linked with somatic complaints. Tricyclic Antidepressants can cause side effects such as dry mouth. These are no longer in common usage due to cardiac monitoring issues. MAO Inhibitors are not in common usage as they require a special diet to be safe.

Anxiety disorders

The different types of anxiety disorders are:
<u>Panic disorder</u>—recurrent brief but intense fear in the form of panic attacks with physiological or psychological symptoms.
<u>Specific phobia</u>—fear of specific situations or objects
<u>Generalized anxiety disorder</u>—chronic physiological and cognitive symptoms of distress, excessive worry lasting at least 6 months of duration.
<u>Separation anxiety disorder</u>- excessive anxiety related to being separated from someone the client is attached to
<u>Selective mutism</u>- unable to speak in social settings (when it would seem appropriate) though normally able to speak
<u>Social anxiety disorder</u>- anxiety about social situations
<u>Agoraphobia</u>- anxiety of being outside of the home or in open places

- 34 -

Treatment of anxiety disorders include:
- Short-acting anti-anxiety medications for episodic symptoms (panic attacks) and antidepressants for longer term use (ex. OCD, social phobia)
- Psychotherapy such as supportive therapy, cognitive-behavioral therapy (systematic desensitization), DBT (Dialectical Behavioral Therapy),
- Group therapy
- Inpatient hospitalization (when a threat to self or others)

Drugs used for anxiety are Benzodiazepines:

- Ativan (Lorazepam)
- Xanax
- Klonopin
- Valium

Can be addicting

Benzodiazepines are effective, short acting, and quickly relieve anxiety. They should be used for as short a time as possible and in conjunction with appropriate therapeutic intervention because of their addiction potential. In the elderly, long term-use of these drugs can cause psychotic symptoms that can be reversed by discontinuing their usage.

Somatoform disorders

All somatoform disorders are marked by multiple physical/somatic symptoms that cannot be explained medically. Symptoms impair social or work functioning and cause distress.
- Somatic symptom disorder – Somatic symptoms (including pain) that are persistent and distressing about which feelings regarding these symptoms take up an extremely large amount of time and energy.
- Illness anxiety disorder – Preoccupation with getting or currently having an illness
- Factitious disorder – Falsely presenting oneself or someone else as ill, even when there are no obvious gains in doing so.
- Conversion disorder (functional neurological symptom disorder): Motor or perceptual symptoms suggesting physical disorder, but actually reflect emotional conflicts.
- Psychological factors affecting other medical conditions – the client has a medical condition that is adversely affected by psychological behavior.

The treatment of somatoform disorders includes the following:
- No definitive treatment, but goal is early diagnosis in order to circumvent unnecessary medical/surgical intervention.
- Attempt to move attention from symptoms to problems of living.
- Supportive Therapy to help individual cope with symptoms.
- Long-term relationship with single physician.
- No medication.

Dissociative disorders

Dissociative disorders are characterized by a disturbance in the normally integrative functions of identity, memory, consciousness, or environmental perception.
- Dissociative identity disorder (previously multiple personality disorder): Two or more personalities exist within one person. Each personality is dominant at a particular time.
- Dissociative amnesia: Inability to recall important personal data, more than forgetfulness. Is not due to organic causes and comes on suddenly.
- Depersonalization/derealization disorder: Feeling detached from one's mental processes or body, as if one is an observer.

Treatment is primarily done via psychotherapy, with the goals of working through unconscious conflict or recovering traumatic memories, and integrating feeling states with memories or events.

Feeding and Eating disorders

- Pica
- Rumination disorder
- Anorexia nervosa
- Avoidant/restrictive food intake disorder
- Bulimia nervosa
- Binge eating disorder

Anorexia Criteria:
Criteria A: Extreme restriction of food, lower then requirements, leading to low body weight.
Criteria B: An irrational fear of gaining weight or behaviors that prevent weight gain, though at low weight.
Criteria C: Distorted body image or a lack of acknowledgement of gravit of current weight.

Treatment
Treatment for eating disorders includes:
- Psychopharmacology
- Individual therapy
- Family therapy
- Medical supervision to monitor weight, vital signs, and blood values
- Hospitalization when necessary for close behavioral and medical supervision

Pica
Pica is persistent eating of non-food substances such as paint, hair, sand, cloth, pebbles, etc. Those with pica do not show an aversion to food.

Rumination disorder
Rumination disorder is the regurgitation and re-chewing of food.

Avoidant/restrictive food intake disorder
Criteria A: A disruption in eating evidence by not meeting nutritional needs and failure to gain expected weight or weight loss, nutritional deficiency, requires nutritional supplementation, or interpersonal interference.
Criteria B: This disruption is not due to lack of food or culture.
Criteria C: There does not appear to be a problem with the clients's body perception.
Criteria D: The disturbance can't be explained by another medical condition.

Bulimia nervosa criteria
Criteria A: Cyclical periods of binge eating:
1. Discretely consuming an amount of food that is larger than most individuals would eat eat in the same time period and situation.
2. The client feels a lack of control over the eating.
Criteria B: Characterized by binge eating followed by purging via self-induced vomiting/laxatives/fasting/vigorous exercise in order to prevent weight gain.
Criteria C: At least one binge eating episodes per week for three months.
Criteria D: It is marked by a persistent over-concern with body shape and weight.
Criteria E: The eating and compensatory behaviors do not only occur during periods of anorexia nervosa.

[handwritten note: one binge eating episode per week for 3 months!]

Elimination disorders

Encopresis is the involuntary fecal soiling in children who have already been toilet trained.
Enuresis is the repeated voiding of urine during the day or night in bedding or clothes. It occurs in those old enough to be expected to exercise bladder control.
Encopresis and enuresis make up the two major categories of elimination disorders.

Personality disorders

Personality disorders are characterized by a long-term and inflexible pattern of maladaptive personality traits. These traits cause subjective distress and/or significant impairment in social or work functioning. These disorders are believed to operate as coping and defensive mechanisms due to ego deficits and early developmental problems.

Personality disorders criteria
Criteria A: Long-term pattern of maladaptive personality traits and behaviors that do not align with the client's culture. These traits and behaviors will be found in at least two areas:
Impulse Control
Inappropriate emotional intesity or responses
Inappropriately interpreting people, events, and self
Inappropriate social functioning
Criteria B: The traits and behaviors are inflexible and exist despite changing social situations.
Criteria C: The traits and behaviors cause distress and impair functioning.
Criteria D: Onset was adolescence or early adulthood and has been enduring.
Criteria E: The behaviors and tratis are not due to another mental disorder.
Criteria F: The behaviors and traits are not due to a substance.

Cluster A personality disorders

The following are Cluster A personality disorders:

- Paranoid personality disorder: pervasive and inappropriate interpretation of others' actions as threatening or demeaning. Does not cause psychotic symptoms.
- Schizoid personality disorder: lack of concern for social relationships and a restricted range of emotional experience and expression. Incapacity to form intimate social relationships/experience affection for others, and lack of caring about others' responses.
- Schizotypal personality disorder: characterized by deficits in interpersonal connectedness; peculiarities in various thought, perception, speech and behavior patterns (i.e. magical thinking, ideas of reference, recurrent illusions).

Cluster B personality disorders

The following are Cluster B personality disorders:

- Antisocial personality disorder: a history of chronic irresponsible and antisocial behavior, beginning in childhood or adolescence. Violations of others' rights and occupational failure over several years. Early lying/stealing can lead to acting out sexual behavior, drinking, drugs, and later failure at work and home and adult violations of social norms.
- Borderline personality disorder: instability in relationships, mood, and self-image. Unpredictable and impulsive acting-out, which can be self-destructive. Strong mood shifts from normal state to rage. Chronic fear of being alone, dread of feeling emptiness. May have short-lived paranoid or dissociative symptoms.
- Histrionic personality disorder: excessive emotionality and attention seeking. Constant seeking of reassurance, approval, or praise. Overly dramatic and intense behavior.
- Narcissistic personality disorder: grandiose sense of self-importance, fantasies of unlimited success, chronic exhibitionism, difficulty dealing with criticism, indifference to others. Relationship difficulties—feeling entitled, taking advantage of/exploiting others, polarizing others by idealizing or devaluing.

Cluster C personality disorders

The following are Cluster C personality disorders:

- Avoidant personality disorder: characterized by social discomfort, fear of criticism, timidity, extreme sensitivity to possibility of social rejection, fear of social relationships, desire for closeness but withdrawing socially, low self-esteem.
- Dependent personality disorder: characterized by a persistent pattern of dependent and submissive behavior, a lack of self-confidence, and an inability to function independently.
- Obsessive-compulsive personality disorder: characterized by a persistent pattern of perfectionism and inflexibility. Limited ability to demonstrate positive emotions. Perfectionism and an over-concern for trivial detail. Demand others comply. Preoccupation with work; tight with money.

Treatment

The treatment of personality disorders includes the following:
- Intervention's purpose is to alleviate symptoms, decrease social/emotional disability, or deal with interpersonal/societal need for symptom management.
- Psychotherapy is used to promote recognition of the client's covert dependence and unexpressed fearfulness.
- Worker should place importance on awareness of countertransference issues because of treatment-resistant behaviors, among others, such as mistrust of the worker, lack of boundaries, and lack of recognition of the worker as a person.
- Psychopharmacology is not generally used.

Disruptive, impulse-control, and conduct disorders

The components of the disruptive, impulse-control, and conduct disorders classification are:
- Oppositional defiant disorder
- Intermittent explosive disorder
- Conduct disorder
- Pyromania
- Kleptomania

Pattern of negative, hostile, and defiant behavior and vindictiveness, but with less serious violations of the basic rights of others that characterize conduct disorders. Behavior is motivated by interpersonal reactivity or resentful power struggle with adults.

Conduct disorder

Criteria A: Persistent pattern of behavior in which significant age-appropriate rules or societal norms are ignored, and others' rights and property are violated (theft, decietfulness); aggression to people and animals and destruction of property are common.
Criteria B: The patterns of behavior cause academic, social or other impairments.
Criteria C: The behaviors couldn't better be classified as antisocial personality disorder.

Major and minor neurocognitive disorders

Delirium

Criteria A: A disturbance in consciousness or attention.
Criteria B: Develops over a short period of time, and fluctuates throughout the day
Criteria C: There are also changes in cognition.
Criteria D: Not better explained by another condition.
Criteria E: Is caused by a medical condition or is substance related.

Major and minor neurocognitive disorders (NCD) which may be due to:
- Alzheimer's disease
- Frontotemporal lobar degeneration
- Lewy body disease
- vascular disease
- traumatic brain injury
- substance/medication use
- HIV Infection
- prion Disease

- Parkinson's disease
- Huntington's disease
- another medical condition
- multiple etiologies

Criteria A: A change in cognitive ability from baseline. This information can be determined by the client, a well-informed significant other, family member, or caretaker, or it can be determined by neuropsychology testing.
Criteria B: For a major neurocognitive disorder, the cognitive change interferes with ADLs and independence. For a minor neurocognitive disorder, the cognitive change doesn't interfere with normal ADLS and independence, if accommodations are used.
Criteria C: The cognitive change cannot be defined as delirium only.
Criteria D: The cognitive change is not better described as another mental disorder.

Obsessive-compulsive and related disorders

Criteria A: The client exhibits obsessions, compulsions, or both.
Obsession- continuous, repetitive thoughts, compulsions, or things imagined that are unwanted and cause distress. The client will try to suppress thoughts, ignore them, or do a compulsive behavior.
Compulsion- recurrent behavior or thought the client feels obliged to perform after an obsession to decrease anxiety, however, the compulsion is usually not connected in an understandable way to an observer.
Criteria B: The obsessions/compulsions take at least one hour per day and cause distress.
Criteria C: The behavior is not caused by a substance.
Criteria D: The behavior could not better be explained by a different mental disorder.

Note if the criteria is met with good insight (client realizes OCD beliefs are not true), poor insight (client thinks the OCD beliefs are true), or absent insight (client is delusional, truly believing OCD beliefs are true). Note if the client has ever had tic disorder.

Other Obsessive-Compulsive and related disorders include:
Body dysmorphic disorder
Hoarding disorder
Trichotillomania (hair-pulling disorder)
Excoriation (skin-picking disorder)

Trauma- and stressor-related disorders

Reactive attachment disorder – child rarely seeks or responds to comfort when upset, usually due to neglect of emotional needs by caregiver (e.g. foster and institutionalized children)
Disinhibited social engagement disorder – child has decreased hesitations regarding interacting with unfamiliar adults. Does not question leaving normal caregiver to go off with a stranger.
Posttraumatic stress disorder - persistently re-experiencing a severe trauma for more than one month. Individual exhibits arousal-anxiety symptoms, and avoidance of things associated with the trauma or numbness.

<u>Acute stress disorder</u> - anxiety and dissociative symptoms develop within one month of experiencing a trauma.

<u>Adjustment disorder</u> – the client has behavior/emotional changes occurring within 3 months of a stressor. These changes cause distress for the client and are disproportional to the actual stressor.

Sleep-wake disorders

<u>Insomnia disorders</u> - Difficulty falling asleep, staying asleep, or early rising without being able to go back to sleep.

<u>Hypersomnolence disorder</u> –sleepiness despite getting at least 7 hours with difficulty feeling awake when suddenly awoke, lapses of sleep in the day, feeling unrested after long periods of sleep.

<u>Narcolepsy</u> – uncontrollable lapses into sleep, occurring at least three times each week for at least 3 months.

<u>Obstructive sleep apnea hypopnea</u> – Breathing related sleep disorder with obstructive apneas or hypopneas.

<u>Central sleep apnea</u> – Breathing related sleep disorder with central apnea.

<u>Sleep-related hypoventilation</u> – Breathing related sleep disorder with evidence of decreased respiratory rate and increased CO_2 level.

<u>Circadian rhythm sleep-wake disorder</u> – sleep wake disorder with the primary cause being a mismatch between the circadian rhythm and the sleep required by the person

<u>Non-rapid eye movement sleep arousal disorder</u>- awakening during the first third of the night associated w/ sleep walking/sleep terrors.

<u>Nightmare disorder</u>- Recurring distressing dreams that are well remembered and cause distress.

<u>Rapid eye movement sleep behavior disorder</u>- arousal during REM sleep associated with motor movements and vocalizing.

<u>Restless legs syndrome</u>- the need to move the legs due to uncomfortable sensations, usually relieved by activity.

Substance related disorders

<u>Substance related disorders</u> may be caused by abusing a drug, by medication side-effects, or by exposure to a toxin.

<u>Substance intoxication or withdrawal</u>—the behavioral, psychological, and physiological symptoms due to effects of the substance. It will vary depending on type of substance. Substance related disorders includes the following classes: caffiene; hallucinogens; alcohol; cannabis; stimulants; tobacco; inhalants; opioids; other; and sedatives, hypnotics and anxiolytics. The severity of the particular substance use disorder can be determined by the presence of the number of symptoms.

Also present may be substance induced delirium, dementia, psychosis, mood disorders, anxiety disorder, sexual dysfunction, or sleep dysfunction.

Treatment should focus first on the substance. Treatment options include outpatient or inpatient; residential or day care; group, individual, and/or family counseling; methadone maintenance (for opiates); detoxification; self-help groups; or a combination of therapies and medication.

Substance-related and addictive disorders now includes gambling disorder, as evidence shows that the behaviors of gambling trigger simliar reward systems as drugs.

Alcohol abuse

<u>Challenges with diagnosis and treatment</u>
The particular challenges of alcohol abuse in the context of diagnosis and treatment are as follows:
- Alcohol is the most available and widely used substance.
- Progression of alcoholism dependence often occurs over an extended period of time, unlike some other substances whose progression can be quite rapid. Because of this slow progression, individuals can deny their dependence and hide it from employers for long periods.
- Most alcohol dependent individuals have gainful employment, live with families, and are given little attention until their dependence crosses a threshold, at which time the individual fails in their familial, social, or employment roles.
- Misuse of alcohol represents a difficult diagnostic problem as it is a legal substance. Clients, their families, and even clinicians can claim that the client's alcohol use is normative.
- After friends, family members, or employers tire of maintaining the fiction that the individual's alcohol use is normative, the alcoholic will be more motivated to begin the process of accepting treatment.

Substance use and abuse

<u>Dangers</u>
The following are possible injuries or illnesses that often result from the use of substances:
- Physical damage
- Brain damage
- Organic failure
- Fetal damage when used by pregnant women
- Birth of drug exposed babies who require intensive therapy throughout childhood
- Altering of brain chemistry/permanent brain damage
- Effects on dopamine in brain, which directly effects mood

The harm that may come from the use of illegal drugs due to their method of administration is as follows:
- Doses can be unknown, which can lead to drug overdose and death.
- Using contaminated needles can cause staph infections, Hepatitis, or HIV/AIDS.
- Inhalants are frequently toxic and can cause brain damage, heart disease, and kidney or liver failure.

The harm that can result from the behaviors that substance use/abuse can generate is as follows:
- Substances that are illegally obtained are often associated with minor crimes, crimes against family members and the community, and prostitution.
- Alcohol is associated with domestic violence, child abuse, sexual misconduct, and serious auto accidents.
- All substances promote behavioral problems that may make it difficult for the individual to obtain/retain employment, or to sustain normal family relationships.

Treatment
The components of treatment for individuals with substance use disorders are:
- An assessment phase
- Treatment of intoxication and withdrawal when necessary
- Development of a treatment strategy.

The three general treatment strategies used with individuals with substance use disorders are:
- Total abstinence (drug-free)
- Substitution, or use of alternative medications that inhibit the use of illegal drugs
- Harm reduction

The goals of substance use disorder treatment are:
- Reducing use and effects of substances
- Abstinence
- Reducing the frequency and severity of relapse
- Improvement in psychological and social functioning

- Tolerance—needing clearly increasing amounts of the substance to achieve desired effect; or clearly diminished effect with continued use of the same amount of the substance
- Withdrawal—typical withdrawal syndrome for the substance; or the same or a similar substance is taken to relieve/avoid withdrawal symptoms

Remission
The type of remission is based on whether any of the criteria for abuse/dependence have been met and over what time frame:
Early Remission: After the criteria for a substance use disorder have been met, none of those criteria are fulfilled (except for the criteria for craving) for at least three months but not more than 1 year.
Sustained Remission: After the criteria for a substance use disorder have been met, none of those criteria are fulfilled (except for the criteria for craving) for 1 year or longer.
If the client is in remission in a controlled environment, this should be specified.
Maintenance Therapy- a replacement medication that can be taken to avoid withdrawal symptoms. The client could still be considered in remission from a substance use disorder if while using maintanance therapy, they do no meet any criteria for that substance use disorder except for craving. For tobacco use disorder this would include using nicotine replacement systems. For opioid use disorder this could include medications such as methadone.

Clinical disorders
The following clinical disorders are commonly found in clients with substance use disorders:
- Conduct disorders, particularly the aggressive subtype
- Depression
- Bipolar disorder
- Schizophrenia
- Anxiety disorders
- Eating disorders

- 43 -

- Pathological gambling
- Antisocial personality disorder
- PTSD
- Other personality disorders

Medical problems
Some medical problems that may be directly related to substance use include:
- Cardiac problems (acute cocaine intoxication)
- Respiratory depression and coma (severe opioid overdose and alcohol abuse)
- Hepatic cirrhosis (prolonged heavy drinking)
- Malnutrition (from poor self-care)
- Physical trauma (risk-taking behavior)
- HIV infection (risk-taking behavior)

Conditions associated with those who administer substances by injection:
- Bacterial infections
- HIV
- hepatitis

Predicting factors
Some factors that contribute to and predict substance use are:
- Early or regular use of "gateway" drugs (alcohol, marijuana, nicotine)
- Early aggressive behavior
- Intra-familial disturbances
- Associating with substance-using peers

Drug of choice
The following factors influence an individual's preference for a "drug of choice":
- Current fashion
- Availability
- Peer influences
- Individual biological and psychological factors
- Genetic factors (especially with alcoholism)

Treatment of substance use disorders

Objectives of clinical management
The following are the objectives of clinical management in treatment for clients with substance use disorders:
- Establish and maintain a therapeutic alliance.
- Monitor the client's clinical status.
- Arrange and monitor services/programs for the client and family.
- Assess the need for continued services, monitor their effectiveness.
- Provide direct clinical social work services.
- Remain alert to states of intoxication and withdrawal.
- Facilitate client's following the treatment plan.

- Prevent relapse.
- Provide education about substance use disorders.
- Insure availability of medical care.

Pharmacologic treatments
Pharmacologic treatments are used for clients with substance use disorders in the following ways:
- To treat intoxication and withdrawal.
- To decrease reinforcing effects of abused substances.
- To discourage the use of substances by causing unpleasant consequences through a drug-drug interaction or by pairing substance use with an unpleasant drug-induced condition.
- Agonist substitution therapy (i.e. methadone).
- Medications to treat clinical conditions.

Effective treatment
The psychosocial treatments that have been found to be most effective for clients with substance use disorders are:
- Cognitive behavioral therapies
- Behavioral therapies
- Psychodynamic/interpersonal therapies
- Group and family therapies
- Participation in self-help groups

Treatment plan
The components of a treatment plan for a client with a substance use disorder are:
- A strategy to achieve abstinence or to reduce the effects or use of substances.
- Efforts to increase ongoing compliance with the treatment program, prevent relapse, and enhance functioning.
- Clinical management.
- If necessary, additional treatments for clients with associated conditions.

Hospitalization
Hospitalization is appropriate for:
- Those with a drug overdose who can't be adequately treated in outpatient or emergency room settings.
- Those at risk for severe or medically complicated withdrawal.
- Those with medical conditions that make ambulatory detoxification unsafe.
- Those with a documented record of not engaging in or benefitting from treatment in a less restrictive setting.
- Those with mental health problems that would markedly impair their ability to participate in, comply with, or benefit from treatment. Also, those whose associated disorder would on its own require hospital level care.
- Those who have not responded to less intensive treatments and whose substance use disorder poses an ongoing threat to their physical and mental health. Also those who exhibit behaviors that constitute an acute danger to self or others.

Residential treatment
Residential treatment is appropriate for those who do not meet the clinical criteria for hospitalization, but whose lives and social interactions focus primarily on substance use, and who do not have adequate social and vocational skills and drug-free social supports to maintain abstinence in an outpatient setting.

Outpatient treatment
Outpatient treatment is appropriate for those whose clinical condition or environmental circumstances don't require a more intensive level of care.

Management of alcohol intoxication and withdrawal
The following are considerations in the management of alcohol intoxication and withdrawal in clients being treated for alcohol use disorders:
- Clients who are acutely intoxicated need to be monitored and kept in a safe environment.
- Within 4-12 hours after stopping or reducing alcohol use symptoms of alcohol withdrawal typically begin. These symptoms peak during the second day of abstinence, and settle within 4-5 days.
- There can be serious complications of alcohol withdrawal including seizures, hallucinations, and delirium.
- For clients with moderate to severe withdrawal, treatment includes medical attention to reduce the physical effects of withdrawal.

Cocaine
The recommended treatment setting for most clients with cocaine use disorders includes:
- Intensive outpatient treatment (meetings more than twice/wk).
- Variety of treatment modalities used simultaneously.
- Focus of treatment is the maintenance of abstinence.

The following should be considered in the management of cocaine intoxication and withdrawal in clients being treated for substance use disorders:
- Intoxication (by cocaine) can cause hypertension, tachycardia, seizures, and paranoid delusions. Usually only supportive care is required, but some acutely agitated clients may benefit from sedation.
- After stopping cocaine use, craving and depression are common.

Opioid use disorders
Clients who have a history of at least one year of dependence on opioids, maintenance on methadone or LAAM (l-a-acetylmethadol or levomethadyl acetate) can be appropriate. One goal of treatment is to achieve a stable maintenance dose. Some clients will be able to attain abstinence from all opioid drugs. Some clients will require long-term maintenance with opioid agonists (methadone or LAAM). Abstinence can never be achieved for some clients. In these cases the goal of treatment is reduction in morbidity and mortality through reducing the effects of opioid use.

The strategies effective in the treatment of opioid withdrawal are:
- Methadone substitution with gradual tapering.
- Abrupt cessation of opioids, with medications to suppress symptoms of withdrawal.

Because the concurrent use of or withdrawal from other substances can complicate the treatment of opioid withdrawal, monitoring for the presence of other substances is imperative.

The clinical aspects that may influence treatment of opioid use disorders are:
- Mental illness. Many clients who are opioid-dependent also have mental illnesses that must be identified and treated alongside the substance use disorders.
- Injection. Using opioids by injection is linked with a high risk of medical complications such as bacterial endocarditis, hepatitis, HIV infection, and tuberculosis.
- Treating pregnant women with opioid use disorders is complicated by the increased risks to the fetus and the urgency of minimizing the intake of opioids. These risks include low birth weight, prematurity, neonatal abstinence syndrome, stillbirth, and sudden infant death syndrome.

Narcotics

Narcotics are:
- Drugs used medicinally to relieve pain.
- They have a high potential for abuse.
- They cause relaxation with an immediate rush.
- Possible effects are restlessness, nausea, euphoria, drowsiness, respiratory depression, constricted pupils.

The following are symptoms of overdose of narcotics:
- Slow, shallow breathing
- Clammy skin
- Convulsions
- Coma
- Possible death

The withdrawal syndrome for narcotics includes:
- Watery eyes
- Runny nose
- Yawning
- Cramps
- Loss of appetite
- Irritability
- Nausea
- Tremors
- Panic
- Chills
- Sweating

The following are indications of possible misuse of narcotics:

- Scars (tracks) caused by injections
- Constricted pupils
- Loss of appetite
- Sniffles
- Watery eyes
- Cough
- Nausea
- Lethargy
- Drowsiness
- Nodding
- Syringes, bent spoons, needles, etc.
- Weight loss or anorexia

Depressants

Depressants are:

- Drugs used medicinally to relieve anxiety, irritability, or tension.
- They have a high potential for abuse and development of tolerance.
- They produce a state of intoxication similar to that of alcohol.
- When combined with alcohol, their effects increase and their risks are multiplied.

The possible effects of depressants are:

- Sensory alteration, reduction in anxiety, intoxication
- In small amounts, can cause relaxed muscles and calmness
- In larger amounts—slurred speech, impaired judgment, loss of motor coordination
- In very large doses—respiratory depression, coma, death
- Newborn babies of abusers may exhibit dependence, withdrawal symptoms, behavioral problems, and birth defects.

The symptoms of overdose of depressants include:

- Shallow respiration
- Clammy skin
- Dilated pupils
- Weak and rapid pulse
- Coma
- Death

Withdrawal syndrome for depressants includes:

- Anxiety
- Insomnia
- Muscle tremors
- Loss of appetite
- Abrupt cessation or a greatly reduced dosage may cause convulsions, delirium, or death.

The indications of possible misuse of depressants are:
- Behavior similar to alcohol intoxication (without the odor of alcohol)
- Staggering, stumbling, lack of coordination
- slurred speech
- Falling asleep while at work
- Difficulty concentrating
- Dilated pupils

Stimulants

Stimulants are drugs used to increase alertness, relieve fatigue, feel stronger and more decisive, for euphoric effects, to counteract the "down" feeling of depressants or alcohol.

The possible effects of stimulants are:
- Increased heart rate
- Increased respiratory rate
- Elevated blood pressure
- Dilated pupils
- Decreased appetite

With high doses:
- Rapid or irregular heartbeat
- Loss of coordination
- Collapse
- Perspiration
- Blurred vision
- Dizziness
- Feelings of restlessness, anxiety, delusions

The symptoms of overdose of stimulants include:
- Agitated behavior
- Increase in body temperature
- Hallucinations
- Convulsions
- Possible death

The withdrawal syndrome for stimulants includes:
- Apathy
- Long periods of sleep
- Irritability
- Depression
- Disorientation

The following are the indications of possible misuse of stimulants:
- Excessive activity, talkativeness, irritability, argumentativeness, nervousness.
- Increased blood pressure or pulse rate, dilated pupils
- Long periods without sleeping or eating
- Euphoria

Hallucinogens

Hallucinogens are:
- Drugs that cause behavioral changes that are often multiple and dramatic.
- No known medical use, but some block sensation to pain and their use may result in self-inflicted injuries.
- "Designer drugs," which are made to imitate certain illegal drugs, can be many times stronger than the drugs they imitate.

The possible effects of hallucinogens are:
- Rapidly changing mood/feelings, immediately and long after use.
- Hallucinations, illusions, dizziness, confusion, suspicion, anxiety, loss of control.
- Chronic use—depression, violent behavior, anxiety, distorted perception of time.
- Large doses—convulsions, coma, heart/lung failure, ruptured blood vessels in the brain.
- Delayed effects—"flashbacks" occurring long after use.
- Designer drugs—possible irreversible brain damage.

The symptoms of overdose of hallucinogens include:
- Longer, more intense episodes
- Psychosis
- Coma
- Death

The indications of possible misuse of hallucinogens include:
- Extreme changes in behavior and mood
- Sitting/reclining in a trance-like state
- Individual may appear fearful
- Chills, irregular breathing, sweating, trembling hands
- Changes in sensitivity to light, hearing, touch, smell, and time
- Increased blood pressure, heart rate, blood sugar

Cannabis

Cannabis is the hemp plant from which marijuana (a tobacco like substance) and hashish (resinous secretions of the cannabis plant) are produced.

The possible effects of cannabis are:
- Euphoria followed by relaxation
- Impaired memory, concentration, and knowledge retention
- Loss of coordination
- Increased sense of taste, sight, smell, hearing
- Irritation to lungs and respiratory system
- Cancer
- With stronger doses: fluctuating emotions, fragmentary thoughts, disoriented behavior

The symptoms of overdose of cannabis include:
- Fatigue
- Lack of coordination
- Paranoia

The withdrawal syndrome for cannabis includes:
- Insomnia
- Hyperactivity
- Sometimes decreased appetite

The following are indications of possible misuse of cannabis:
- Animated behavior and loud talking, followed by sleepiness.
- Dilated pupils
- Bloodshot eyes
- Distortions in perception
- Hallucinations
- Distortions in depth and time perception
- Loss of coordination

Alcohol

Alcohol:
- A liquid distilled product of fermented fruits, grains, and vegetables.
- Can be used as a solvent, an antiseptic, and a sedative.
- Has a high potential for abuse.
- Small to moderate amounts taken over extended periods of time have no negative effects and may have positive health results.

The possible effects of alcohol use are:
- Intoxication
- Sensory alteration
- Reduction in anxiety

Some symptoms of overdose of alcohol use include:
- Staggering
- Odor of alcohol on breath
- Loss of coordination
- Dilated pupils
- Slurred speech
- Coma
- Respiratory failure
- Nerve damage
- Liver damage
- Fetal alcohol syndrome (in babies born to alcohol abusers)

The withdrawal syndrome for alcohol includes:
- Sweating
- Tremors
- Altered perception
- Psychosis
- Fear
- Auditory hallucinations

The following are some indications of possible misuse of alcohol:
- Confusion
- Disorientation
- Loss of motor control
- Convulsions
- Shock
- Shallow respiration
- Involuntary defecation
- Drowsiness
- Respiratory depression
- Possible death

Steroids

Steroids are synthetic compounds closely related to the male sex hormone, testosterone, and are available legally and illegally. They have a moderate potential for abuse, particularly among young males.

The following are possible effects of steroids:
- Increase in body weight
- Increase in muscle mass and strength
- Improved athletic performance
- Improved physical endurance.

The symptoms of overdose of steroids include:
- Rapid gains in weight and muscle
- Extremely aggressive behavior
- Severe skin rashes
- Impotence, reduced sexual drive
- In female users, development of irreversible masculine traits

Withdrawal syndrome for steroids includes the following symptoms:
- Considerable weight loss
- Depression
- Behavioral changes
- Trembling

The following are indications of possible misuse of steroids:
- Increased aggressiveness
- Increased combativeness
- Jaundice
- Purple or red spots on body
- Unexplained darkness of skin
- Unpleasant and persistent breath odor
- Swelling of feet, lower legs

Viewing change in clients

There are three different ways to view how change occurs (in clients), as seen in the varied approaches to social work:
- Psychological (e.g., psychodynamic, behavioral, cognitive, etc.)
- Sphere of change (e.g. individual, couple, family, social system, etc.)
- Goal of change (e.g. personality, behavioral, social system, etc.)

Differences in approach to social work

Focus of social work assessment
The different approaches to social work have different aims for assessment. The following are different focuses that social work assessment can have:
- Intrapsychic dynamics, strengths, and problems
- Interpersonal dynamics, strengths, and problems
- Environmental strengths and problems
- The interaction and intersection of intrapsychic, interpersonal, and environmental factors.

Time needed to reach goals
The approach to social work practice will affect the length of time needed to accomplish goals. Extended periods of time for treatment are needed for those approaches that focus on personality change. Shorter-term treatment is called for in those approaches that focus on behavioral change, cognitive change, or problem solving. Examples are crisis intervention, task-centered treatment, cognitive, and behavioral treatment.

Treatment relationship
The way of viewing the treatment relationship is influenced by the approach to social work practice. One view of the treatment relationship sees the therapeutic relationship as the main channel for promoting change and providing support. Another view sees the worker's role as ally, teacher, or coach. In this view, a here-and-now approach is taken. This can be seen in behavioral, cognitive, or crisis intervention models for practice.

Psychosocial approach

Assessment
Assessment in the psychosocial approach to social work practice outlines client's presenting problem and client's resources for addressing it. It determines if there is an appropriate match between presenting problem and available services. Assessment begins in first interview and continues throughout treatment. Components include:
- Dynamic: Determining how different characteristics of client and client's important relationships interact to influence his or her total functioning.
- Etiological: Determining the causative factors that produced the presenting problem and that influence the client's previous attempts to deal with it.
- Clinical: articulation of the client's functioning (i.e., mental status, coping strategies/style, if pertinent a clinical diagnosis).

Treatment planning
In the psychosocial approach to social work practice, the components of treatment planning are as follows:
- Development of a unique treatment plan based on the client's situation.
- Client goals and their practicality, given the client's abilities, strengths, and weaknesses, as well as availability of relevant services.
- Treatment plan is directed at changing the individual, the environment, or the interaction between the two.

Problem-solving approach assessment

Assessment in the problem-solving approach to social work practice is described below:
- Focus first on identifying the problem and the aspects of the person/environment that can be involved in problem solving.
- Assess motivation, capacity, and opportunity (MCO) of the client to resolve the problem.
- Include a statement of the problem (objective facts and subjective responses to them), precipitating factors, and prior efforts to resolve it.
- A combined activity of worker and client.

Important terms

Partialization — Helping client to break down problems/goals into smaller, more manageable elements in order to decrease client's sense of overwhelm and increase client's empowerment. Discrete elements of problem/goal can then be prioritized as more manageable or more important.

Supporting/sustaining — Worker conveys confidence in, interest in, and acceptance of client in order to decrease client's feelings of anxiety poor self-esteem and low self confidence. Worker uses interest, sympathetic listening, acceptance of client, reassurance, and encouragement.

Psychotherapy, Clinical Interventions, and Case Management

Theoretical approaches

The *Crisis Intervention* approach is brief treatment of reactions to crisis in order to restore client's equilibrium.

Family Therapy treats entire family system and sees the individual symptom bearer as indicative of a problem in the family as a whole.

Group Therapy is a model in which group members help and are helped by others with similar problems, receive validation for their own experiences, and test new social identities and roles.

In the *Narrative Therapy* approach the stories clients tell about their lives reveal how they construct perceptions of their experiences. The worker helps client construct alternative, more affirming stories.

The *Ecological or Life Model* focuses on life transitions, environmental pressures, and maladaptation between individual and family/ environment. Focuses on interaction and interdependence of people and environments.

The *Task Centered* approach focuses on completing tasks to strengthen self-esteem and restore usual capacity for coping.

Psychosocial approach

Theoretical base
The theoretical base for the psychosocial approach to social work practice is as follows:
- Psychoanalytic theory (Sigmund Freud)
- Ego Psychology: psychoanalytic base, with focus on ego functions and adaptation; defense mechanisms (Anna Freud); adaptations to an average "expected" environment (Hartmann); ego mastery and development through the life cycle (Erikson); separation/individuation (Margaret Mahler)
- Social Science Theories: role, family and small group, impact of culture, communication theory, systems theory
- Biological theories: ecological, homeostasis, behavioral genetics, health, illness

Basic tenets
The basic tenets of the psychosocial approach are:
- Psychosocial
- Problem-solving
- Crisis intervention
- Task-centered casework
- Planned short-term treatment

Human behavior
The assumptions about human behavior that the Psychosocial approach to practice makes are:
- The individual always seen in the context of environment, interacting with social systems (such as family), and influenced by earlier personal experiences.
- Conscious, unconscious, rational, and irrational motivations govern individual behavior.
- Individuals can change and grow under fitting conditions throughout the life cycle.

Change
In the Psychosocial approach to Social Work practice, the means through which change occurs are:
- Development of insight and resolution of emotional conflicts.
- Corrective emotional experience in relationship with the worker.
- Changes in affective, cognitive, or behavioral patterns that induce changes in interpersonal relationships.
- Changes in the environment.

The motivations for change are:
- Disequilibrium induces anxiety and releases energy to change.
- Conscious and unconscious needs and wishes.
- Relationship with the worker (or group in group treatment).

Therapeutic relationship
The role of the therapeutic relationship in the psychosocial approach is as follows:
- Mindful use of the relationship can motivate and create energy to change.
- Corrective emotional experience.
- Client and client's needs are central. Self-disclosure by worker is used purposefully and only for client's benefit.
- Some transference dynamics may hamper treatment, but generally they should be seen and used as potential vehicles for promoting client self-understanding and changing problematic interpersonal patterns.
- To deal with possible countertransference, worker should be self aware, seek supervision and consultation to decrease countertransference reactions, and use his or her own therapy for dealing with countertransference.
- Worker should be aware that he or she may be perceived as more competent than the client and as the expert who is there to "fix" the client's problems. This can be disempowering to the client and works against a strengths perspective.

Treatment phases
The phases of treatment in the psychosocial approach are:
1. Engagement/assessment (applicant becomes client; increasing motivation; initial resistance; establishing work relationship, assessment; informed consent re: confidentiality; client/worker's roles, rights, responsibilities)
2. Contracting/goal setting (client/worker's mutual understanding re: goals, treatment process, nature of relationship/roles, intended time of treatment)

3. Ongoing treatment/interventions (working toward improving previously agreed upon problems; major focus: current functioning/conscious experience; dealing with ongoing resistance, transference, countertransference)
4. Termination (potential for growth, reiterate major themes of treatment, experience feelings about relationship ending)

Problem-Solving approach

Theoretical base
The theoretical base for the Problem-Solving approach to social work practice is as follows:
- Psychodynamic, with major influence from Ego psychologists: Erik Erikson (capacity for change throughout life), Robert White (coping, adaptation, mastery of environment), Heinz Hartmann (use of the conflict-free ego).
- Social science theory: role theory, problem solving theory (John Dewey).

Treatment planning
In the Problem-Solving approach to social work practice, the following are the components of treatment planning:
- Psychosocial: derived from an evaluation of the problem and the client's Motivation, capacity, and opportunities (MCO).
- Functional: the function of the agency serves a boundary of service (i.e., adoption agency, mental health service)
- Interagency: using resources from other agencies in a network of services designed to help the client.

Phases of treatment
The four Ps are the basic elements involved in treatment: A *person* has a *problem*, comes to a *place* for help given through a *process.*
1. Clearly identify the problem and the client's subjective response to it.
2. Select a part of the problem that has possibility for resolution, identify possible solutions, asses their achievability in light of MCO.
3. Engage client's ego capacities.
4. Determine steps/actions to be taken by worker and client to resolve or alleviate the problem.
5. Help client carry out problem-solving activities and determine their effectiveness.
6. Termination.

Human behavior
The assumptions that the Problem-Solving approach to social work practice makes about human behavior are as follows:
- Individuals are engaged in life-long problem-solving and adaptation to maintain, rebuild, or achieve stability, even as circumstances change.
- The individual is viewed as a whole person; the focus, however, is on the person in relation to a problem.
- Individuals have or can develop the motivation and ability to change.
- This perspective does not see the individual as sick or deficient, but instead as in need of help to resolve life problems.

- Each individual has a "reachable moment" at a time of disequilibrium, at which point he or she can most successfully mobilize motivation and capacity
- An individual's cognitive processes can be engaged to solve problems, to achieve, and to grow emotionally
- An individual has both rational/irrational, conscious/unconscious processes, but cognitive strengths can control irrationality.

Change
In the Problem-Solving approach to Social Work practice, the motivations for change are:
- Disequilibrium between reality and what the client wants.
- Conscious desire to achieve change.
- Positive expectations based on new life possibilities.
- The strength of a supportive relationship and positive expectations of the worker.

The means through which change occurs are:
- Improved problem-solving skills. These may produce changed in personality or improved functioning, but these are secondary to problem resolution.
- Gratification, encouragement, and support which result from improvement in the problem situation. This and the worker's emotional support increase the possibility of change.
- Repetition and practice (drilling) of the problem-solving method increases possibility for replication of effective strategies in new situations.
- Insight, resolution of conflicts, and changes in feelings.
- Problem resolution concerning changes in the individual, the environment, and/or the interaction between the two.

Therapeutic relationship
The role of the therapeutic relationship in the Problem-Solving approach to Social Work practice is as follows:
- Mindful and continual use of the supportive social work relationship to motivate clients to engage in problem resolution.
- The worker is an expert in problem-solving methodology and guides clients through steps of problem resolution. The relationship grows as worker and client work on problems jointly.
- Work is focused on practical problem solving, therefore transference/countertransference are less likely. These are only addressed if interfering with the work.

Crisis Intervention approach

The theoretical base for the Crisis Intervention approach to social work practice is as follows:
- Psychodynamic, particularly ego psychology (Freud, Erikson, Rapoport) and Lindemann's work on loss and grief.
- Intellectual development (Piaget)
- Social Science: stress theory, family structure, role theory

Human behavior

The following are assumptions that the Crisis Intervention approach makes about human behavior:

- The individual has a tendency to a natural progressive growth that prevails over forces of regression.
- Stress during a crisis induces disequilibrium and anxiety that allow therapeutic accessibility. Crisis can create opportunities to develop new coping mechanisms and growth or can give rise to dysfunctional behavior.
- Crisis occurs when established coping skills do not resolve stress adequately. A crisis inflicts an array of affective, cognitive, and behavioral tasks. A crisis can reactivate old problems.
- An individual in crisis is not ill, but rather is dealing with a challenge that is a part of the human condition. The crisis counselor does not necessarily assume the presence of a pathological condition or DSM disorder.
- An individual in crisis is affected by the past, but the present situation is more relevant.

Change

The motivations for change in the Crisis Intervention approach are as follows:

- Disequilibrium caused by a stressful event or situation.
- Energy, which is made available by anxiety about the situation.
- A supportive relationship.

Change occurs through:

- Challenging old coping patterns and a reorganization of coping skills.
- Growth, which occurs as the ego develops a larger repertoire of coping skills and organizes them into more complex pattern.

Therapeutic relationship

The role of the therapeutic relationship in the Crisis Intervention approach to practice is described below:

- The relationship remains reality based in the face of the client's often intense attachment. Regression is discouraged even as the crisis evokes a sense of helplessness.
- The worker's role is based on expertise; it is authoritative and directive.
- The client is encouraged to be active, to be reality oriented, and to work toward finding new methods of coping with crisis.
- Use of the relationship as a corrective experience is not emphasized. There is a minimal focus on transference/ countertransference.

Treatment phases

The following are the phases of treatment in the Crisis Intervention approach to practice:

1. Identify events that brought on the crisis.
2. Promote awareness of impact of crisis, both cognitive and emotional.
3. Manage affect leading to tension discharge and mastery.
4. Seek resources in networks (individual, family, social) and in community.
5. Identify specific tasks associated with healthy resolution of crisis.

Treatment skills and techniques
The treatment skills or techniques used in the Crisis Intervention approach are:
- Brief treatment. Like the crisis itself, treatment is time limited.
- Present- and future-oriented. Treatment can deal with the past, however, to resolve old conflicts if they prevent work on the present crisis.
- Uses all psychosocial and problem-solving techniques, but reorders them; clinician is active, directive, and at times authoritative.

Behavior Modification approach

Theoretical base
The theoretical base of the Behavior Modification approach to social work practice is:
- Early classical conditioning research (Pavlov)
- Behavior modification theory—operant conditioning (Skinner, Thorndike, Watson, Dollard & Miller, Thomas)
- Social learning theory—observing, imitating, modeling (Bandura)

Human behavior
The following are the assumptions that the Behavior Modification approach makes about human behavior:
- One can know a person only through the observable. Behavior can be explained by learning theory. Theory of the unconscious is unnecessary.
- A person has learned dysfunctional behaviors rather than emotional illness. No presumptions about psychiatric illness.
- One expresses dysfunctional behavior in symptoms. Definition of symptoms: observed individual behaviors that are labeled as deviant or problematic. Once the symptoms are removed, there are no remaining underlying problems.
- High priority goes to research and empirically based knowledge.

Change
The Behavioral Modification approach sees the following as the motivations for change:
- Disequilibrium
- Anxiety
- Conscious desire to eliminate a symptom
- Agreement to follow a behavior modification program

In the Behavioral Modification approach to Social Work practice, the means through which change occurs are:
- Operant/voluntary behavior which is 1) increased by positive or negative reinforcement and 2) decreased by withholding reinforcement or punishing.
- Involuntary behavior which is increased or decreased by conditioning.
- Change depends upon environmental conditions or events that precede, are connected with, or follow the behavior.
- As a result of observing and imitating in a social context, modeling occurs; this is not learned by reward and punishment.

<u>Therapeutic relationship</u>
The role of the therapeutic relationship in the Behavioral Modification approach to practice is as follows:
- The relationship is warm, empathic, and facilitating.
- The relationship is not the focus nor is it used as part of the treatment.

Cognitive Therapy approach

<u>Theoretical base</u>
The theoretical base for the Cognitive Therapy approach to social work practice includes:
- Albert Ellis' rational-emotive behavior therapy
- Aaron Beck's cognitive theory

<u>Human behavior</u>
The following are assumptions the Cognitive Therapy approach makes about human behavior:
- Mental distress is caused by the maladaptive and rigid ways we construe events, not by the events themselves.
- Negative automatic thoughts are generated by dysfunctional beliefs. These beliefs are set in motion by activating events and they trigger emotional consequences. Future events are interpreted through the filter of these belief systems.
- Negative affect and symptoms of psychological disorders follow negative automatic thoughts, biases, and distortions.
- Irrational thinking carries the form of systematic distortions.

<u>Change</u>
The motivations for change in the Cognitive Therapy practice approach are:
- Disequilibrium
- Anxiety
- Desire to live without a symptom
- Agreement to work toward changing thought patterns.

In the Cognitive Therapy approach to social work practice, the means through which change occurs are:
- Structured sessions
- Exploring and testing cognitive distortions and basic beliefs
- Homework between sessions which allows client to practice changes in thinking in the natural environment.
- Changes in feelings and behaviors in the future come about through changes in the way the client interprets events.

<u>Therapeutic relationship</u>
The role of the therapeutic relationship in the Cognitive Therapy approach is:
- Worker is teacher, ally, coach
- Worker is active, directive, didactic

Treatment skills/techniques

Some treatment skills/techniques used in the Cognitive Therapy approach are:
- Short term treatment
- A focus on symptom reduction
- Using a rational approach, focus on concrete tasks in sessions and for homework.
- Per Albert Ellis—Be forcefully confrontive in order to reveal client's thought system, get client to see how that system defeats him or her, and work to change the thoughts that make up that system.
- Per Aaron Beck—A gentler, more collaborative approach. Help client restructure interpretations of events. "What is the evidence for this idea?" or "Is there another way to look at this situation?" Social skill building, group therapy, milieu treatment.

Task-Centered approach

Theoretical base

The theoretical base of the Task-Centered approach to social work practice is as follows:
- Learning theory
- Cognitive and behavioral theory
- High priority on research-based practice knowledge

Human behavior

The assumptions that the Task-Centered approach makes about human behavior are as follows:
- An individual is not influenced solely by internal/unconscious drives, nor controlled solely by environmental forces.
- The client usually is able to identify his or her own problems/goals.
- The client is the primary agent of change and is a consumer of services.
- The worker's role is to help the client achieve the changes that he or she decides upon and is willing to work on.

Change

The motivations for change according to the Task-Centered approach to practice are:
- Temporary breakdown in coping influences client to seek help.
- A conscious wish for change.
- Strengthening of self-esteem through task completion.

In the Task-Centered approach to social work practice, the means through which change occurs are:
- Clarification of problem/problems
- Steps taken to resolve or alleviate problems.
- Changes in environment.

Therapeutic relationship
The role of the therapeutic relationship according to the Task-Centered approach to practice is as follows:
- The relationship is not an objective in itself, but is a means of augmenting and supporting problem solving. Transference/ countertransference aspects are minimized.
- Worker expects that client will work on agreed upon tasks and activities to resolve problems, and also provides acceptance respect and understanding.
- Collaborative relationship. Worker seeks client's input at all stages. Client is consumer and worker is the authority with expertise who works on the client's behalf.

Inappropriate clients
For the following clients, the Task-Centered approach to practice is not appropriate:
- Clients who are interested in existential issues, life goals, and/or discussion on stressful events.
- Clients who are unwilling or unable to use the structured approach to tasks.
- Clients who have problems that are not subject to resolution or improvement by problem-solving.
- Clients who are involuntary, where treatment is mandated.

 Systems Theory approach

Theoretical base
The theoretical base to the Systems Theory approach to social work practice is as follows:
- This approach is based on general system theory applied to social work treatment.
- Systems Theory is a framework that a worker can use with any of the practice approaches in order to help the client establish and maintain a steady state.

Human behavior
The assumptions the Systems Theory approach makes about human behavior are:
- Individuals have potential for growth and adaptation throughout life. They are active, problem solving and purposeful.
- Individuals can be understood as open systems which interact with other living systems and the nonliving environment.
- All systems are interdependent. Change in one system brings about changes in the others. Additionally, change in a subsystem brings about changes in other subsystems.

Change
The motivations for change according to the Systems Theory approach to practice are changes in the individual, environment, or in the interaction between the individual and the environment.

<u>Therapeutic relationship</u>
The role of the therapeutic relationship according to the Systems Theory approach is as follows:
- Depending on the problem and target of change, the relationship may be supportive, facilitative, collaborative, or adversarial. The worker may intervene on behalf of the client with individuals, the social support network, or the larger system.
- The relationship offers feedback to the client and to other systems.

<u>Definitions</u>
- Boundary—organizational means by which the parts of a system can be differentiated from their environment and which differentiates subsystems
- Open/Closed system—indicates whether boundary between a system and its environment is open or closed.
- Subsystem—subset of the entire system
- Entropy—randomness, chaos, disorder in a system. Causes a system to lose energy faster than it creates or imports it.
- Homeostasis—a system will make changes in order to maintain an accustomed balance.

Ecological or Life Model approach

<u>Theoretical base</u>
The theoretical base for the Ecological or Life Model approach to social work practice is as follows:
- Ecology
- Systems Theory
- Stress, coping, and adaptation theory
- Psychodynamic, behavioral, and cognitive theory

This approach follows a conceptual framework that has its focus on the interaction and interdependence of people and environments. It provides service to individuals, families, and groups within a community, organizational, and cultural environment.

<u>Human behavior</u>
The assumptions the Ecological or Life Model approach to practice makes about human behavior are:
- The individual is active, purposeful, and problem solving. He or she has potential for growth and adaptation throughout life.
- There are three areas of life experience in which problems occur: life transitions, environmental pressures, and/or maladaptive lack of "fit" between the individual and a larger entity (the family, the community).
- Each individual client system depends upon or is interdependent with other systems.

<u>Change</u>
Motivation for change in this approach stems from changes that the individual wants in relation to him or herself, the environment, or the interplay between the two.

<u>Therapeutic relationship</u>
The role of the therapeutic relationship in the Ecological/Life model approach is as follows:
- The worker's relationship with the client is based on mutuality, trust, and authenticity.
- Depending on the goal of the intervention, the worker/client relationship may be supportive, collaborative, or adversarial.

Family Systems Theory

<u>Human behavior</u>
The following are the assumptions that the Family Systems Theory approach to practice makes about human behavior:
- Change in one part of the family system brings about change in other parts of the system.
- The family provides the following to its members: unity, individuation, security, comfort, nurturance, warmth, affection, and reciprocal need satisfaction.
- Where family pathology is present, the individual is socially and individually disadvantaged.
- Behavioral problems are a reflection of communication problems in the family system.
- Treatment focuses on the family unity; changing family interactions is the key to behavioral change.

<u>Change</u>
Disequilibrium of the normal family homeostasis is the primary motivation for change according to this perspective. The family system is made up of three subsystems: the marital relationship, the parent-child relationship, and the sibling relationship. Dysfunction that occurs in any of these subsystems will likely cause dysfunction in the others.
The means for change in the Family Systems theory approach is the family as an interactional system.

<u>Therapeutic relationship</u>
The worker interacts in the "here and now" with the family in relation to current problems. The worker is a consultant to the family. The role differs according to school of thought:
- Structural—dysfunctional interaction is actively challenged
- Strategic and Systemic—worker is very active
- Milan School—male/female clinicians are co-therapists; a team observes from behind a one-way mirror, consults and directs their co-therapists with the clients
- Psychodynamic—worker facilitates self-reflection and understanding of multi-generational dynamics, conflicts
- Satir—Worker models caring, acceptance, love, compassion, nurturance in order to help clients face fears and increase openness

<u>Murray Bowen's family systems theory</u>
Bowen's theory focused on:
- The role of thinking versus feeling/reactivity in relationship/family systems.
- Role of emotional triangles. The three-person system or triangle is viewed as the smallest stable relationship system and forms when a two-person system experiences tension.

- Generationally repeating family issues. Parents transmit emotional problems to a child. (Ex: parents fear something wrong with a child and treat child as if something is wrong, interpret child's behavior as confirmation.)
- Undifferentiated family ego mass—family's lack of separateness, fixed cluster of egos of individual family members as if all have a common ego boundary
- Emotional cutoff—way of managing emotional issues with family members (cutting off emotional contact)
- Consideration of thoughts and feelings of each individual family member as well as seeking to understand the family network.

Haley and Madanes' Strategic Family Therapy
This therapy seeks to learn what function the symptom serves in the family, i.e., what "payoff" is there for the system in allowing the symptom to continue?
Problem-focused behavioral change, emphasis of parental power and hierarchical family relationships, focus on role of symptoms as an attribute of the family's organization. Helplessness, incompetence, illness all provide power positions within the family; child uses symptoms to change the behavior of parents.

Psychodynamic theory's contributions to Family System's theory, via work of Nathan Ackerman, Don Jackson, Olga Silverstein
Emphasizes multi-generational family history. Earlier family relations and patterns determine current ones. Distorted relations in childhood lead to patterns of miscommunication and behavioral problems. Interpersonal and intrapersonal conflict beneath apparent family unity results in psychopathology. Social role functioning influenced by heredity and environment. Jackson focuses on power relationships. He developed a theory of "double-bind" communication in families. Double-bind communication occurs when two conflicting messages communicated simultaneously create/maintain a "no-win," pathological symptom.

Salvador Minuchin's Structural family therapy
This therapy seeks to strengthen boundaries when family subsystems are enmeshed, or seeks to increase flexibility when these systems are overly rigid. Minuchin emphasizes that the family structure should be hierarchical and that the parents should be at the top of the hierarchy.

Milan School's systemic family therapy
The Milan School makes the assumption that symptoms serve a purpose: to maintain the family structure within dysfunctional families. In this understanding, a family member is sacrificed to maintain the family structure.

Virginia Satir and the Esalen Institute's Experiential Family Therapy
This perspective draws on sociology, ego concepts, and communication theory to form role theory concepts. Satir examined the roles of "rescuer" and "placatory" that constrain relationships and interactions in families. This perspective seeks to increase intimacy in the family and improve self-esteem of family members by using awareness and communication of feelings. Emphasis on individual growth in order to change family members and deal with developmental delays. Particular importance is given to marital partners and on changing verbal and non-verbal communication patterns that lower self-esteem.

<u>Definitions</u>
- Boundaries - means of organization through which system parts can be differentiated both from their environment and from each other. They protect and improve the differentiation and integrity of the family, subsystem, and individual family members.
- Collaborative Therapy - therapy in which separate worker sees each spouse or member of the family
- Complementarity of needs - circular support system of a family, in which reciprocity is found in meeting needs; can be adaptive or maladaptive
- Complementary family interaction - type of family relationship in which members present opposite behaviors that supply needs or lacks in the other family member
- Double-bind communication - communication in which two contradictory messages are conveyed concurrently, leading to a no-win situation
- Enmeshment - obscuring of boundaries in which differentiation of family subsystems and individual autonomy are lost. Similar to Bowen's "undifferentiated family ego mass." Characterized by "mind reading" (partners speak for each other, complete each other's sentences)
- Family of origin - family into which one is born
- Family of procreation - the family which one forms with a mate and one's own children
- Homeostasis - state of systemic balance (of relationships, alliances, power, authority)
- Identified patient - "symptom bearer" in the family
- Multiple family therapy - Therapy in which three or more families form a group with one or more clinicians to discuss common problems. Group support is given and problems are universalized.
- Scapegoating - unconscious, irrational election of one family member for a negative, demeaned, or outsider role

Narrative Therapy

<u>Theoretical base</u>
The theoretical base for the Narrative Therapy approach to social work practice is as follows:
- Draws on the work of Michael White of the Dulwich Centre in Australia.
- Utilizes a variety of individual and personality theories, as well as social psychological approaches.
- Focuses on the stories people tell about their lives. These stories are interpreted through their subjective personal filters.
- Interventions are designed to reveal and reframe the way clients structure their perceptions of their experiences.

Human behavior

The assumptions about human behavior that the Narrative Therapy approach to practice makes are as follows:

- Individuals' behaviors come from their interpretations of experiences.
- Subjective meanings influence actions. Meanings derived from interpretations of experience determine specifics of action.
- Narrative therapy is concerned with the telling and re-telling of the preferred stories of people's lives, as well as the performance and re-performance of these stories.

Therapeutic relationship

The role of the therapeutic relationship in the Narrative therapy approach is as follows:

- Worker is co-constructor of new narratives.
- The relationship is a partnership; authority of therapist is minimized. Partnership does not use techniques that result in clients feeling coerced or manipulated.
- Relationship seeks and is an agent of client empowerment. Worker offers an optimistic, future-oriented perspective that builds on client's abilities and strengths in moving toward change. Emphasizes client's possibilities, strengths, resources.
- Worker guides therapeutic conversations to create new possibilities, fresh options, and opportunities to reframe the client's realities.

Geriatric Social Work

Theoretical base

The theoretical base of Geriatric Social Work is as follows:

- Psychodynamic theory
- Ego psychology
- Family systems theory
- Life-span development theory (Wieck)
- Continuity theory
- Normal aging and demographics of the aging population
- Impact of chronic illness and physical/cognitive limitations

Human behavior

The assumptions about human behavior in Geriatric Social Work are as follows:

- Growth occurs throughout the life span, including during old age.
- Individuals are inherently adaptive and are capable of managing the disruptions, discontinuities, and losses that are characteristic of old age.
- Our culture demands and values independence. This can present a conflict with accepting the increasing need for help in old age.
- The younger generation's caring for the older may be seen as role reversal and may be challenging to both generations. Dependency in the aged, however, has a different meaning than dependency in childhood.
- Supportive services are preferable to institutional care whenever possible.
- Ageist assumptions or an individual's living in an institutional setting are not reasons to compromise self-determination or confidentiality.
- Individuals age in different ways.

Change

Geriatric Social Work sees the following as motivations for change:

- The need for individuals to adapt to longer periods of old age and retirement as life expectancy increases. With longer period of old age comes increased risk for chronic illness and physical/cognitive limitations.
- Greater need for multiple types of social services, supported housing, and care options.
- Adult children are also affected by their parents' aging and may need help dealing with the emotional impact or with care planning.

The means through which change occurs in Geriatric Social Work are:

- Individual, couples, family treatment
- Support groups or group therapy
- Recreational programs
- Education

Therapeutic relationship

The role of the therapeutic relationship in Geriatric Social Work is as follows:

- Individual, couple, or multi-generational family therapist
- Case manager
- Advocate
- Care planning—working with older adult and/or his or her children to determine level of care needed and options
- Social worker for institution—in this role worker may experience conflict in defining who is client and whose needs have precedence (institution or individual)
- Guardian for older adult who the court has declared mentally incompetent or conservator for older adult who the court has declared incompetent to handle his or her own financial affairs
- Educator
- Group therapist or leader
- Program planner

Assessment and treatment planning

Assessment is concerned with:

- Presenting problem and client's resources for resolving it
- When adult children involved, intergenerational dynamics/resources, relevance and impact of family history on present functioning
- Presence and effect of chronic illness and physical/cognitive limitations
- Home safety
- Medications, their influence on functioning, and negative side effects
- Need for supportive services or institutional care
- ADLs (activities of daily living—e.g., bathing, dressing, etc.) and IADLs (instrumental activities of daily living—e.g., cooking, driving)

Treatment planning is concerned with:
- Interventions, solutions that offer choice and support the older adult's highest level of functioning
- Promoting independence by planning home modifications through home-safety assessment and planning for assistive devices through assessing physical/cognitive limitations

Maltreated/traumatized children

The role of the therapeutic relationship in social work practice with maltreated/traumatized children is as follows:
- The worker is to establish trust and a working relationship with the family and built parental self esteem.
- Treatment issues include the parents confusing the worker's clinical role with the role of child protective services and the parents viewing the clinician as a hostile part of the legal system, rather than as a trusted helper.
- Communication can be inhibited by the perception of coercion, which can also limit the treatment's effectiveness. Both parent and child may become unwilling to reveal potentially damaging facts.
- Worker should openly discuss mandated reporting obligations and responsibility to inform child protective services.

Trauma-Related social work

Theoretical base
The theoretical base of Trauma-Related social work practice with adults is as follows:
- The trauma victim experiences a threat to his or her physical integrity or life. The trauma experience confronts a person with an extreme situation of fear and helplessness.
- Trauma may be chronic and repeated or may take the form of one event of short duration.
- Many of the symptoms related to PTSD and domestic violence are self-protective attempts at coping with realistic threats.

Human behavior
The assumptions about human behavior in Trauma-Related social work practice are as follows:
- Most individuals experience the world as a basically safe place in which they are worthy participants.
- Trauma can challenge or reverse these assumptions about the world and oneself.
- Resilience is defined as an innate capacity to self-regulate after experiencing a stressor so extreme as to be traumatic.
- Resilience can be derived from both internal and environmental resources.
- Resilience can be more difficult to achieve or sustain when the trauma is more severe, is chronic, and/or when the perpetrator is someone who should be a caretaker or trusted protector.

<u>Change</u>
The motivations for change in Trauma-Related practice are:
- Reality-based fear and the need for protection.
- Symptoms including depression, anxiety, dissociation, low self-esteem.

<u>Therapeutic relationship</u>
The role of the therapeutic relationship in Trauma-Based social work practice is as follows:
- For clients with PTSD, the worker is a protective presence. The worker guides the pace of treatment in order to avoid flooding the client with too much affect and traumatic memories that would promote regression. The worker creates an emotionally safe therapeutic space in which to remember and process the trauma.
- For clients who have experienced domestic violence, the worker may be therapist, case manager, court-based victim's advocate, or broker to obtain services.

Treatment for domestic violence

For domestic violence, develop a safety plan for safe shelter, etc. to protect victim from perpetrator. Do not assess or treat domestic violence in marital or family therapy sessions as this may increase risk to the victim, inhibit revealing the violence history, and enrage the perpetrator.

Clinical work with children

Children are typically referred to treatment for symptoms or behavioral problems. The child's underlying conflicts reveal themselves through play and verbally in free expression. Play is the child's form of symbolic communication, an emulation of the real world, and the child's psychological reality.

<u>Theoretical base</u>
The theoretical base for clinical work with children in social work practice is as follows:
- Normal child development theory
- Psychosocial development theory (S. Freud, Anna Freud, Erikson)
- Attachment theory
- Object relations theory

<u>Change</u>
The following are motivations for change in the child-treatment (age related treatment) approach to practice:
- If child is in alternative placement (foster care, etc.), child's behavior may be seen as problematic by the agency or worker and treatment interventions may be sought.
- Child is unhappy with peer relations, may be socially immature.
- Unsatisfactory school adjustment (grades, problems with authority)
- Conflict with parents (struggle to cope with dysfunctional family or problems in parents' marriage)
- Feelings of anger, unhappiness
- Self-destructive behaviors such as cutting or eating disorders.

<u>Therapeutic relationship</u>
The role of the therapeutic relationship when treating children in social work practice is as follows:
- Worker as therapist—provides a safe environment in which worker can follow child's lead, show child acceptance, create environment for free expression
- Worker as advocate
- Worker as case manager, care coordinator
- Worker as protective service worker
- Worker as adoption and foster care specialist
- Worker as school guidance counselor

Sigmund Freud's Psychoanalytic Theory

<u>Topographical Theory</u>
Unconscious
- Repressed fantasies and experiences of childhood/adolescence
- Primary process functioning—immediate discharge of mental energies
- Inaccessibility to consciousness
- Wish fulfillment—wishes are the motivation behind dreams
- Infantile—guided by pleasure principle

Preconscious
- Accessibility to consciousness
- Censor which blocks the unconscious
- Operates according to reality principle

Consciousness
- Sensations from the outer world and from inner events such as thoughts, emotions, memories
- Reality principal functioning

<u>Structural theory</u>
- Id is the source of all motives, energies, and instincts. Cathexes of the id are mobile, press for immediate and rapid discharge.
- Ego is the rational, reality-oriented personality system.
- Superego moral and ethical standards, ambitions, and ego ideals (conscience). Seeks to inhibit id impulses.
- Personality development—infants are pure id (driven by pleasure principle). Id collides with reality, which leads to ego development. Ego builds practical coping strategies, including capacity to delay gratification. Ego is then governed by reality principle. Reality oriented thinking is referred to as secondary process thought. Finally, the oedipal complex occurs in early childhood. Out of that process develops he superego.

Group work

The values underlying social work practice with groups are:
- Dignity and work of every individual.
- All people have a right and a need to realize their full potential.
- Every individual has basic rights and responsibilities.

- The social work group acts out democratic values and promotes shared decision making.
- Every individual has the right of self-determination in setting and achieving goals.
- Positive change is made possible by honest, open, and meaningful interaction.

Some advantages of group work are as follows:
- Members can help others dealing with the same issues and can identify with others in the same situation.
- Sometimes people can more easily accept help from peers than from professionals.
- Through consensual validation, members feel less violated and more reassured as they discover that their problems are similar to those of others.
- Groups give opportunities to members for experimentation and testing new social identities/roles.
- Group practice is not a replacement for individual treatment. Group work is an essential tool for many workers and can be the method of choice for some problems.
- Group practice can complement other practice techniques.

Purposes and goals

Group practice takes a multiple-goals perspective to solving individual and social problems and is based on the recognition that group experiences have many important functions and can be designed to achieve any or all of the following:
- Providing restorative, remedial, or rehabilitative experiences.
- Helping prevent personal and social distress or breakdown.
- Facilitating normal growth and development, especially during stressful times during the life-cycle.
- Achieving greater degree of self-fulfillment and personal enhancement.
- Helping individuals become active, responsible participants in society through group associations.

Types of social work groups

The different types of social work groups are:
- Educational groups, which focus on helping members learn new information and skills.
- Growth groups, which provide opportunities for members to develop deeper awareness of their own thoughts, feelings, and behavior as well as develop their individual potentialities (i.e. values clarification, consciousness-raising, etc.)
- Therapy groups, which are designed to help members change their behavior by learning to cope and improve personal problems and to deal with physical, psychological, or social trauma.
- Socialization groups, which help members learn social skills and socially accepted behaviors and help members function more effectively in the community.
- Task groups, which are formed to meet organizational, client, and community needs and functions.

Relationships

The importance of relationships in group work methodology is described below:

- Establishing meaningful, effective, relationships is essential and its importance cannot be overemphasized. The worker will form multiple and changing relationships with individual group members, with sub-groups, and with the group as a whole.
- There are multiple other parties who have a stake in members' experiences, such as colleagues of the worker, agency representatives, relatives, friends, and others. The worker will relate differently to all of these.

Contracting work agreements

The process and importance of contracting working agreements in group work is explained as follows:

- Only if group members are involved in clarifying and setting their own personal and common group goals can they be expected to be active participants in their own behalf.
- Working agreements consider not only worker-member relationships, but also others with a direct or indirect stake in the group's process. Examples would be agency sponsorship, collaborating staff, referral and funding sources, families, caretakers, and other interested parties in the public at large.

Influencing group process

The worker's ability to recognize, analyze, understand, and influence group process is necessary and vital. The group is a system of relationships rather than a collection of individuals. This system is formed through associations with a unique and changing quality and character (this is known as group structures and processes). Processes that the worker will be dealing with include understanding group structures, value systems, group emotions, decision-making, communication/interaction, and group development (formation, movement, termination).

Individualizing group work methodology

The process of individualizing in group work methodology is as follows:

- The worker must be prepared to help individual members profit from their experiences in and through the group.
- Ultimately, what happens to group members and how they are influenced by the group's processes determines the success of any group experience, not how the group itself functions as an entity.

Externalizing

The worker should give attention to helping members relate beyond the group, to encouraging active participation and involvement with others in increasingly wider spheres of social living. This should occur even when the group is relatively autonomous.

Programming

The importance of programming in group work methodology is explained below:

- The worker uses activities, discussion topics, task-centered activities, exercises, and games as a part of a planned, conscious process to address individual and group needs while achieving group purposes and goals.
- Programming should build on the needs, interests, and abilities of group members and should not necessitate a search for the unusual, esoteric, or melodramatic.
- Social work skills used in implementing programs include the following: initiating and modifying program plans to respond to group interests, self-direction and responsibility, drawing creatively upon program resources in the agency and environment, and developing sequences of activities with specific long-range goals.
- Using program activities is an important feature of group practice.

Group formation

Key elements of the group formation process:

- The worker makes a clear and uncomplicated statement of purpose, of both the members' stakes in coming together and the agency's (and others') stakes in serving them.
- Describing the worker's part in as simple terms as possible.
- Reaching for member reaction to worker's statement of purpose. Identifying how the worker's statement connects to the members' expectations.
- The worker helps members do the work necessary to develop a working consensus about the contract.
- Recognizing goals and motivations, both manifest and latent, stated and unstated.
- Re-contracting as needed.

The worker's role in "contracting" during group formation is as follows:

- Setting goals (contracting)
- Determining membership
- Establishing initial group structures and formats.
- All three of these elements require skillful management by the worker.

The worker's process of selecting members for a group is as follows:

- Worker explains reasons for meeting with group applicants.
- Worker elicits applicants' reactions to group participation. Worker assesses applicants' situations by engaging them in expressing their views of the situation and goals in joining the group.
- Worker determines appropriateness of applicants for group, accepts their rights to refuse membership, and provides orientation upon acceptance into the group.

The issues of heterogeneity vs. homogeneity in group formation are explained as follows:

- A group ought to have sufficient homogeneity to provide stability and generate vitality.
- Groups that focus on socialization and developmental issues or on learning new tasks are more likely to be homogeneous.
- Groups that focus on disciplinary issues or deviance are more likely to be heterogeneous.
- Composition and purposes of groups are ultimately influenced or determined by agency goals.

- 75 -

Closed groups
- Convened by workers.
- Members begin the experience together, navigate it together, and end it together at a predetermined time (set number of sessions).
- Closed groups afford better opportunities than open groups for members to identify with each others.
- Give greater stability to the helping situation; stages of group development progress more powerfully.
- Greater amount and intensity of commitment due to same participants being counted on for their presence.

Open groups
- Open groups allow participants to enter and leave according to their choice.
- A continuous group can exist, depending on frequency and rate of membership changes.
- Focus shifts somewhat from the whole group process to individual members' processes.
- With membership shifts, opportunities to use group social forces to help individuals may be reduced. Group will be less cohesive, less available as a therapeutic instrument.
- Worker is kept in a highly central position throughout the life of the group, as he or she provides continuity in an open structure.

Short-term groups
- Short term groups are formed around a particular theme or in order to deal with a crisis.
- Limitations of time preclude working through complex needs or adapting to a variety of themes or issues.
- The worker is in the central position in a short term group.

Formed groups
- Deliberately developed to support mutually agreed-upon purposes.
- Organization of group begins with realization of need for group services.
- Purpose is established by identification of common needs among individuals in an agency or worker caseload.
- Worker guided in interventions and timing by understanding of individual and interpersonal behavior related to purpose.
- It is advisable to have screening, assessment, and preparation of group members.
- Different practice requirements for voluntary and non-voluntary groups as members will respond differently to each.

Beginning phase
Intervention skills: The interventive skills the worker will use in the beginning work phase of a group are as follows:
- Worker must tune into the needs and concerns of the members. Member cues may be subtle and difficult to detect.
- Seeking members' commitment to participate through engagement with members.

- Worker must continually asses:
  - members' needs/concerns
  - any ambivalence/resistance to work
  - group processes
  - emerging group structures
  - individual patterns of interaction
- Facilitate the group's work.

Stress: The stress that the worker might experience in beginning phases of a group's process includes:
- Anxiety regarding gaining acceptance by the group.
- Integrating group self-determination with an active leadership role.
- Fear of creating dependency and self-consciousness in group members which would deter spontaneity.
- Difficulty observing and relating to multiple interactions.
- Uncertainty about worker's own role.

Middle phase
The middle phase of group work:
- Relatively clear agreement of purpose.
- Members are engaged in group tasks.
- Members allow worker to facilitate group efforts toward achieving goals.

The interventive skills the worker will use in the middle phase of group work include:
- Being able to judge when work is being avoided.
- Being able to reach for opposites, ambiguities, and what is happening in the group when good and bad feelings are expressed.
- Supporting different ways in which members help each other.
- Being able to partialize larger problems into more manageable parts.
- Being able to generalize and find connections between small pieces of group expression and experience.
- Being able to facilitate purposeful communication that is invested with feelings.
- Identifying and communicating the need to work and recognizing when work is being accomplished by the group.

Intervention and development stages
The intervention and development stages of the worker in work with groups are:
- Power and control stage—consists of limit setting, clarification, use of the program
- Intimacy stage—consists of handling transference, rivalries, degree of uncovering
- Differentiation stages—consist of clarification of differential and cohesive processes, group autonomy
- Separation—consists of a focus on evaluation, handling ambivalence, incorporating new resources

<u>Facilitating group work</u>
The worker's tasks in facilitating the group's work are as follows:
- Promote member participation and interaction.
- Bring up real concerns in order to begin the work.
- Help the group keep its focus.
- Reinforce observance of rules of the group.
- Facilitate cohesiveness and focus the work by identifying emerging themes.
- Establish worker identity in relation to group's readiness.
- Listen empathically, support initial structure and rules of the group, and evaluate initial group achievements.
- Suggest ongoing tasks or themes for the subsequent meeting.

<u>Termination</u>
Group members may have feelings of loss and may desire to minimize the painful feelings they are experiencing. Members may experience ambivalence about ending. The worker will:
- Examine his or her own feelings about termination.
- Focus the group on discussing ending.
- Help individuals express their feelings of loss, relief, ambivalence, etc.
- Review achievements of the group and members.
- Help members prepare to cope with next steps.
- Assess members' and group's needs for continued services.
- Help members with transition to other services.

The following are group members' methods of forestalling or dealing with termination:
- Simple denial—member may forget ending, act surprised, or feel "tricked" by termination
- Clustering—physically drawing together, also called super-cohesion
- Regression—reaction can be simple-to-complex. Earlier responses reemerge, outbursts of anger, recurrence of previous conflicts, fantasies of wanting to begin again, attempts to coerce the leader to remain, etc.
- Nihilistic flight—rejecting and rejection-provoking behavior
- Reenactment and review—recounting or reviewing earlier experiences in detail or actually repeating those experiences
- Evaluation—assessing meaning and worth of former experiences
- Positive flight—constructive movement toward self-weaning. Member finds new groups, etc.

Small group work

<u>System Analysis and Interactional Theory</u>
The System Analysis and Interactional Theory of small groups is as follows:
- This is a broadly used framework for understanding small groups. In this framework, small groups are living systems that consist of interacting elements which function as a whole.
- In this framework, a social system is a structure of relationships or a set of patterned interactions.

- System concepts help maintain a focus on the whole group, and explain how a group and its sub-groups relate functionally to larger environments.
- This framework describes how interaction affects status, roles, group emotions, power and values.

Social System Concepts
- Boundary maintenance: maintaining group identities and separateness
- System linkages: two or more elements combine to act as one
- Equilibrium: maintaining a balance of forces within the group

General Systems Concepts
- Steady state: tendency of an open system to remain constant but in continuous exchange
- Equifinality: final state of a system that can be reached from different initial conditions
- Entropy: tendency of a system to wear down and move toward disorder

Symbolic Interactionism
- Emphasizes the symbolic nature of people's relationships with others and with the external world, versus social system analysis that emphasizes form, structures, and functions.
- Group members play a part in determining their own actions by recognizing symbols and interpreting meaning.
- Human action is accomplished mainly through the process of defining and interpreting situations in which people act. The worker uses such concepts to explain how individuals interact with others, and to understand the role of the individual as the primary resource in causing change; the significance of social relationships; the importance of self-concept, identification, and role identity in group behavior; and the meanings and symbols attributed to group interactions.

Gestalt orientations and Field Theory
- Gestalt psychology played major part in development of group dynamics. Contrasting with earlier psychologies that stressed elementary sensations and associations, Gestalt theorists viewed experiences not in isolation, but as perpetually organized and part of a field comprised of a system of co-existing, interdependent factors.
- Group dynamics produced a plethora of concepts and variables: goal formation, cohesion, group identification and uniformity, mutual dependency, influences and power, cooperation and competition, and productivity.
- Group dynamics (or group process) provide a helpful framework of carefully defined and operationalized relevant group concepts.

Cognitive Consistency Theory and Balance Theory
The Cognitive Consistency Theory and Balance Theory in relation to small group practice are summarized below:
- Basic assumption of cognitive consistency theory is that individuals need to organize their perceptions in ways that are consistent and comfortable. Beliefs and attitudes are not randomly distributed but rather reflect an underlying coherent

system within the individual that governs conscious processes and maintains internal and psychosocial consistency.
- According to balance theory, processes are balanced when they are consistent with the individual's believes and perceptions. Inconsistency causes imbalance, tensions, and stress, and leads to changing perceptions and judgments which restore consistency and balance.
- The group worker incorporates varying ideas from these orientations. Some stress the need for the group to be self-conscious, to study its own processes, emphasizing that cognition is apparent in contracting, building group consciousness, pinpointing or eliminating obstacles, and sharing data.

Sociometry

- Inspired by J. L. Moreno's work.
- Both a general theory of human relations and a specific set of practice techniques (psychodrama, sociodrama, role playing).
- Sociometric test are devised to measure the "affectivity" factor in groups.
- Quality of interpersonal attraction in groups is a powerful force in rallying group members, creating feelings of belonging, and making groups sensitive to member needs.

Social Reinforcement and Exchange theory

- Social exchange theorists propose that members of groups are motivated to seek profit in their interactions with others, i.e. to maximize rewards and minimize costs.
- Analysis of interactions within groups is done in terms of a series of exchanges or tradeoffs group members make with each other.
- The individual member is the primary unit of analysis. Many of the core concepts of this theory are merely transferred to the group situation and do not further understanding of group processes.

Group properties

Group properties are attributes that characterize a group at any point in time. They include:
- Formal vs. informal structure
- Primary group (tight-knit family, friendship, neighbor)
- Secondary relationships (task centered)
- Open vs. closed
- Duration of membership
- Autonomy
- Acceptance-rejection ties
- Social differentiation and degrees of stratification
- Morale, conformity, cohesion, contagion, etc.

Analyzing group processes

The major categories for analyzing group processes are:
- Communication processes
- Power and influence
- Leadership
- Group norms and values
- Group emotion
- Group deliberation and problem solving

Group development

Group development is summarized as follows:
- Group processes that influence the progress of a group, or any of its sub-groups, over time. Group development typically involves changing structures and group properties that alter the quality of relationships as groups achieve their goals.
- Understanding group development gives workers a blueprint for interventions that aid the group's progression toward attaining goals. A danger in using development models is in the worker's forcing the group to fit the model, rather than adapting interventions for what is occurring in the group.
- A complex set of properties, structures, and ongoing processes influence group development. Through processes that are repeated, fused with others, modified and reinforced, movement occurs.

Stages
The stages in the different linear stage models of group development are:
- Tuckman's Five stages:
    - form
    - storm
    - norm
    - perform
    - adjourn
- Boston Model (Garland, Jones, & Kolodny):
    - Preaffiliation
    - Power and Control
    - Intimacy
    - Differentiation
    - Separation
- Relational Model (feminist, Schiller):
    - Preaffiliation
    - Establishing a Relational Base
    - Mutuality & Interpersonal Empathy
    - Challenge & Change
    - Separation & Termination

Models of group practice

Social Goals Model
The Social Goals Model of group practice is described below:
- Primary focus—to influence a wide range of small group experiences, to facilitate members' identifying and achieving of their own goals, and to increase social consciousness and social responsibility.
- Assumes a rough unity between involvement in social action and psychological health of the individual. Early group work was concerned with immigrant socialization and emphasized principles of democratic decision making, in addition to tolerance for difference.
- Methodology—focus on establishing positive relationships with groups and members, using group processes in doing with the group rather than for the group, identification of common needs and group goals, stimulation of democratic group participation, and providing authentic group programs stemming from natural types of "group living."

Remedial/Rehabilitative Models
Remedial/Rehabilitative Models of group practice are explained below:
- Uses a medical model and the worker is focused primarily on individual change.
- Structured program activities and exercises.
- More commonly found in organizations concerned with socialization, such as schools, and in those concerned with treatment and social control (inpatient mental health treatment, etc.).

Practice techniques in this model focus on stages of treatment:
- Beginning stage—intake, group selection, diagnosis of each member, setting specific goals
- Middle stage—planned interventions. Worker is central figure and uses direct means to influence group and members. Worker is spokesperson for group values and emotions. Worker motivates and stimulates members to achieve goals.
- Ending stage—group members have achieved maximum gains. Worker helps clients deal with feeling about ending. Evaluation of work, possible renegotiation of contract.

Reciprocal Interactional or Mediating Model
Worker is not called a therapist but a mediator and participates in a network of reciprocal relationships. Goals are developed mutually through contracting process. The interaction and insight of group members is the primary force for change in what is seen as a "mutual aid" society.
Worker's task—help search for common ground between group members and the social demands they experience, help clients in their relationships with their own social systems, detect and challenge obstacles to clients' work, and contribute data.

Phases of intervention:
- Tuning in/preparation for entry—worker helps the group envision future work, but makes no diagnosis. Worker is sensitive to members' feelings.
- Beginnings—worker engages group in contracting process; group establishes clear expectations.

- Middle phase—searching for common ground, discovering/challenging obstacles, data contribution, sharing work visions, defining limits/requirements
- Endings—worker sensitive to own and members' reactions and helps members evaluate the experience and consider new beginnings

Freudian/Neo-Freudian approach
The Freudian/Neo-Freudian approach to group practice is described below:
- Groups of 8-10 members.
- Interaction mainly through discussion.
- Group members explore feelings and behavior and interpret unconscious processes.
- The worker uses interpretation, dream analysis, free association, transference relations, and working through.
- This approach aims to help group members re-experience early family relationships, uncover deep-rooted feelings, and gain insight into the origins of faulty psychological development.

Tavistock "Group as a Whole" group-centered models
The Tavistock "Group as a Whole" group-centered models for practice with groups are described below:
- This approach derives from Bion's work with Leaderless Groups. Bion developed analytic approaches that focused on the group as a whole.
- Latent group feelings are represented through the group's prevailing emotional states or "basic assumption cultures."
- Groups are sometimes called S groups (Study groups).
- Therapist is referred to as a consultant. The consultant does not suggest an agenda, establishes no rules/procedures, but rather acts as an observer. Major role of the consultant is to alert members to ongoing group processes and to encourage study of these processes.
- Consultant encourages members to explore their experiences as group members through interaction.

Irvin Yalom's "Here-and-Now" or Process Groups
Irvin Yalom's "Here-and-Now" or Process Groups are described below:
- Yalom stressed using clients' immediate reactions and discussing members' affective experiences in the group.
- Relatively unstructured and spontaneous sessions.
- Groups emphasize therapeutic activities, like imparting information, or instilling hope, universality, and altruism.
- The group can provide a rehabilitative narrative of primary family group development, offer socializing techniques, provide behavior models to imitate, offer interpersonal learning, and offer an example of group cohesiveness and catharsis.
- Two inpatient group methods based on the interpersonal approach are the Interactional Agenda group and Focus Groups.

Moreno's Psychodrama

Moreno's Psychodrama group therapy is described below:

- Powerful therapy for groups that uses spontaneous drama techniques to aid in the release of pent-up feelings, and to provide insight and catharsis to help participants develop new and more effective behaviors.
- Five primary instruments used are the stage, the patient or protagonist, the director or therapist, the staff of therapeutic aides or auxiliary egos, and the audience.
- Can begin with a warm-up. Uses an assortment of techniques such as self-presentations, interviews, interaction in the role of the self and others, soliloquies, role reversals, doubling techniques, auxiliary egos, mirroring, multiple doubles, life rehearsals, and exercises.

Behavioral group therapies

Behavioral group therapies are as follows:

- Main goals: to help group members eliminate maladaptive behaviors and learn new behaviors that are more effective. Not focused on gaining insight into the past, but rather on current interactions with the environment.
- Among few research-based approaches.
- Worker utilizes directive techniques, providing information, and teaching coping skills and methods of changing behavior.
- Worker arranges structured activities. Primary techniques used—restructuring, systematic desensitization, implosive therapies, assertion training, aversion techniques, operant-conditioning, self-help reinforcement and support, behavioral research, coaching, modeling, feedback, and procedures for challenging and changing conditions.

Group types and purposes

Seriously mentally ill clients

Group work with seriously mentally ill clients is described below:

- Clearly defined programs that use psychosocial rehabilitation approaches (not psychotherapeutic).
- Focus on making each group session productive and rewarding to group members.
- Themes addressed include dealing with stigma, coping with symptoms, adjusting to medication side effects, dealing with problems (family, relationships, housing, employment, education, etc.), real/imagined complained about mental health treatment organizations.
- Many groups in community-based settings focus on helping members learn social skills for individuals with limited or ineffective coping strategies.
- Mandated groups in forensic settings are highly structured and focus on basic topics such as respect for others, responsibility for one's behavior, or staying focused.

Chemical dependency

Groups are the treatment of choice for substance use disorder.

Guidelines for these groups include maintaining confidentiality, using "I" statements, speaking directly to others, never speaking for others, awareness of one's own thoughts and feelings, honesty about thoughts and feelings, taking responsibility for one's own behavior.

Types of groups used include

- Orientation groups that give information regarding treatment philosophy/protocols.
- Spiritual groups that incorporate spirituality into recovery.
- Relapse prevention groups that focus on understanding and dealing with behaviors and situations that trigger relapse.
- AA and NA self- help groups utilize the principles and philosophies of 12-step programs. For family and friends, Nar-Anon and Al-Anon groups provide support.

Parent education

Parent education groups:

- These groups are used in social agencies, hospitals and clinics.
- Often labeled as Psycho Ed groups or Parent training groups.
- Use a cognitive-behavioral approach to improve the parent-child relationship.
- Often structured to follow manuals or curricula.
- Focus is helping parents improve parent-child interactions, parent attitudes, and child behaviors.

Abused women

Abused women's groups:

- Provide warm, accepting, caring environment in which members can feel secure.
- Structured for consciousness raising, dispelling false perceptions, and resource information.
- Common themes these groups explore include the use of power which derives from the freedom to choose, the need for safety, the exploration of resources, the right to protection under the law, and the need for mutual aid.
- Basic principles of these groups: respect for women, active listening and validation of members' stories, insuring self-determination and individualization, and promoting group programs that members can use to demonstrate their own strength and achieve empowerment.
- For post-group support, groups typically seek to utilize natural supports in the community.

Spouse abusers

Groups for spouse abusers (perpetrators of domestic violence):

- Work with this population is typified by resistance and denial.
- Clients have difficulty processing guild, shame, or abandonment anxiety and tend to convert these feelings into anger.
- These clients have difficulties with intimacy, trust, mutuality, and struggle with fear of abandonment and diminished self-worth.
- Mandatory group treatment is structured. It is designed to challenge male bonding that often occurs in such groups. Including spouses/victims in these groups is quite controversial in clinical literature.

<u>Sex offenders</u>
Groups for sex offenders:
- Typically, membership in these groups is ordered by the court. No assurance of confidentiality, as workers may have to provide reports to the courts, parole officers, or other officials.
- Clients typically deny, test workers, and are often resistant.
- In groups with voluntary membership, confidentiality is extremely important, as group members often express extreme fear of exposure.
- Prominent themes include denial, victim-blaming, blaming behavior on substances, blaming behavior on uncontrollable sex drives/needs.
- Treatment emphasizes the importance of conscious control over drives/needs, regardless of their strength or if they are "natural."
- Culture of victimization strongly discouraged.

<u>Children of alcoholic families</u>
Individuals who grow up with parents who abuse alcohol and/or drugs often learn to distrust others as a survival strategy. They become used to living with chaos and uncertainty and with shame and hopelessness. These individuals commonly experience denial, secrecy, and embarrassment. They may have a general sense of fearfulness, especially if they faced threats of violence, and tend to have rigid role attachment. Treatment in these groups requires careful planning, programming, and mutual aid in the form of alliances with parental figures and other related parties in order to create a healthy environment that increases the individual's safety and ability to rely on self and others.

<u>Sexually abused children</u>
Groups for sexually abused children:
- Group treatment typically used with child victims of sexual abuse.
- Worker must pay particular attention to his or her own attitudes toward sexuality and the sexual abuse of children.
- Important in these groups are contracting, consistent attendance, and clearly defined rules and expectations.
- Clients may display control issues and may challenge the worker's authority.
- Confidentiality is not guaranteed.
- Termination can be a particularly difficult process.
- Common themes that come up include fear, anger, guilt, depression, anxiety, inability to trust, delayed developmental/socialization skills.
- Programming can include ice breaking games, art, body drawings, letter writing, and role playing.

Relapse prevention therapy

This is an approach to treatment that uses cognitive behavioral techniques to help clients develop greater self-control to avoid relapse. Strategies used:
- Discussing ambivalence
- Identifying emotional and environmental triggers
- Developing and reviewing specific coping strategies
- Exploring the decision chain that leads to resuming substance use
- Learning from brief relapses (slips) about triggers that lead to relapse and developing effectual techniques for early intervention.

Motivational enhancement therapy

This therapy is based on cognitive behavioral, client-centered, systems, and social-psychological persuasion techniques.
Is a brief treatment modality.
Includes an empathic approach in which the worker helps to motivate the client through asking about the pros and cons of specific behaviors, through exploring the client's goals and related indecision about reaching those goals, and through listening reflectively.

Substance use disorder treatment

Operant behavioral therapy
This therapy involves operant rewarding or punishing of clients for desirable or undesirable behaviors, such as treatment compliance or relapse. Rewards may include vouchers or other prizes awarded for drug-free testing or community reinforcement in which family members or peers reinforce abstinence.

Contingency management therapy
This is a behavioral treatment which is based on the use of predetermined consequences (both positive and negative) to reward abstinence or punish drug-related behaviors. Examples of negative consequences are notification of courts, employers, or family members. The effectiveness of this treatment requires the use of frequent, random, supervised urine monitoring for substance use. If negative contingencies are based upon the expected response of others, the worker must obtain the written informed consent of the client at the initiation of the contract.

Aversion therapy
This involves combining substance use with an unpleasant experience, such as a mild electric shock or pharmacologically induced vomiting. It is used in specialized facilities and controlled trials have had mixed results.

Cue exposure treatment
This treatment is based on Pavlov's extinction paradigm and involves exposure of the individual to cues that stimulate drug craving, at the same time preventing actual drug use and the experience of drug-related enforcement. It can also be combined with relaxation techniques and drug refusal training to ease the disappearance of classically conditioned craving.

Group therapy
The advantages of group therapy in substance use disorder treatment are:
- Can be a supportive, therapeutic, and educational experience that helps motivate and sustain participants.
- Gives clients opportunities to identify with others.
- Helps participants understand the impact of substance use on their lives.
- Helps participants to learn more about their own and others' feelings and reactions.
- Commonly regarded as the preferred mode of psychotherapeutic treatment for substance-dependent clients.

Family interventions

When abstinence disrupts a previously well-established maladaptive style of family interaction and family members need help adjusting to a new set of individual and familial goals, attitudes, and behaviors.

Family/couple therapy can be useful to promote psychological differentiation of individual family members, to provide a forum for the exchange of information and ideas about the treatment plan, to develop behavioral management contracts for continued family support, and to reinforce behaviors that prevent relapse and enhance recovery prospects.

Clinical risks

Clinical risks in substance use disorder treatment include:

- Suicide attempts and completions are substantially higher with substance use disorders than in the general population, with completed suicides 3-4 times that in the general population.
- Increased risks for homicide and other violence.
- Impaired reality testing, anxiety, irritability, increased aggressiveness, and impaired impulse control.

Important terms

Catharsis — The release of tension or anxiety through reliving and intentionally examining early life, repressed, or traumatic experiences.

Clarification — Worker questions, repeats, or rephrases material client discusses. Worker must use sensitivity to client's defensiveness.

Confrontation — Worker continually seeks to understand the client's view of self and situation

Direct influence — Worker offers advice, suggestions in order to influence client

Exploration — Worker challenges client to deal with inconsistencies between his or her words and actions, maladaptive behaviors, or resistance to treatment or change

Structure — The patterned interactions, network of roles and statuses, communications, leadership, and power relationships that distinguish a group at any point in time.

Universalization — Normalization of problems; problems are presented as a part of the human condition in order to help the client see them as less pathological.

Ventilation — Client's airing of feelings associated with the information presented about self and the situation. May alleviate intensity of client's feelings or feeling that he or she is alone with them. Worker may need to help client distinguish times when ventilation is useful and when it may increase intensity of feelings.

Professional Ethics and Values 27%

Core social work values

The following are core social work values held across the board by major social work theorists:
- Worth of the individual
- Right of individuals to access to services
- Right of individuals to fulfill potential without regard to class, race, gender, or sexual orientation
- Self determination
- Confidentiality

Core social work goals

Core social work goals held across the board by major social work theorists are to help clients:
- improve social functioning
- resolve problems
- achieve desired change
- meet self-defined goals

Confidentiality

Social work privilege does not have the same force as that of attorneys and clergy. Unlike clergy and attorneys, social workers may be compelled to testify in court under certain circumstances.

Organizational policies should reflect the expectation of confidentiality:
- Records must be secured and locked.
- Policies should be in place that insure that records not be left where unauthorized persons are able to read them.
- Computerized records should be secured with the same attention given to written records (hard copies).
- Agencies must provide spaces that permit private conversations so that conversations about clients can be held where they cannot be overheard.

Informed consent

A client may provide consent for the worker to share information with family members, or with other professionals or agencies for purposes of referral. When the client provides this consent, he or she has reason to expect that shared information is in his or her best interest, and designed to improve his or her situation.

Reporting child abuse

Every state in the U.S. has laws that mandate that social workers report the mere suspicion of child abuse to the appropriate authorities. A good faith report gives the worker immunity from civil or criminal liability if the report is not verified as social workers cannot be found liable for following the law. Informing clients of the worker's decision to make a report is determined situationally, particularly if there is a concern of the client's violent reaction to self or others.

Reporting incidents or suspicions of sexual abuse

Perpetrators of these crimes can be highly motivated to obtain retractions and may threaten or use violence to do so. A major concern in developing immediate and long term strategies for protection and treatment is the role of the non-abusing parent and his or her ability to protect the child. The victim may be safer if the worker does not notify the family when making the report. Great care must be taken by the worker with these cases.

Reporting client as a danger

The following are circumstances under which a social worker must report that a client is a danger to self or others:
- The client's mental state is such that he or she may deliberately or accidentally cause harm to self.
- The client makes a direct threat to harm another person and there is a reasonable possibility that he or she can carry out the threat.
- Duty to warn: All mental health professionals have a duty to warn individuals who are threatened. This principle was established by the Tarasoff Decision (*Tarasoff vs. Regents of University of California, 1976*).

Confidentiality if sued for malpractice

A worker who is sued for malpractice may reveal information discussed by clients. The worker should aim to limit the discussion of the content of clinical discussions to those statements needed to support an effective defense.

Liability

Liability for social workers is as follows:
- Clients can sue social workers for malpractice.
- The chain of liability extends from the individual worker to supervisory personnel to the director and then to the board of directors of a nonprofit agency.
- Most agencies carry malpractice insurance, which usually protects individual workers, however, workers may also carry personal liability and malpractice insurance.
- Supervisors can be named as parties in a malpractice suit as they share vicarious liability for the activities of their supervisees.

NASW Code of Ethics

Misrepresentation

Social workers should make clear distinctions between statements made and actions engaged in as a private individual and as a representative of the social work profession, a professional social work organization, or of the social worker's employing agency.

Social workers who speak on behalf of professional social work organizations should accurately represent the official and authorized positions of the organization.

Social workers should ensure that their representations to clients, agencies, and the public of professional qualifications, credentials, education, competence, affiliations, services provided, or results to be achieved are accurate. Social workers should claim only those relevant professional credentials they actually possess and take steps to correct any inaccuracies or misrepresentations of their credentials by others.

(see section 4.06 of the Code of Ethics)

Solicitations

Social workers should not engage in uninvited solicitation of potential clients who, because of their circumstances, are vulnerable to undue influence, manipulation, or coercion.

Social workers should not engage in solicitation of testimonial endorsements (including solicitation of consent to use a client's prior statement as a testimonial endorsement) from current clients or other persons who, because of their particular circumstances are vulnerable to undue influence.

(see section 4.07 of the Code of Ethics)

Acknowledging credit

Social workers should take responsibility and credit, including authorship credit, only for work they have actually performed and to which they have contributed. Social workers should honestly acknowledge the work of and the contributions made by others.

(see section 4.08 of the Code of Ethics)

Dishonesty, fraud, and deception

Social workers should not participate in, condone, or be associated with dishonesty, fraud, or deception.

(see section 4.04 of the Code of Ethics)

Impairment

Social workers should not allow their own personal problems, psychosocial distress, legal problems, substance use disorder, or mental health difficulties to interfere with their professional judgment and performance or to jeopardize the best interests of people for whom they have a professional responsibility. Social workers whose personal problems, psychosocial distress, legal problems, substance use disorder, or mental health difficulties interfere with their professional judgment and performance should immediately seek consultation and take appropriate remedial action by seeking professional help, making adjustments in workload, terminating practice, or taking any other steps necessary to protect clients and others.

(see section 4.05 of the Code of Ethics)

Core values of social work

The core values of the social work profession, according to the NASW Code of Ethics, are:

- Service
- Social justice
- Dignity and worth of the person
- Importance of human relationships
- Integrity
- Competence

Purpose

The purposes of the NASW Code of Ethics are to:

- Identify core values on which social work's mission is based.
- Summarize broad ethical principles that reflect the profession's core values.
- Establish a set of specific ethical standards that should be used to guide social work practice.
- Provide ethical standards to which the general public can hold the social work profession accountable.
- Socialize practitioners new to the field to social work's mission, values, ethical principles, and ethical standards.
- Articulate standards that the profession can use to assess whether social workers have engaged in unethical conduct.

Commitment to clients

Social workers' primary responsibility is to promote the well-being of clients. In general, client interests are primary. However, social workers' responsibility to the larger society or specific legal obligations may on limited occasions supersede the loyalty owed clients, and clients should be so advised.
(see section 1.01 of the Code of Ethics)

Self-determination

Social workers respect and promote the right of clients to self-determination and assist clients in their efforts to identify and clarify their goals. Social workers may limit clients' right to self-determination when, in the social workers' professional judgment, clients' actions or potential actions pose a serious, foreseeable, and imminent risk to themselves or others.
(see section 1.02 of the Code of Ethics)

Informed consent

The implications of informed consent, per the NASW Code of Ethics, are as follows:

- Social workers should use clear, understandable language to inform clients of the purpose of their services, risk related to those services, any limits to services, relevant costs, reasonable alternatives, clients' right to refuse or withdraw consent, and the time frame covered by the consent. Workers should provide clients an opportunity to ask questions.
- If clients are not literate or have difficulty understanding the language used in the practice setting, the worker should take steps to ensure their comprehension (detailed verbal explanation or providing an interpreter/translator when possible).
- For clients lacking capacity to provide informed consent, workers should seek permission from an appropriate third party while informing the client and seeking

to ensure that the third party acts in a manner consistent with the client's wishes and interests.
- When clients receive services involuntarily, workers should provide information about the nature and extent of services and about the extent of the client's right to refuse services.
- Workers who provide services via electronic media should inform clients of the limitations and risks associated with such services.
- Informed consent should be obtained before audio or videotaping clients or permitting observation by a third party.

(see section 1.03 of the Code of Ethics)

Competence
Competence, as discussed in the NASW Code of Ethics:
- Social workers should provide services and represent themselves as competent only within the boundaries of their education, training, license, certification, consultation received, supervised experience, or other relevant professional experience.
- Social workers should provide services in substantive areas or use intervention techniques or approaches that are new to them only after engaging in appropriate study, training, consultation, and supervision from people who are competent in those interventions or techniques.
- When generally recognized standards do not exist with respect to an emerging area of practice, social workers should exercise careful judgment and take responsible steps (including appropriate education, research, training, consultation, and supervision) to ensure the competence of their work and to protect clients from harm.

(see section 1.04 of the Code of Ethics)

Cultural competence and social diversity
The NASW Code of Ethics addresses cultural competence and social diversity as follows:
- Social workers should understand culture and its function in human behavior and society, recognizing the strengths that exist in all cultures.
- Social workers should have a knowledge base of their clients' cultures and be able to demonstrate competence in the provision of services that are sensitive to clients' culture and to differences among people and cultural groups.
- Social workers should obtain education about and seek to understand the nature of social diversity and oppression with respect to race, ethnicity, national origin, color, sex, sexual orientation, age, marital status, political belief, religion and mental or physical disability.

(see section 1.05 of the Code of Ethics)

Conflicts of interest
Social workers should be alert to and avoid conflicts of interest that interfere with the exercise of professional discretion and impartial judgment. Social workers should inform clients when a real or potential conflict of interest arises and take reasonable steps to resolve the issue in a manner that makes the clients' interests primary and protects clients' interests to the greatest extent possible. Occasionally, protecting clients' interests may require termination of the professional relationship with proper referral of the client.

Social workers should not take unfair advantage of any professional relationship or exploit others to further their personal, political, or business interests.
(see section 1.06 of the Code of Ethics)

Dual or multiple relationships
Social workers should not engage in dual or multiple relationships with clients or former clients in which there is a risk of exploitation or potential harm to the client. In instances when dual or multiple relationships are unavoidable, social workers should take steps to protect clients and are responsible for setting clear, appropriate, and culturally sensitive boundaries. (Dual or multiple relationships occur when social workers relate to clients in more than one relationship, whether professional, social, or business. Dual or multiple relationships can occur simultaneously or consecutively.)
(see section 1.06 of the Code of Ethics)

Providing services to two or more people who have a relationship with each other
When social workers provide services to two or more people who have a relationship with each other (for example, couples, family members), social workers should clarify with all parties which individuals will be considered clients and the nature of social workers' professional obligations to the various individuals who are receiving services. Social workers who anticipate a conflict of interest among the individuals receiving services or who anticipate having to perform in potentially conflicting roles (for example, when a social worker is asked to testify in a child custody dispute or divorce proceedings involving clients) should clarify their role with the parties involved and take appropriate action to minimize any conflict of interest.
(see section 1.06 of the Code of Ethics)

Clients' right to privacy
Social workers should respect clients' right to privacy. Social workers should not solicit private information from clients unless it is essential to providing service, or conducting social work evaluation, or research. Once private information is shared, standards of confidentiality apply.
(see section 1.07 of the Code of Ethics)

Disclosing confidential information
Social workers may disclose confidential information when appropriate with a valid consent from a client, or a person legally authorized to consent on behalf of a client. Social workers should protect the confidentiality of all information obtained in the course of professional service, except for compelling professional reasons. The general expectation that social workers will keep information confidential does not apply when disclosure is necessary to prevent serious, foreseeable, and imminent harm to a client or other identifiable person or when laws or regulations require disclosure without a client's consent. In all instances, social workers should disclose the least amount of confidential information necessary to achieve the desired purpose; only information that is directly relevant to the purpose for which the disclosure is made should be revealed.
(see section 1.07 of the Code of Ethics)

Social workers should inform clients, to the extent possible, about the disclosure of confidential information and, when feasible, before the disclosure is made. This applies whether social workers disclose confidential information as a result of a legal requirement or based on client consent.

Social workers should discuss with clients and other interested parties the nature of confidentiality and limitations of clients' right to confidentiality. Social workers should review with clients circumstances where confidential information may be requested and where disclosure of confidential information may be legally required. This discussion should occur as soon as possible in the social worker-client relationship and as needed throughout the course of the relationship.
(see section 1.07 of the Code of Ethics)

Confidentiality with families, couples, or groups
When social workers provide counseling services to families, couples, or groups, social workers should seek agreement among the parties involved concerning each individual's right to confidentiality and obligation to preserve the confidentiality of information shared by others. Social workers should inform participants in family, couples, or group counseling that social workers cannot guarantee that all participants will honor such agreements. Social workers should inform clients involved in family, couples, marital, or group counseling of the social worker's, employer's, and agency's policy concerning the social worker's disclosure of confidential information among the parties involved in counseling.
(see section 1.07 of the Code of Ethics)

Client access to records
Social workers should provide clients with reasonable access to records concerning the clients. Social workers who are concerned that clients' access to their records could cause serious misunderstanding or harm to the client should provide assistance in interpreting the records and consultation with the client regarding the records. Social workers should limit clients' access to their records, or portions of their records, only in exceptional circumstances when there is compelling evidence that such access would cause serious harm to the client. Both clients' requests and the rationale for withholding some or all of the record should be documented in clients' files.
When providing clients with access to their records, social workers should take steps to protect the confidentiality of other individuals identified or discussed in such records.
(see section 1.08 of the Code of Ethics)

Sexual relationships with clients or clients' relatives
Social workers should under no circumstances engage in sexual activities or sexual contact with current clients, whether such contact is consensual or forced. Social workers should not engage in sexual activities or sexual contact with clients' relatives or other individuals with whom clients maintain a close personal relationship when there is a risk of exploitation or potential harm to the client. Sexual activity or sexual contact with clients' relatives or other individuals with whom clients maintain a personal relationship has the potential to be harmful to the client and may make it difficult for the social worker and the client to maintain appropriate professional boundaries. Social workers—not their clients, their clients' relatives, or others with whom the client maintains a personal relationship— assume the full burden for setting clear, appropriate, and culturally sensitive boundaries.
(see section 1.09 of the Code of Ethics)

Sexual relationships with former clients
Social workers should not engage in sexual activities or sexual contact with former clients because of the potential for harm to the client. If social workers engage in conduct contrary to this prohibition or claim that an exception to this prohibition is warranted because of extraordinary circumstances, it is social workers—not their clients—who assume the full

burden of demonstrating that the former client has not been exploited, coerced, or manipulated, intentionally or unintentionally.
(see section 1.09 of the Code of Ethics)

Prior sexual relationships
Social workers should not provide clinical services to individuals with whom they have had a prior sexual relationship. Providing clinical services to a former sexual partner has the potential to be harmful to the individual and is likely to make it difficult for the social worker and individual to maintain appropriate professional boundaries.
(see section 1.09 of the Code of Ethics)

Physical contact
Social workers should not engage in physical contact with clients when there is a possibility of psychological harm to the client as a result of the contact (such as cradling or caressing clients). Social workers who engage in appropriate physical contact with clients are responsible for setting clear, appropriate, and culturally sensitive boundaries that govern such physical contact.
(see section 1.10 of the Code of Ethics)

Derogatory language
Social workers should not use derogatory language in their written or verbal communications to or about clients. Social workers should use accurate and respectful language in all communications to and about clients.
(see section 1.12 of the Code of Ethics)

Payment for services
Social workers should ensure that their fees are fair, reasonable, and commensurate with the service performed. Consideration should be given to the client's ability to pay.
Social workers should avoid accepting goods or services from clients as payment for professional services. Bartering arrangements, particularly involving services, create the potential for conflicts of interest, exploitation, and inappropriate boundaries in social workers relationships with clients. Social workers should explore and may participate in bartering only in very limited circumstances when it can be demonstrated that such arrangements are an accepted practice among professionals in the local community, considered to be essential for the provision of services, negotiated without coercion, and entered into at the client's initiative and with the client's informed consent. Social workers who accept goods or services from clients as payment for professional services assume the full burden of demonstrating that this arrangement will not be detrimental to the client or the professional relationship.
Social workers should not solicit a private fee or other remuneration for providing services to clients who are entitled to such available services through the worker's employer or agency.
(see section 1.13 of the Code of Ethics)

Clients who lack decision-making capacity
When social workers act on behalf of clients who lack the capacity to make informed decisions, social workers should take reasonable steps to safeguard the interests and rights of those clients.
(see section 1.14 of the Code of Ethics)

Interruption of services
Social workers should make reasonable efforts to ensure continuity of services in the event
that services are interrupted by factors such as unavailability, relocation, illness, disability,
or death.
(see section 1.15 of the Code of Ethics)

Termination of services
Social workers should terminate services to clients, and professional relationships with
them, when such services and relationships are no longer required or no longer serve the
clients' needs or interests.
Social workers in fee-for-service settings may terminate services to clients who are not
paying an overdue balance if the financial contractual arrangements have been made clear
to the client, if the client does not pose an imminent danger to self or others, and if the
clinical and other consequences of the current nonpayment have been addressed and
discussed with the client.
Social workers who anticipate the termination or interruption of services to clients should
notify clients promptly and seek the transfer, referral, or continuation of services in relation
to the clients' needs and preferences.
Social workers who are leaving an employment setting should inform clients of all available
options for the continuation of service and their benefits and risks.
(see section 1.16 of the Code of Ethics)

Social workers should not terminate services to pursue a social, financial, or sexual
relationship with a client.
(see section 1.16 of the Code of Ethics)

Terminating services with clients who still need services
Social workers should take reasonable steps to avoid abandoning clients who are still in
need of services. Social workers should withdraw services precipitously only under unusual
circumstances, giving careful consideration to all factors in the situation and taking care to
minimize possible adverse effects. Social workers should assist in making appropriate
arrangements for continuation of services when necessary.
(see section 1.16 of the Code of Ethics)

Respect to colleagues
Social workers should treat colleagues with respect and represent accurately and fairly the
qualifications, views, and obligations of colleagues.
Social workers should avoid unwarranted negative criticism of colleagues with clients or
with other professionals.
Social workers should cooperate with social work colleagues and with colleagues of other
professions when it serves the well-being of clients.
(see section 2.01 of the Code of Ethics)

Confidentiality with colleagues
Social workers should respect confidential information shared by colleagues in the course
of their professional relationships and transactions. Social workers should ensure that such
colleagues understand social workers' obligation to respect confidentiality and any
exceptions related to it.
(see section 2.02 of the Code of Ethics)

Interdisciplinary collaboration

Social workers who are members of an interdisciplinary team should participate in and contribute to decisions that affect the well-being of clients by drawing on the perspectives, values, and experiences of the social work profession. Professional and ethical obligations of the interdisciplinary team as a whole and of its individual members should be clearly established.

Social workers for whom a team decision raises ethical concerns should attempt to resolve the disagreement through appropriate channels. If the disagreement cannot be resolved social workers should pursue other avenues to address their concerns, consistent with client well-being.

(see section 2.03 of the Code of Ethics)

Disputes involving colleagues

Social workers should not take advantage of a dispute between a colleague and employer to obtain a position or otherwise advance the social workers' own interests.

Social workers should not exploit clients in disputes with colleagues or engage clients in any inappropriate discussion of conflicts between social workers and their colleagues.

(see section 2.04 of the Code of Ethics)

Consultation

Social workers should seek advice and counsel of colleagues whenever such a consultation is in the best interests of clients.

Social workers should keep informed of colleagues' areas of expertise and competencies. Social workers should seek consultation only from colleagues who have demonstrated knowledge and competence related to the subject of the consultation.

When consulting with colleagues about clients, social workers should disclose the least amount of information to achieve the purposes of the consultation.

(see section 2.05 of the Code of Ethics)

Referral for services

Social workers should refer clients to other professionals when other professionals' specialized knowledge or expertise is needed to serve clients fully, or when social workers believe they are not being effective or making reasonable progress with clients and additional service is required.

Social workers who refer clients to other professionals should take appropriate steps to facilitate an orderly transfer of responsibility. Social works who refer clients to other professionals should disclose, with clients' consent, all pertinent information to the new service providers.

Social workers are prohibited from giving or receiving payment for a referral when no professional service is provided by the referring social worker.

(see section 2.06 of the Code of Ethics)

Sexual relationships between colleagues

Social workers who function as supervisors or educators should not engage in sexual activities or contact with current supervisees, students, trainees, or other colleagues over whom they exercise professional authority.

Social workers should avoid engaging in sexual relationships with colleagues where there is potential for a conflict of interest. Social workers who become involved in, or anticipate becoming involved in, a sexual relationship with a colleague have a duty to transfer professional responsibilities, when necessary, in order to avoid a conflict of interest.
(see section 2.07 of the Code of Ethics)

Impairment of colleagues
Social workers who have direct knowledge of a social work colleague's impairment which is due to personal problems, psychosocial distress, substance use disorder, or mental health difficulties, and which interferes with practice effectiveness, should consult with that colleague and assist the colleague in taking remedial action.
Social workers who believe that a social work colleague's impairment interferes with practice effectiveness and that the colleague has not taken adequate steps to address the impairment should take action through appropriate channels established by employers, agencies, NASW, licensing and regulatory bodies, and other professional organizations.
(see section 2.09 of the Code of Ethics)

Incompetence of colleagues
Social workers who believe that a social work colleague is incompetent should consult with that colleague when feasible and assist the colleague in taking remedial action.
Social workers who believe that a social work colleague is incompetent and has not taken adequate steps to address the incompetence should take action through appropriate channels established by employers, agencies, NASW, licensing and regulatory bodies, and other professional organizations.
(see section 2.10 of the Code of Ethics)

Reporting unethical conduct
Social workers should take adequate measures to discourage, prevent, expose, and correct the unethical conduct of colleagues.
Social workers should be knowledge about established policies and procedures for handling concerns about colleagues' unethical behavior. Social workers should be familiar with national, state, and local procedures for handling ethics complaints.
Social workers who believe that a colleague has acted unethically should seek resolution by discussing their concerns with the colleague when feasible and when such discussion is likely to be productive.
Social workers should defend and assist colleagues who are unjustly charged with unethical conduct.
(see section 2.11 of the Code of Ethics)

Supervision and consultation
Social workers who provide supervision or consultation should have the necessary knowledge and skill to supervise or consult appropriately and should do so only within their areas of knowledge and competence.
Social workers who provide supervision or consultation are responsible for setting clear, appropriate, and culturally sensitive boundaries.
Social workers should not engage in any dual or multiple relationships with supervisees in which there is a risk of exploitation or of potential harm to the supervisee.
Social workers who provide supervision should evaluate supervisees' performance in a manner that is clear and respectful.
(see section 3.01 of the Code of Ethics)

Performance evaluation
Social workers who have responsibility for evaluating the performance of others should fulfill such responsibility in a fair and considerate manner and on the basis of clearly stated criteria.
(see section 3.03 of the Code of Ethics)

Client records
Social workers should take reasonable steps to ensure that documentation in records is accurate and reflects the services provided.
Social workers should include sufficient and timely documentation in records to facilitate the delivery of services and to ensure continuity of services provided to clients in the future.
Social workers' documentation should protect clients' privacy to the extent that is possible and appropriate and should include only information that is directly relevant to the delivery of services.
Social workers should store records following the termination of service to ensure reasonable future access. Records should be maintained for the number of years required by state statutes or relevant contracts.
(see section 3.04 of the Code of Ethics)

Billing
Social workers should establish and maintain billing practices that accurately reflect the nature and extent of services provided, and specifically by whom the service was provided in the practice setting.
(see section 3.05 of the Code of Ethics)

Resource allocation
Social workers should advocate for resource allocation procedures that are open and fair. When not all clients' needs can be met, an allocation procedure should be developed that is nondiscriminatory and based on appropriate and consistently applied principles.
(see section 3.07 of the Code of Ethics)

Continuing education and staff development
Social work administrators and supervisors should take reasonable steps to provide or arrange for continuing education and staff development for all staff for whom they are responsible. Continuing education and staff development should address current knowledge and emerging developments related to social work practice and ethics.
(see section 3.08 of the Code of Ethics)

Labor-Management disputes
Social workers may engage in organized action, including the formation of and participation in labor unions to improve services to clients and working conditions.
The actions of social workers who are involved in labor-management disputes, job actions, or labor strikes should be guided by the professions' values, ethical principles, and ethical standards. Reasonable differences of opinion exist among social workers concerning their primary obligation as professionals during an actual or threatened labor strike or job action. Social workers should carefully examine relevant issues and their possible impact on clients before deciding on a course of action.
(see section 3.10 of the Code of Ethics)

Competence

Social workers should accept responsibility or employment only on the basis of existing competence or the intention to acquire the necessary competence.

Social workers should strive to become and remain proficient in professional practice and the performance of professional functions. Social workers should critically examine, and keep current with, emerging knowledge relevant to social work. Social workers should routinely review professional literature and participate in continuing education relevant to social work practice and social work ethics.

Social workers should base practice on recognized knowledge, including empirically based knowledge, relevant to social work and social work ethics.

(see section 4.01 of the Code of Ethics)

Discrimination

Social workers should not practice, condone, facilitate, or collaborate with any form of discrimination on the basis of race, ethnicity, national origin, color, age, religion, sex, sexual orientation, marital status, political belief, or mental or physical disability.

(see section 4.02 of the Code of Ethics)

Social workers

Social workers should not permit their private conduct to interfere with their ability to fulfill their professional responsibilities.

(see section 4.03 of the Code of Ethics)

Practice Test

Practice Questions

1. A social worker has been called to conduct a mental status exam (MSE) with an 86-year-old elderly man who is suspected of having early symptoms of dementia. At one point you ask him to interpret the idiom, "People who live in glass houses shouldn't throw stones." He responds, "Someone living in a glass house has to be careful, because stones can break glass." This response represents an example of:
   a. Formal operational thought
   b. Pre-operational thought
   c. Sensorimotor interpretation
   d. Concrete operational thought

2. The human and development and behavior theorist most closely associated with Functionalism is:
   a. John B. Watson
   b. William James
   c. Alfred Adler
   d. Lev Vygotsky

3. The theorist in human development and behavior who is most focused on moral development is:
   a. Lawrence Kohlberg
   b. Margaret Mahler
   c. Carol Gilligan
   d. John Bowlby

4. A key difference between the theorists Wilhelm Wundt and William James regarding cognitive and emotional responses to experiences is:
   a. James felt cognitive processing precedes emotions, while Wundt felt that emotions emerge prior to cognitive understanding.
   b. James felt emotional reactions precede cognitive processing, while Wundt felt that cognitive processing precedes emotional reactions.
   c. James felt that cognitive processing and emotions occur simultaneously, while Wundt felt emotions emerge before cognitive processing.
   d. James felt that cognitive processing precedes emotions, while Wundt felt that cognitive processing and emotions occur simultaneously.

5. Sigmund Freud proposed the concepts of *preconscious* and *unconscious* to describe thoughts, feelings and ideas that are outside of conscious awareness but that nevertheless influence behavior and thinking. The primary difference between preconscious and unconscious thought is:

    a. Unconscious thoughts can never be brought to conscious awareness, while preconscious thoughts can only be brought to awareness with great difficulty.

    b. Preconscious thoughts can never be brought to conscious awareness, while unconscious thoughts can be brought to awareness only with great difficulty.

    c. Unconscious thoughts can be brought to awareness relatively easily, while preconscious thoughts are much more difficult to bring to awareness.

    d. Preconscious thoughts can be brought to awareness relatively easily, while unconscious thoughts are much more difficult to bring to awareness.

6. An 11-year-old boy is seen in clinic for multiple episodes of stealing behavior, exclusively involving the theft of inexpensive toys from a local store. From the perspective of Freud's structure of personality, describe the driving personality force in this behavior and the MOST immediately effective intervention:

    a. The driving force is the Superego, and the most effective intervention would be an appeal to the child's sense of empathy for the needs of the store's owner.

    b. The driving force is the Ego, and the most effective intervention would be to discuss acceptable ways to meet the desire for toys.

    c. The driving force is the Id, and the most effective intervention would be to cite the negative consequences of the behavior.

    d. The driving force is the Life Instinct, and the most effective intervention would be to examine the role of altruism in proper behavior.

7. A 46-year-old woman is referred for treatment for nicotine and alcohol addiction. She is also some 150 pounds overweight. The client claims to "like smoking" with no desire to quit, denies the extent of her alcoholism, and suggests that she doesn't "really eat very much." From a Freudian perspective, the client may have a fixation in the following stage of Freud's five stages of psychosexual development:

    a. Latency Period

    b. Phallic Stage

    c. Anal Stage

    d. Oral Stage

8. A couple comes to see you. Married just two years, they're having difficulty adjusting. He's the youngest in his family and she's the oldest, which seems at the root of some of their problems. For example, she feels he's being irresponsible, and he feels she's being harsh and uncaring of his situation. Specifically, he has been out of work for several months, and she's working a marginal, late-night waitressing job just to make ends meet. She's tired and upset, and wants him to take any of a number of jobs he has passed up. He's pushing for something even better than any in his past. To make matters worse, he's been making troubling purchases "just for fun," which have caused more financial burden. From an Adlerian perspective, which of the following would BEST explain their situation:

    a. Needs hierarchy and separation-individuation

    b. Ego vs Superego conflicts

    c. Birth order and guiding fiction

    d. Inferiority vs superiority

9. An 8-year-old girl is brought to see you by referral from a school counselor. The referral indicates the child is inordinately afraid of being outdoors, refusing recess periods and other normal play experiences. Accompanied by her mother, she seems quite shy and reserved. During the child's intake interview, the mother repeatedly interrupts questions about the child's various fears. Comments such as, "Well, of course she won't want to be on the playground! It's a dangerous place!" frequently emerge, along with voiced concerns about physical activity ("she could fall"), being outside on the sidewalk with friends ("a car could come by and hit them"), etc. Noting the mother's marked overprotective posture, you draw upon the following theorist in considering a possible etiology of the problem:
   a. B. F. Skinner
   b. Ivan Pavlov
   c. Jean Piaget
   d. John B. Watson

10. A man comes in to see you about a compulsion that is troubling him. Whenever someone brings up something very serious (a family death, grave illness, loss of a crucial job, or other major misfortune) he finds himself compelled to resort to humor to minimize the intense feelings involved. This has offended many people. During exploration of the problem, it is learned that his father was violently intolerant of any expression or display of negative emotion. Drawing upon Pavlovian theory, the client's compulsion can best be described as a/an:
   a. Unconditioned stimulus
   b. Unconditioned response
   c. Conditioned stimulus
   d. Conditioned response

11. When evaluating a 16-year-old girl's depression you discover that she's distressed, in part, because she has never learned to drive. Consequently, she's passed up occasional babysitting jobs, social events, and other activities. She feels inferior to others. Pointing this out to the parents, her father states, "She just can't learn. I've taken her driving and shown her what to do many times, but she isn't able to cut it." You recommend enrollment in a professional driving class, but the father resists, saying, "There's nothing some driving instructor knows that I can't teach her." To overcome his resistance you note the unique driving tools available to an instructor and explain the concept of:
   a. Behavior modification
   b. Interactive scaffolding
   c. Defense mechanisms
   d. Anaclitic depression

12. Which of the following concepts from social psychologist Kurt Lewin would be MOST helpful in understanding the powerful role of peer pressure:
   a. The behavioral equation
   b. Force field analysis
   c. Sensitivity training
   d. Leadership climates

13. As a hospital social worker, you are assigned to work with families in an intensive care unit. A husband was recently told that his wife is terminally ill. In speaking with him, you attempt to discuss his feelings about the impending loss of his wife and how he and his family are coping. However, you find the conversation persistently returning to recent medical tests, current physical indicators, and potential changes in her medications. This is an example of the following defense mechanism:
    a. Projection
    b. Compensation
    c. Intellectualization
    d. Rationalization

14. A 32-year-old single woman comes to see you about depression. You notice that she wears an excessive amount of makeup, dresses in teen-style attire, wears her hair in a faddish fashion, and uses a mixture of old and new era teen terms and language. As you talk, she narrates activities dominated by associations at teen and young adult clubs and haunts, and describes attempted relationships with individuals much younger than herself. When you ask about peer relationships, she indicates that she avoids those her age as she does not want to become "old before her time," and sees herself as much more youthful that others her age. The defense mechanism she employs is BEST described as:
    a. Avoidance
    b. Fixation
    c. Devaluation
    d. Affiliation

15. You are counseling a man at a walk-in community clinic. He had moved in with his girlfriend, but was recently evicted from her home. His way to work was by riding with her, and he now is unsure how to keep his job given the loss of transportation. This has left him with no stable living situation and in danger of unemployment. He has no family or close friends in the area. Emotionally, however, he is preoccupied with the loss of his relationship and the security and affection he found through it, which is all he wants to talk about. According to the theorist Abraham Maslow, the BEST response to this situation is to:
    a. Go where the client wants to be, and work on his feelings about the relationship loss.
    b. Refuse to talk about relationship issues until immediate needs regarding housing, transportation, and employment are met.
    c. Permit some discussion on feelings of loss, but keep the focus on his immediate housing, transportation, and employment needs.
    d. Explain to him that his needs are beyond what you have to offer and refer him to a shelter program.

16. A 38-year-old man is being seen in an STI (sexually transmitted infections) clinic for treatment of chlamydia. You have been called to discuss his sexual history with a focus on safe-sex practices, particularly while being treated. You learn that he has a history of short-term sexual relationships with women, with many involving "one-night" encounters. He also admits to occasionally paying for sexual favors. According to the ego psychology theorist Erik Erikson, this client is struggling with master of the following stage of personality development:
    a. Stage 1: trust vs mistrust
    b. Stage 5: identity vs identify diffusion
    c. Stage 6: intimacy vs isolation
    d. Stage 8: integrity vs despair

17. A 28-year-old woman comes to see you with complaints about rejection by her new boyfriend. They've been dating for about 6 weeks, and she notes that he's just no longer being as attentive as he was. She wants to know what to do to "win him back." Upon further inquiry you learn that she's experienced this in all her prior dating relationships. You further learn that she calls, texts, drops by, and otherwise attempts to stay in contact throughout every day. She voices great fear that he will soon leave her "like the others." As she talks, you note high lability in her emotions, ranging from fear and anxiety to intense anger. She also uses frequent criticism of herself, suggesting she is "not worth" having a relationship with, etc. You quickly recognize symptoms of likely borderline personality disorder. In considering a treatment approach, you draw upon Margaret Mahler's work, which posits that this disorder likely occurs from problematic experiences during:
    a. Normal autism phase
    b. Symbiosis phase
    c. Differentiation (hatching) phase
    d. Rapprochement phase

18. A normally well-behaved 15-year-old girl is being seen for her recent onset of conflict and behavior problems. The parents are overwhelmed and in need of direction. They have used a variety of behavioral modification techniques (e.g., lectures, restrictions, grounding, loss of privileges) without success. The behavior has become so problematic that it has impeded the father's normal overseas travel for work. With further inquiry, you learn that the father's employment has taken him away for extensive periods in the child's life, but that she now has his nearly undivided attention. Drawing upon the operant conditioning work of B.F. Skinner, you identify the problem as one of:
    a. Positive reinforcement
    b. Negative reinforcement
    c. Punishment
    d. Extinction

19. The difference between Ivan Pavlov's conditioning and B.F. Skinner's operant conditioning is:
    a. Pavlovian conditioning deals with the modification of voluntary behavior via consequences, while Skinner's operant conditioning produces behavior under new antecedent conditions.
    b. Skinner's operant conditioning deals with the modification of voluntary behavior via consequences, while Pavlovian conditioning produces behavior under new antecedent conditions.
    c. Pavlovian conditioning deals exclusively with involuntary bodily functions, while Skinner's operant conditioning deals solely with voluntary behaviors.
    d. Skinner's operant conditioning deals exclusively with involuntary bodily functions, while Pavlovian conditioning deals solely with voluntary behaviors.

20. A couple is receiving counseling to overcome identified obstacles and increase marital satisfaction. In the course of several visits, you become aware that the husband often speaks of his "duty" to his family and his obligation to "do right by them." Using Lawrence Kohlberg's multistage model of moral development, you identify the husband's level to be:
   a. Level 1: Stage 2
   b. Level 2: Stage 4
   c. Level 3: Stage 5
   d. Level 3: Stage 6

21. You are a school counselor seeing a 12-year-old middle school boy for consistent misbehavior in class. He resists following instructions and bullies others, and has been accused to taking things belonging to others out of the class coat closet. Meeting with his mother, she indicates an extended history of defiance of home rules, refusal to obey direct instructions, etc. Upon further inquiry you learn that she divorced when the boy was still an infant, after which she had to work long hours. Due to finances, he was bounced from daycare to daycare for some years. Drawing upon the work of John Bowlby and Mary Ainsworth, you recognize problems potentially arising from:
   a. Dysfunctional parenting
   b. Poverty and oppression
   c. Disrupted attachment
   d. Divorce and displacement

22. All of the following are true for the Person-in-Environment (PIE) system EXCEPT:
   a. It diagnostically identifies cause and effect relationships
   b. It was developed specifically for use in social work
   c. It identifies and balances problems and strengths
   d. It evaluates four client domains for a more comprehensive view

23. During what period of child development would evidence of childhood psychopathology most likely become apparent?
   a. Physical development
   b. Cognitive/intellectual development
   c. Sexual development
   d. Language development

24. Failure of an infant to crawl by the following age would be cause for concern:
   a. 6 months
   b. 9 months
   c. 12 months
   d. None of the above

25. A 10-year-old girl is brought in by her parents for evaluation because she has unexpectedly experienced menarche. They are concerned about possible sexual abuse, though they acknowledge that no other symptoms are present. The FIRST and most appropriate social work response would be to:
   a. Refer the child to a qualified pediatrician for examination
   b. Contact local child abuse authorities and make a suspected abuse referral
   c. Interview the child immediately for risks of sexual abuse
   d. Reassure the parents that this is not unexpected for the child's age

26. The term *sandwich generation* refers to:
    a. The prevalence of fast-food consumption in the current era
    b. The loss of whole family–present dinner time meals in the home
    c. The pressure of couples still rearing children while being required to care for aging parents
    d. The pressure between health problems of aging and rising retirement age requirements

27. As a school counselor you are seeing an 8-year-old girl who has symptoms suggestive of reactive attachment disorder (aversion to accepting comfort and affection, even from familiar adults, particularly when distressed), which is strongly correlated with severe abuse and/or neglect. There is no evidence of sexual abuse, but ample evidence of excessive punishment, emotional abuse, and significant neglect. From your social work training, you are aware that the MOST likely perpetrator of such abuse of a child this age would be:
    a. The father
    b. The mother
    c. Older siblings
    d. Another adult relative

28. A home health referral indicates that an elderly client's caregiving needs are not fully met by the live-in caregiving son and daughter-in-law. The client is constantly left in a windowless back bedroom with no television or radio, and virtually never brought out. There are also signs of skin breakdown, isolation-induced depression, and questionable nourishment, all of which were addressed by the referring nurse. The caregivers now openly acknowledge they are not able (or willing) to meet the client's needs, so they openly support placement. However, they emphasize that they have given up employment to provide care, are living on the client's retirement funds, and note that the home (which could be sold to pay for care) has been left to them in a will. Consequently, they are unwilling to make the changes required for placement. The FIRST social work response should be to:
    a. Accept that the caregiver's situation cannot be changed at this time
    b. Refer them to a caregiver education seminar coming up in 2 months
    c. Arrange a prompt extended family meeting to explore options
    d. Contact the local Adult Protective Services to report suspected abuse

29. In describing domestic violence, the cycle of abuse is most commonly framed in four phases. During the reconciliation phase, a perpetrator is likely to express all of the following EXCEPT:
    a. Threats of further abuse
    b. Blaming the victim for the abuse
    c. Apologizing for the abuse
    d. Minimizing the abuse

30. A husband finds his wife is drinking too much. She often apologizes and indicates she'd like to get help, though she refuses to call and make an appointment. Eventually he calls for her, and sets up an appointment with you. In exploring her drinking, you learn that he does most of the shopping for groceries, and for the alcoholic beverages brought into the home. He reveals that he purchases the alcohol to keep peace, and because he knows she would suffer with symptoms of delirium tremens if she was left without any access to alcohol. Worried for the children, he would at times call into work claiming to be sick when he knew she was having a particularly bad drinking binge. His behavior is BEST described as:
    a. Addictive
    b. Codependent
    c. Manipulative
    d. Maladaptive

31. As a hospital social worker you have been called to evaluate a patient who has been dealing with a diagnosis of terminal cancer. Recently he came to his physician and offered him a considerable sum of money to pursue an unorthodox, unproven treatment. The physician tried to explain the problems with such treatment, but the patient remained insistent, and even accused the physician of being unwilling to seek a cure in deference to continuing to bill his insurance for other fruitless procedures and treatments. Deeply disturbed, the physician referred the patient to you. After speaking with the client and confirming the above, you recognized the symptoms as characteristic of:
    a. A psychotic break
    b. Chemotherapy toxicity
    c. Grief bargaining
    d. Acute denial

32. When considering issues of cultural diversity, social workers must be sensitive to all of the following EXCEPT:
    a. Race and ethnicity
    b. Employment class
    c. Gender and orientation
    d. National origin

33. Cultural competence in social work requires a salient understanding of and capacity within all of the following EXCEPT:
    a. Knowledge of diversity
    b. Attitude of accommodation
    c. Cultural skills
    d. Group affiliations

34. A social worker is interviewing a client from a different culture. The client is encouraged to tell stories about his life from a cultural perspective, stories about traditions, history, and culture-specific experiences. Even though the client speaks English, a skilled interpreter is present to capture and elucidate unique idioms, phrases, and terms that have a unique meaning from within the client's cultural context. Listening carefully for underlying feelings and cultural meanings, the social worker restates important concepts, and incorporates the unique terms into the overall narrative. This form of engagement is referred to as:
    a. Conceptual reframing
    b. Ethnographic paraphrasing
    c. Ethnographic interviewing
    d. Conceptual exploration

35. The difference between the *nurturing system* and the *sustaining system* is:
    a. The nurturing system refers to family and intimate supports, while the sustaining system refers to institutional supports and society as a whole.
    b. The sustaining system refers to family and intimate supports, while the nurturing system refers to institutional supports and society as a whole.
    c. The nurturing system refers to educational opportunities and support, while the sustaining system refers to employment opportunities and support.
    d. The sustaining system refers to educational opportunities and support, while the nurturing system refers to employment opportunities and support.

36. Working at a bicultural community counseling center for Southeast Asian families, you encounter a family troubled by sharp divisions between older family members and their young children. In particular, from the parent's viewpoint, the children seem to have lost respect for their elders, often treating their parents and even their grandparents in dismissive ways. According to Robbins, Chatterjee, and Canada (1998) this is evidence of:
    a. Traditional adaptation
    b. Marginal adaptation
    c. Assimilation
    d. Bicultural adaptation

37. All of the following are common characteristics of African American families EXCEPT:
    a. Church membership and spirituality are both important
    b. Individual independence is diligently fostered
    c. Family members feel deeply responsible for each other
    d. Extended kinship relationships are significant

38. Characteristics common to many Hispanic-Latino families include all of the following EXCEPT:
    a. Patriarchal family leadership is emphasized
    b. The family is more important than the individual
    c. Personal problems are to be kept within the family
    d. Religion has no major role in family life

39. As a counselor you are working with a 22-year-old woman who is grappling with her emerging sexual identity as a lesbian. She expresses comfortable acceptance of her lesbianism, and indicates meaningful support from an extended circle of friends in the LGBT community. Even so, she has yet to reveal her sexuality to her heterosexual friends and family, citing fears of rejection and stating that she is embarrassed to take this very difficult step. According to Robins, Chatterjee, and Canada (1998), this client is in the following stage of the Coming Out Process:
   a. Stage 2: Identity recognition
   b. Stage 4: Disclosure
   c. Stage 7: Pride in identity
   d. Stage 8: Increased disclosure

40. In the LGBT community, the term Intersex refers to:
   a. Ambiguous sexual anatomy (hermaphrodite)
   b. Heterosexual orientation
   c. Sexual encounters outside of preference
   d. Sexual attraction to both men and women

41. A 46-year-old woman has come in with complaints of depression. Attempts at exploration of the underlying issues reveal numerous long-standing challenges (work, marriage, children), but no clear precipitating event(s). Along with dysphoria, the client has clear vegetative symptoms as well (anorexia, insomnia, fatigue, anhedonia, and impaired attention). Other than ventilation and support, what should be the social worker's FIRST response in this situation?
   a. Press the client further in seeking a precipitating depressive event
   b. Refer the client to a psychiatrist for antidepressant evaluation
   c. Begin working with the client's denial about depressive issues in her life
   d. Refer the client to a primary care physician for a health evaluation

42. A 72-year-old Caucasian man comes in to see you with symptoms of depression. Although widowed, he has a supportive extended family, is well educated, generally financially solvent, and has only typical age-related health concerns (moderate arthritis, borderline high blood pressure, and a pacemaker). Successful throughout his life, he has a very stable history. During the conversation he makes a passing comment about "wondering if life is worth it anymore." The BEST response to this somewhat offhand comment would be to:
   a. Ignore it as a common phrase that shouldn't be troubling
   b. Note it, but wait to see of similar feelings arise again
   c. Reassure him that life is always worth living, even if challenging
   d. Key in on the phrase and inquire directly about suicidal thoughts

43. The MOST correct answer describing the difference between HIV and AIDS is:
   a. HIV is a virus and AIDS is an illness
   b. HIV is ultimately caused by AIDS
   c. HIV is a precursor to AIDS
   d. There is no difference

44. You are seeing a recently returned 26-year-old male military veteran who had been deployed on active duty in the Middle East. He has obvious symptoms of posttraumatic stress disorder (PTSD) (intrusive memories, flashbacks, hypervigilance, angry outbursts, etc.). You should explore the possibility of all of the following as potential causes of these symptoms EXCEPT:
    a. Combat stress
    b. Disciplinary issues
    c. Mild traumatic brain injury (MTBI)
    d. Sexual assault trauma

45. The National Association of Social Workers (NASW) has established a clear position with regard to undocumented (illegal) immigrants. The position includes all of the following EXCEPT:
    a. Advocating for rights and services for undocumented residents
    b. Transitioning undocumented immigrants back to their homeland
    c. Opposing any mandatory immigration reporting by social workers
    d. Facilitating documentation and benefits for undocumented residents

46. During an intake interview, key areas of data collection include all of the following categories EXCEPT:
    a. Problem areas, strengths, and support systems
    b. Attitude and motivation
    c. Insurance and ability to pay
    d. Relationships, resources, and safety

47. An Observational Assessment involves appraisal of a client in all of the following areas EXCEPT:
    a. Psychiatric status
    b. Physical appearance
    c. Health signs
    d. Life skills

48. In your clinical setting you are asked to assess clients based upon their complaints, deficits, and identified problems. This method of assessment draws upon which of the following assessment models?
    a. Strengths perspective
    b. Medical model
    c. Biopsychosocial model
    d. None of the above

49. An interview that is focused on past and current relationships, community contacts, and interpersonal interactions is known as a:
    a. Family history
    b. Social history
    c. Interpersonal history
    d. Relationship history

50. A client arrives for services at a community counseling clinic. He is pleasant, easily engaged, and discusses the need to work on "some interpersonal problems." When asked about any prior treatment, he notes that he has been seen by another therapist for the past 8 months. However, he now needs to seek services closer to home due to a change in his work schedule. When presented with an information release for contact with his prior therapist he becomes agitated and upset, and refuses to allow the contact. The BEST response in this situation would be to:
    a. Accept the client's need to keep his therapeutic past private
    b. Discuss his concerns and support him, but require the collateral contacts
    c. Refuse services to the client based on his refusal to permit collateral contacts
    d. None of the above

51. During a Friday afternoon counseling visit, a client voices thoughts about suicide. She does not appear to be emotionally overwrought, but rather seems peaceful and calm. She discusses that she feels she has accomplished all she can in life, particularly given the poor relationship she has with her husband and the fact that the last of their children recently left home. She notes having read some online information about a cardiac medication she takes (Digoxin), and believes that an overdose of this medication would precipitate rapid cardiac arrest. She just had the prescription refilled, and is just considering when to act—perhaps when her husband is out golfing the next Sunday morning. The FIRST appropriate response to this information should be to:
    a. Call 911 to ensure the client receives immediate help for her suicidal intent
    b. Call local law enforcement to involuntarily escort the client for further suicide evaluation and hospitalization
    c. Complete a suicide risk evaluation, and then arrange voluntary hospitalization if the client will accept it
    d. Create a very detailed suicide prevention contract with the client, and plan several sessions to address her suicidality

52. You are seeing a married couple, at times individually. During an individual session the husband reveals that he is bisexual. He also reveals a lengthy history of sexual liaisons with other men and discloses that he recently learned he is HIV positive (via confirmatory tests through his primary care physician). Inquiring, you discover that he has not disclosed his HIV status to his spouse and that he does not use any barrier protection when with her. Upon explaining the life-and-death risk to his wife, he still maintains that he won't change this behavior. He first minimizes the risk, and then claims she would "suspect something" if he started using protection. After lengthy counseling he remains unwilling to either reveal his HIV status or to use protection. Your duty now is to:
    a. Maintain confidentiality, but continue this as a priority topic.
    b. Contact the client's physician to disclose the problem.
    c. Contact the wife to inform her of the danger.
    d. State laws vary; know your state's laws.

53. A mental status exam (MSE) covers all the following domains EXCEPT:
    a. Addictions and compulsions
    b. Appearance and attitude
    c. Mood and affect
    d. Insight and judgment

54. The acronym BIRP refers to a record charting method and stands for:
    a. Behavior, intensity, reaction, and plan
    b. Behavior, interpretation, recapitulation, and plan
    c. Behavior, intervention, response, and plan
    d. Behavior, insight, repetition, and plan

55. While the use of the multiaxial system in *DSM-IV* has been removed from *DSM-5*, the use of specifiers continues. The purpose of diagnostic specifiers is to:
    a. Offer clinical justification
    b. Delineate subtypes and severity
    c. Differentiate between related diagnoses
    d. Indicate uncertainty

56. In testing, a 9-year-old male client is given an intelligence quotient (IQ) score of 68. This score correlates with the following degree of intellectual disability:
    a. Profound
    b. Severe
    c. Moderate
    d. Mild

57. In working with an 11-year-old girl, you note that she seems to have limited verbal skills, including problems in word selection and use. Intelligence testing indicates normal cognitive capacity and age-appropriate comprehension of language spoken to her. These early indicators are BEST suggestive of the following tentative diagnosis:
    a. Phonological Disorder
    b. Stuttering
    c. Mixed Receptive-Expressive Language Disorder
    d. Expressive Language Disorder

58. An 8-year-old boy presents with a number of complex developmental deficits. In particular, the child seems to isolate himself as evidenced by an apparent disinterest (or perhaps inability) in communicating with others, an idiosyncratic use of words and language, little imaginative play or social imitation, poor peer relationships, limited responses to others in his presence even if engaged, and odd, repetitive motions, routines, and rituals. The most likely tentative diagnosis would be:
    a. Asperger syndrome
    b. Rett syndrome
    c. Autistic disorder
    d. Childhood disintegrative disorder

59. Parents bring in their 14-year-old son, concerned about his persistent rebellious, disobedient, and argumentative behavior. The problem has been getting progressively worse over the past year, and they feel it is just not tolerable any longer. They note that he is continuing to do well in school and with friends, but he is constantly angry, argumentative, and overly touchy, and he refuses to behave; he ignores family rules and refuses to perform basic household chores or to clean up his own room, etc. There is no evidence of drug use, nor does he appear to be a victim of bullying or other abuse in or out of the home. The most appropriate initial *DSM* diagnosis in this situation is:
  a. Oppositional Defiant Disorder
  b. Conduct Disorder
  c. Bipolar Disorder
  d. Attention Deficit Hyperactivity Disorder (ADHD)

60. As a social worker in a medical clinic, you are called to evaluate a 15-year-old girl who admits to persistent eating of paper products. The problem has persisted for some 6 months, and has led to substantial weight loss and some level of poor nutrition. The preferred paper for ingestion is tissue paper, either toilet roll paper or facial tissues. The parents first noted the problem when tissue products continually disappeared in the home. In further discussion with them, they note that their daughter has also been avoiding regular meals, tending to pick at her food, and leaving the table early. There has also been some evidence of her ingesting other nonfood materials, such as clay, mineral oil, and sand, and obvious evidence of her consuming an inordinate amount of ice chips. The patient is reluctant to talk about any of this, just saying things such as "I don't know" and "maybe" and "I guess" to most any inquiry, and/or growing silent. The MOST LIKELY tentative diagnosis would be:
  a. Pica
  b. Bulimia Nervosa
  c. Anorexia Nervosa
  d. Rumination Disorder

61. When used in reference to an individual who is chronologically at least 4 years old (or, mentally, at least 4 years old), the term *encopresis* refers to:
  a. The voluntary expelling of fecal matter in an inappropriate place
  b. The involuntary expelling of fecal matter in an inappropriate place
  c. The expelling of fecal matter in response to symptoms of stress or anxiety
  d. All of the above.

62. A mother brings in her 8-year-old daughter due to her inability to sleep in her own bed at night. The mother has a history of sleeping with her daughter since about age 2, when she became divorced. She has, however, recently remarried and the daughter's insistence to sleep in the bed with her mother has become extremely problematic. When efforts are made to send the daughter to her own bed (in a room alone) the daughter becomes extremely stressed, tearful, and eventually displays tantrum-like behavior that fully disrupts sleep for the household until she is allowed to sleep with her mother. The MOST LIKELY diagnosis for this behavior would be:
  a. Oppositional-Defiant Disorder
  b. Separation Anxiety Disorder
  c. Agoraphobia
  d. Panic Disorder

63. Delirium differs from encephalopathy in the following:
    a. Delirium has a sudden onset, while encephalopathy is gradual
    b. Delirium involves sepsis, while encephalopathy involves toxins
    c. Delirium has a gradual onset, while encephalopathy is sudden
    d. None of the above

64. You are called to evaluate a 78-year-old man (per his driver's license) found wandering by police, who was seen in the emergency department for "altered mental status." Staff suggest he appears "senile" and is probably in need of placement in a residential care setting. Upon meeting the patient, you screen him using the Folstein Mini-Mental State Exam (MMSE). He is indeed confused, disoriented, forgetful, and otherwise cognitively impaired. Medical staff note he has no emergent condition. He is not febrile (no fever) or septic (only slightly elevated white blood cell count), no respiratory distress (breathes easily), and no cardiac compromise (age-expected elevated blood pressure and heart rate, with normal cardiac sounds and ECG tracing). No family can be reached; no information about prescription medication is available. The BEST social work response in this situation is to:
    a. Record "probable dementia" and arrange out-of-home placement
    b. Arrange patient transportation back home with a home health referral
    c. Delay any response until family or other collateral contact can be made
    d. Advocate for the patient to be admitted for further medical evaluation

65. The most common cause of dementia is:
    a. Alzheimer disease
    b. Stroke
    c. Senility
    d. None of the above

66. As a chemical dependency counselor, you are counseling a 38-year-old married man regarding his ongoing use of alcohol. The client consumes alcohol on weekends and at parties, and tends to drink heavily about twice each month. At times, recovery from significant inebriation has resulted in his being unable to go to work on a Monday, and on one occasion he was given a DUI citation, resulting in this court-ordered counseling. The pattern of the client's alcohol use is best described as:
    a. Alcohol dependency (alcoholism)
    b. Alcohol abuse
    c. Recreational alcohol use
    d. Casual alcohol use

67. In a county psychiatric emergency clinic, you are asked to evaluate a 19-year-old woman for unspecified psychotic behavior. She is accompanied by her parents, who brought her to the clinic. Upon contact you note she is disheveled and unkempt in grooming and hygiene. In talking with you she often pauses inexplicably, rambles about something unrelated, laughs to herself, and then turns her face away. Episodically attending to you, she spontaneously claims that you are controlling her mind, and indicates that she sees odd objects floating around you. There is no recent history of substance abuse (though remotely positive for amphetamines), and her symptoms have been prominent for most of the past year, though particularly acute this evening when she attacked her mother claiming that she was a clone and trying to pull her "real mom" out of the clone's body. The most likely diagnosis for this presentation is:

    a. Bipolar disorder
    b. Schizoaffective disorder
    c. Schizophrenia
    d. Substance-induced psychosis

68. A 34-year-old man makes an appointment to see you for help coping with a difficult relationship in his life. At intake you learn that he feels a famous movie actress has hidden affection for him. He has written her many times through her fan club, and has received letters from club personnel—never from the actress herself. But, he explains, this is just because she's "not currently free to express her feelings openly" due to a waning relationship with a wealthy businessman. When talking about the businessman, there are clear feelings of competition. When asked for greater detail or information to buttress his beliefs he avoids the questions. The MOST appropriate early diagnostic impression would be Delusional Disorder, with the following subtype:

    a. Grandiose type
    b. Jealous type
    c. Persecutory type
    d. Erotomanic type

69. A call is received from a family member about an adult male loved one who is "behaving in an extremely bizarre way." Specifically, he is racing from home to home, claiming that he is being followed by some sort of assault team (SWAT) intent on arresting him. He claims that people are hiding in cars all around him, even going so far as to claim entire parking lots are filled with cars hiding his assailants. He insists on pulling drapes and hiding out in the home for his safety. No evidence corroborates his story. He does have a history of deployment in Middle East combat, as well as a history of substance abuse, though neither presents as proximal to this event. By the next morning he appears fine, and becomes angry if the incident is brought up, suggesting it is all an exaggeration by others. The MOST appropriate diagnostic impression would be:

    a. Posttraumatic stress disorder, acute episode
    b. Brief psychotic disorder
    c. Drug-induced psychosis
    d. Bipolar disorder, manic episode

70. You have been called to evaluate a 28-year-old female client described as "very depressed." Upon assessment you discover that she has been struggling with depression since her late teens. She also admits to periods when she's entirely free of depression, even to the extent of thinking the problem is solved. Further questioning reveals that her depressions are quite deep, though not entirely anhedonic or debilitating, nor are her "up" periods marked by extremes in mood, grandiosity, insomnia, etc. Even so, her up and down phases are significant enough to disrupt relationships, work, and school (e.g., feeling unable to get out of bed when down, and pressured speech and euphoria to the extent to make others uncomfortable). Given this presentation, the MOST appropriate diagnostic impression would be:
   a. Bipolar disorder
   b. Dysthymia
   c. Cyclothymia
   d. Mood disorder NOS

71. A 72-year-old widow comes to see you for help with feelings of bereavement. Her spouse died of a sudden heart attack just over a year ago. There was no prior history of a heart condition, so the loss came as a substantial shock and without forewarning. Since that time the client feels she has been unable to recover emotionally. She notes remaining intensely preoccupied with thinking about her husband, cries more days than not, feels estranged from others in many ways without him (e.g., other friends and couples seem distant), and describes her emotions as generally numb, when not overwhelming. Sometimes she yearns to die so that she can "be with him" again. There is no overt suicidality, but there is a feeling that life without him is meaningless in many ways. The MOST appropriate early diagnostic impression would be:
   a. Major depressive disorder
   b. Posttraumatic stress
   c. Uncomplicated bereavement
   d. Persistent complex bereavement disorder

72. The key difference between Bipolar I and Bipolar II is:
   a. Bipolar I involves mania and Bipolar II involves primarily depression
   b. Bipolar I involves primarily depression and Bipolar II involves mania
   c. Bipolar I involves hypomania and Bipolar II involves dysthymia
   d. None of the above

73. You have been called to evaluate a 23-year-old man in a hospital emergency room. He presented with fear that he was having a heart attack, but medical staff have ruled this out following laboratory and clinical testing. He notes that his symptoms have subsided, but that when he arrived his heart was pounding, he was tremulous, gasping for breath, and had significant tightness in his chest. He recognized the symptoms as being cardiac in nature, as his father died recently from a heart attack when similar symptoms were present. After lengthy discussion he revealed that the symptoms had been coming and going rapidly over the last month, and that he had actually been sleeping in his car outside the hospital for the last several days to ensure he could get help when needed. The symptoms struck and peaked quickly (within minutes), leaving him fearful that help would not be available if he didn't remain close. These symptoms MOST closely resemble:
    a. Anxiety disorder due to a medical condition
    b. Generalized anxiety disorder
    c. Acute stress disorder
    d. Panic disorder without agoraphobia

74. You are called to a medical clinic to evaluate a 56-year-old woman who presents with persistent fears of a new diagnosis of melanoma. She had a small skin lesion removed from her nose approximately 2 years ago, which had precancerous tissue changes upon evaluation by pathology. Since that time she has become intensely preoccupied with the status of her skin, and tends to check and recheck every blemish that occurs. Frequent visits to her dermatologist have not resulted in the identification of any new dermatological problems, and despite reassurances her worries continue unabated. The problem has grown to the point that she regularly asks her spouse to help her monitor her skin and examine her back to ensure no new problems. He has grown increasingly frustrated. She also refuses to go outdoors unless overly swathed to ward off any exposure to the sun. This has resulted in her increasingly avoiding the outdoors altogether. The MOST likely diagnosis for her presentation is:
    a. Malingering Disorder
    b. Factitious Disorder
    c. Illness Anxiety Disorder
    d. Somatic Symptom Disorder

75. A client is brought into a county mental health clinic by law enforcement. He has no personal identification, and cannot recall any personally identifying information. This forgetfulness appears to be genuine, not due to any threat or allegation of any kind. He does have receipts and other papers on his person that indicate he was recently many hundreds of miles away, but he cannot confirm or deny this. There is no history of head trauma, substance abuse, or prior mental illness that can be ascertained. The MOST appropriate initial working diagnosis would be:
    a. Dissociative Identity Disorder
    b. Dissociative Amnesia
    c. Dissociative Fugue
    d. None of the above

76. A newly married 23-year-old woman has been referred for counseling due to her experiences of painful intercourse. She was not sexually active prior to marriage, and so there is no history to draw upon for past experiences. The problem is painful penetration, not involving spasms of the vagina but characterized by marked vaginal dryness. The proper term for her condition is:

    a. Sexual Aversion Disorder

    b. Dyspareunia

    c. Vaginismus

    d. Female Orgasmic Disorder

77. A 26-year-old woman is seeing you regarding her persistent desire to leave her bedroom window blinds open so that she might be seen disrobing by her male neighbor, who participates voyeuristically in an open way. She is aware that the activity is fraught with problems—he is a married man, and potentially other passersby might see in her window from the street. To this point, however, she finds these risks somewhat exciting and stimulating. She also finds herself compulsively thinking about the activity and planning ways to be "caught" by the man in compromising moments. Diagnostically, her behavior is best described as:

    a. Frotteurism

    b. Voyeurism

    c. Exhibitionism

    d. Other specified paraphilia

78. A sleep specialist has referred a 46-year-old male client to you for counseling around lifestyle changes that may help him with his sleep problem. The problem is characterized by sudden, overwhelming sleep episodes that have occurred daily for the better part of a year. The episodes are refreshing, and include components of REM sleep and cataplexy (muscle tone relaxation). As they are unpredictable, they are causing significant problems at his job. The MOST appropriate working diagnosis for this condition would be:

    a. Narcolepsy

    b. Primary insomnia

    c. Primary hypersomnia

    d. Circadian sleep disorder

79. You have been seeing a 26-year-old female client for about 6 months. She originally came to see you about distress over a recent romantic relationship breakup. Over time you have learned that she tends to have serial relationships of short duration, which inevitably end badly. A common theme in the relationships is a pattern of over-idealizing, rejecting, and then clinging and trying to avoid perceived abandonment. Her mood is often labile, and she frequently follows a similar pattern in the counseling relationship: praising you effusively and then later accusing you of neglect, professional incompetence, and bias, etc. You have learned that she had poor childhood attachment with her parents, with a substantial history of physical abuse by them both. It now appears that the early primary diagnosis of adjustment disorder would now be coupled with:

    a. Histrionic Personality Disorder

    b. Narcissistic Personality Disorder

    c. Borderline Personality Disorder

    d. Antisocial Personality Disorder

80. Face-to-face work with clients is often described as:
    a. Direct practice
    b. Clinical practice
    c. Micro practice
    d. All of the above

81. The theoretical perspective that all relationships are interconnected, and that change in any one relational area will produce change in other relational areas is BEST described as:
    a. Conflict theory
    b. Systems theory
    c. Freudian Theory
    d. Individual Theory

82. A crisis is an event that threatens or upends a state of equilibrium in ways that breach the coping capacity of the participants involved—usually a threat or obstacle to important relationships or goals. All of the following are major types of crises that may need to be addressed EXCEPT:
    a. Cultural/Societal
    b. Transitional
    c. Maturational
    d. Situational

83. Roberts (1991) has proposed a widely used Crisis Intervention Model including:
    a. 3 stages
    b. 5 stages
    c. 7 stages
    d. 9 stages

84. The *Premack Principle* refers to:
    a. A guideline for crisis intervention
    b. A tool for managing intra-family conflicts
    c. A process for improving client rapport
    d. A method for increasing desired behaviors

85. A contingency contract is used in behavior modification to:
    a. Ensure a specific response for a specific behavior
    b. Provide a reward for specific behavior
    c. Provide a punishment for a specific behavior
    d. All of the above.

86. There is strong empirical evidence that the therapeutic approach and treatment of choice for depression should be:
    a. Cognitive-behavioral therapy
    b. Reality therapy
    c. Behavior modification
    d. Critical Incident Stress Management

87. A client comes to see you, citing problems with choosing a career. Working collaboratively you assist in clarifying the problem and identifying outcome goals, with specific steps to engage and achieve the goals and concluded by feedback and evaluation of client progress. From this process it is clear that the model of intervention being used is BEST described as:
   a. Dialectical Behavioral Therapy
   b. Reality Therapy
   c. Solution-Focused Therapy
   d. None of the above

88. The Neo-Freudian psychotherapist that differed from Freud's views primarily on the root origins of anxiety was:
   a. Erich Fromm
   b. Karen Horney
   c. Harry Stack Sullivan
   d. None of the above

89. A 32-year-old male veteran has come to see you over troubling dreams that have persisted long after his return to the United States. The dreams involve reliving combat experiences in which he sees the deaths of important colleagues. Together, you work to relieve and psychologically reconcile these events, allowing the client to discharge the pent-up emotions associated with them. This psychotherapeutic approach is known as:
   a. Reorientation
   b. Catharsis
   c. Purging
   d. Abreaction

90. The term introjection is used differently between psychoanalysis and Gestalt therapy. Specifically, in Gestalt therapy the term refers to:
   a. Failing to produce a boundary that defines a unique sense of self
   b. Modeling oneself after relationally important caregiving adults
   c. Living into the labels that others place on us
   d. Gradually defining oneself, by rejection or integration of outside ideas

91. You have been asked to facilitate an ongoing group experience for young married couples. The goals are relationship enrichment, with a particular focus on marital success after the birth of their children and in the press of career development. The group meets weekly, with no set termination date. This group is best described as:
   a. An open-ended socialization group
   b. An ongoing support group
   c. An open educational group
   d. An ongoing growth group

92. Types of transference common to group work include all of the following EXCEPT:
   a. Transference to quiet members (self-figures)
   b. Transference to the social worker (parental figure)
   c. Transference to individual members (sibling figures)
   d. Transference to the group entity (mother-womb symbol)

93. In seeing a couple with significant conflict issues, a number of hot-point issues begin to emerge. In avoiding taking sides, you are seeking to prevent:
    a. Coaching
    b. Triangulation
    c. Identity fusion
    d. Emotional cutoff

94. In Communications/Experimental Therapy, the idea that the same results can be secured in different ways is referred to as:
    a. Circular Causality
    b. Relational Symmetry
    c. Equifinality
    d. Complementary Conclusion

95. All of the following communication styles are dysfunctional EXCEPT:
    a. Super-reasonable
    b. Irrelevant distractor
    c. Congruent communicator
    d. Placater-pleaser

96. A couple in their 40s have come in to manage conflict issues in their marriage and family. In particular, neither can agree on basic roles as a couple. Both work outside the home; both tend to retain their income independently; each feels the other should be paying a greater portion of the bills; neither wants to be responsible for cooking, shopping, or housecleaning. According to Salvador Minuchin's Structural Family Theory, the couple is struggling with:
    a. Complementarity
    b. Alignments
    c. Power hierarchies
    d. Disengagement

97. A 16-year-old boy is acting out in ways that are regularly disruptive of the family's home life and social relationships. It soon becomes clear to the social worker that he feels misunderstood, unappreciated, and isolated from much of the family. To encounter this, the social worker asks each of the other family members, "Why do you think he is behaving in these ways?" This is an example of Mara Selvini Palazzoli's Milan Systemic Therapy known as:
    a. Hypothesizing
    b. Counter-paradox
    c. Positive connotation
    d. Circular questioning

98. In community organizing, the fundamental client is:
    a. Individual community members
    b. Institutional community members
    c. The community itself
    d. Informal community organizations

99. A community member approaches a social worker/community organizer and reveals that a Latino factory owner has been hiring illegal immigrants and then denying them basic breaks and overtime benefits while threatening them with reporting and deportation. In seeking change, the FIRST step the citizen is encouraged to take is as a:
    a. Negotiator
    b. Whistleblower
    c. Litigant
    d. Protestor

100. In pursuing change for individuals or a community, potential social work roles include of the following EXCEPT:
    a. Client advocate
    b. Legal advisor
    c. Mediator
    d. Broker

101. Given that social workers are generally trained to work with voluntary clients (e.g., those who come seeking help), it can be difficult to work with involuntary (e.g., court or employment ordered) clients. Common mechanisms of resistance by involuntary clients include all of the following EXCEPT:
    a. Aggression
    b. Diversion
    c. Humor
    d. Withdrawal

102. The primary objective of supervision is:
    a. Keeping the agency running
    b. Meeting the clients' individual needs
    c. Developing the supervisee's skills
    d. Making sure that work is completed

103. The purpose of clinical/professional consultation in an agency is to:
    a. Share expertise
    b. Obtain alternate leadership
    c. Receive direction
    d. Defer to an expert

104. The concept of productive conflict management is drawn from which of the following types of management theories?
    a. Bureaucratic
    b. Administrative
    c. Participative
    d. Structuralist

105. A method of program evaluation that examines the extent to which goals are achieved and how well the outcomes can be generalized to other settings and populations is known as:
   a. Cost-Benefit Analysis
   b. Formative Program Evaluation
   c. Summative Program Evaluation
   d. Peer Review

106. The purpose of the Americans with Disabilities Act of 1990 was to:
   a. Prevent discrimination based upon disability in employment
   b. Ensure access to public services, including transportation
   c. Include telecommunication options for the disabled
   d. All of the above.

107. Each state's Division of Child and Family Services (DCFS) commonly provides all of the following services EXCEPT:
   a. Child Protective Services
   b. Domestic Violence Shelters
   c. Employment training
   d. Education referrals

108. At a transitional family shelter, a newly arrived mother and her three children are being reviewed during an interdisciplinary team consultation. The team consists of the social worker, a housing specialist, and an education and employment specialist. The mother lost her job in another city and was attempting to find work in your larger city. They were living in her car when it was burgled of all possessions. All seem unwell and congested. The oldest child, a 4-year-old boy, has severe asthma and needs a sheltered setting. The 3-year-old girl seems expressively vacant and emotionally detached. The 9-month-old female infant is clearly hungry and lacks diapers and other basic necessities. Food is being obtained for them all. Prior to presenting to the agency director, the FIRST social work step should be to:
   a. Complete a psychosocial assessment for mental health issues
   b. Inquire about the availability of extended family support
   c. Obtain clean, warmer clothing from a local clothes closet
   d. Promptly refer the asthmatic boy to a medical doctor

109. The case recording/progress record acronym SOAP stands for:
   a. Subjective, Overview, Analysis, Prognosis
   b. Subjective, Observation, Acuity, Proposal
   c. Subjective, Objective, Assessment, Plan
   d. Subjective, Orientation, Acceptance, Posits

110. Social work Case Management is BEST defined as follows:
   a. The process of assembling relevant information to meet clients' needs
   b. The coordination of services in harmony with clients' goals and desires
   c. The evaluation and monitoring of services to meet clients' needs
   d. All of the above

111. The National Association of Social Workers (NASW) sets the following number of standards for the practice of Social Work Case Management:
    a. 10 standards
    b. 12 standards
    c. 14 standards
    d. 16 standards

112. Another term for Explanatory Research is:
    a. Formulative Research
    b. Causal Comparative Research
    c. Experimental Research
    d. Correlational Research

113. Social work ethics may best be defined as:
    a. Standards of nonmaleficence
    b. Key professional values
    c. Conduct standards based on values
    d. Standards of beneficence

114. The ethical concept of Self-Determination refers to:
    a. The right to do anything one wants to do
    b. The right to require others to help one achieve goals
    c. The right to make choices dangerous to others
    d. The right to personal autonomy and decision making

115. All of the following relate to the concept of confidentiality EXCEPT:
    a. The lack of signage on a substance abuse treatment facility
    b. Installing password protections on clinical computers
    c. Sharing client information only with written permission
    d. Guarding against discussing a client in a public place

116. In treating a client, you discover that she had been sexually involved with her last licensed social work therapist. Further questioning revealed that the therapeutic relationship was terminated specifically to allow a relationship, and that sexual contact did not occur until a full year had elapsed after the termination. The client seems fine with how things were handled, and cites her right to confidentiality in an effort to ensure you will not report the issue, even adding that she would deny the information if asked. Your BEST response to the information would be to:
    a. Ignore it as they are consenting adults, she's no longer his client, and the client has cited confidentiality and intent to deny it
    b. Double-check state laws to see how much time must elapse after termination of a client status before a relationship is possible
    c. Consult with your supervisor or legal counsel to ensure a proper response to the situation
    d. Note the NASW ban on all relationships with clients, current and former, and report, but keep the client's name confidential

117. A client approaches his social work therapist and asks to see his case files. However, the therapist is concerned that exposure to some sensitive parts of the case record would be harmful to the client. Therefore, the MOST appropriate response to this request would be to:

a. Refuse, as the case records are the property of the therapist or the agency
b. Refuse, as the case records are the property of the agency
c. Allow the review, but with assistance to understand sensitive notes
d. Allow only a partial review, withholding portions deemed too sensitive

118. During a couple's therapy session they approach you about their 3-year-old daughter's intensely frightening dreams at night. At first it sounds like they are discussing nightmares, but then you recognize the symptoms as *sleep terrors* (also known as *night terrors* or *pavor nocturnus*). They ask you for advice on how to manage the symptoms. You are a fully licensed therapist, but with no significant pediatric sleep disorder experience. The BEST response would be to:

a. Refer the child to a counselor with experience in pediatric sleep disorders
b. Tell the family you will get back with them once you've done some research
c. Complete a quick Internet search and offer a printout of reputable material
d. Set up an appointment to see the child, and consult a colleague on the issue

119. At the conclusion of a presentation on safe sex practices with teens, a social worker takes the remaining materials back to the main office for storage. Another coworker passes by while she's talking with the office secretary, and she playfully tosses a condom his way saying, "Here's a little something for you." He catches it, laughs, and continues on by. This action would BEST be characterized as:

a. A playful gesture with no untoward meaning or intent.
b. A gesture potentially constituting sexual harassment
c. A failure of appropriate respect between colleagues
d. All of the above

120. A client has a concern that warrants consultation. A consulting therapist has expertise in the required area. The BEST way to secure the consult is to:

a. Share the problem and leave the file with the coworker for review
b. Ask the coworker to review the file, especially recent notes, and offer direction
c. Set up a formal consultation appointment to discuss the issue(s) in the office
d. Discuss the concern with the coworker in the cafeteria over lunch

121. A social worker becomes aware that her colleague has a substance abuse problem. It has become increasingly severe over time, to the extent that the colleague occasionally shows up after lunch breaks clearly compromised and under the influence. The FIRST responsibility of the social worker in this situation is to:

a. Contact a supervisor and report the problem internally
b. Contact the licensing board and report the problem
c. Contact the colleague and discuss treatment options
d. Contact local law enforcement to have them intervene

122. A social worker discovers that his agency is not following the NASW Code of Ethics as related to secure recordkeeping. In particular, file cabinets are not kept locked, laptop computers used in the field are not password protected, and local university students are regularly permitted to sit in on group therapy sessions without the agreement of group participants and without securing commitments of confidentiality from them. The BEST social work response would be to:
    a. Tender a resignation rather than work outside the NASW's standards
    b. Seek to bring the agency's policies and procedures into compliance
    c. Refuse to work with those resources and conditions outside compliance
    d. None of the above.

123. A licensed clinical social worker possesses a master's degree in social work (MSW) as well as a PhD in history from an accredited university. In professional practice, he could properly refer to himself as all of the following EXCEPT:
    a. A therapist or clinician
    b. A master's level social worker
    c. A doctor with a doctoral degree
    d. A licensed clinical social worker

124. In conducting social work research, the concept of *informed consent* refers to:
    a. Possessing of a meaningful understanding of relevant information
    b. Knowledge of both the risks and the benefits of participation in a study
    c. Information that a reasonable person would want to make decisions
    d. All of the above

125. The presence of a strong therapeutic relationship is fundamental to making positive life changes. Among the most important features of a meaningful therapeutic bond is:
    a. Compassion
    b. Empathy
    c. Sympathy
    d. Condolence

126. In a conversation with a case manager she describes some of her caseload as consisting of "numerous schizophrenics, several bipolars, and some borderlines," after which she proceeds to discuss some of the unique challenges the caseload presents. A primary problem with describing a caseload in this way is that it:
    a. Depersonalizes the clients
    b. Stereotypes the clients
    c. Diminishes the clients
    d. All of the above

127. In situations of long-term case management, clients should be encouraged to openly share their emotions and feelings. All of the following are benefits to this sharing EXCEPT:
    a. Allowing judgment of how acceptable or not the feelings are
    b. Reducing the emotional burdens the client feels
    c. Offering insights into the client's emotional state and coping.
    d. Helping the client and worker to see problems more clearly

128. A social worker is a case manager for a 26-year-old man with a diagnosis of paranoid schizophrenia. In seeking to allow him to ventilate feelings, the client taps into a reservoir of anger about the board and care facility where he resides, and about the operator and his co-residents. His emotions begin to escalate quickly, and a marked sense of lability is present. The BEST response is to:
    a. Confront him about his anger and label it as inappropriate
    b. Join him in expressing anger and frustration about his situation
    c. Evaluate him for homicidality and the possible need for intervention
    d. Seek to understand his feelings while soothing/deescalating them

129. When offering a client short-term and/or very narrow services, the best way to handle client's expression of feelings is to:
    a. Encourage the deep expression of feelings
    b. Limit the expression of intense or deep feelings
    c. Refuse to communicate about feelings in any way
    d. None of the above

130. Appropriate and professional social work responses to a client's expression of feelings include all of the following EXCEPT:
    a. Offering analysis and critique
    b. Offering sensitivity and receptivity
    c. Offering understanding and empathy
    d. Offering a meaningful response

131. There are circumstances in which clients reveal a significant role in producing the situation they find themselves in (e.g., addiction, criminal behavior, violence). In such circumstances the FIRST role of the social worker is to:
    a. Point out important societal standards and expectations
    b. Cite relevant legal and moral standards and expectations
    c. Ensure a nonjudgmental attitude, regardless of the client's past
    d. Discuss the consequences of choices and the need for change

132. A social worker is contracted to work in a probation-sponsored drug rehabilitation setting with court-mandated clients. The program has an information release form that specifies the release of "any relevant information" to "any interested party" for "any requested purpose" without termination date. Staff explain that, given the clientele, information must at times be released to legal authorities or others on an urgent basis, making this broad form necessary. The safety of the public or others could be at stake. The proper social work response would be to:
    a. Use the form as directed, given the circumstances
    b. Use the form, but note concerns with administration
    c. Meet with administration to address the use of the form
    d. Refuse to use the form on grounds that it is unethical

133. Exceptions to Confidentiality and Release of Information requirements include all of the following EXCEPT:
    a. In situations of actively expressed suicidal ideation
    b. When a law enforcement official formally requests information
    c. Where a client leads a therapist to suspect harm to others
    d. Where a client discloses abuse to a minor or dependent adult

134. Confidentiality is BEST managed in group counseling sessions by:
   a. Telling participants that confidentiality cannot be assured
   b. Committing group members to keep confidentiality
   c. Having group members sign confidentiality agreements
   d. All of the above

135. A social worker at a community counseling agency receives a subpoena to testify in court about one of her clients. The information outlined in the subpoena includes information that could easily be psychologically damaging to her client. The BEST response to this subpoena would be to:
   a. Comply with the subpoena, as no other options exist
   b. Refuse to testify, even if contempt of court charges could result
   c. Request the court withdraw the order, or limit its scope
   d. None of the above

136. In situations of the death of either the client or the therapist, confidentiality agreements:
   a. Remain in full force and effect
   b. Become null and void
   c. Pass on to family members and/or the holder of the client's records
   d. Remain in effect for the client, but not for but not the therapist's records

137. In working with a client, you discover him to be manipulative, confrontational, at times deceptive, and otherwise very difficult to work with. Over time you find it increasingly difficult to work with him, and find yourself struggling to contain anger and even expressions of contempt. Concerned that you may not be able to maintain therapeutic clarity and requisite positive regard to support the change process, your FIRST step should be to:
   a. Refer him to another therapist
   b. Share your feelings with the client
   c. Seek supervision and/or consultation
   d. Ignore the problem, as it may improve

138. A social worker is providing counseling services to a Southeast Asian family. After several sessions, the family presents her with a gift of a carefully crafted piece of folk art that they produced themselves. Although the materials involved are of little value, the overall value of the handcrafted item is unclear. In this situation, the social worker should FIRST:
   a. Explore the meaning of the gift with the family
   b. Accept the gift graciously, but cite ethical standards for the future
   c. Reluctantly accept the gift, expressing ethical uncertainty
   d. Decline the gift while citing ethical standards as the reason

139. A social worker provides services to an auto mechanic. At one point the social worker required auto repair work, and the client offered to perform the work in lieu of direct payment for services. The BEST response to this would be to:
    a. Accept the request, as it offers mutual advantages
    b. Accept the offer, but set clear boundaries
    c. Decline the offer, suggesting the need for boundaries
    d. Decline the offer, citing professional ethics

140. A social worker bumps unexpectedly into an old client at a civic event in a large town. Both are surprised to see each other. In this situation it would be BEST for the social worker to:
    a. Take any cue the client offers as to how to respond
    b. Smile and quietly and discretely nod a greeting
    c. Smile and openly voice a greeting in passing
    d. Warmly greet the client, walking up to shake hands

141. A hospice social worker has had an extended relationship with a terminally ill client and his family. After the client's death, the family extends an invitation to attend the funeral and a family-only luncheon following the service. In this situation the BEST response by the social worker would be to:
    a. Decline to attend either the funeral or the luncheon
    b. Decline the funeral invitation, but attend the luncheon
    c. Attend the funeral, but decline the luncheon invitation
    d. Attend both the funeral and the luncheon as invited

142. In social work communication, a term that refers to restatements of a client's message in one's own words is known as:
    a. Furthering Response
    b. Seeking Consensus
    c. Summarizing
    d. Paraphrasing

143. Social work communication is facilitated through meaningful client questioning. Questions that possess the underlying goal of securing client agreement are known as:
    a. Leading Questions
    b. Stacked Questions
    c. Open-ended Questions
    d. Close-ended Questions

144. A social worker is seeing a client under mandatory court orders following conviction for a protracted period of sexual offenses with a minor. In the dialogue process, the client repeatedly refers to her offenses as "a mistake I made" and "when that happened," as well as, "he said he wanted it" and "he kept coming back for more," even after repeatedly being redirected. Recognizing that planned behavior does not just "happen mistakenly" and that a minor can never consent to such behavior, the MOST appropriate therapeutic response would be:
    a. Empathic Responding
    b. Reflective Listening
    c. Confrontation
    d. None of the above

145. The concept of *transference* is BEST defined as:
   a. An effort to shift blame for one's own wrongdoing from oneself to another individual
   b. An emotional reaction toward another, drawn from prior experiences with someone else
   c. The awareness of how an individual's appearance, mannerisms, language, or behaviors is a reminder of someone difficult from one's past
   d. A therapist's feeling about a client based upon prior experiences from the therapist's own background

146. A social worker receives a subpoena ordering him to testify in court and to reveal his case notes about his client. The social worker refuses, and bases his right to refuse upon the state's statutes regarding:
   a. Privacy
   b. Confidentiality
   c. Informed consent
   d. Privileged communication

147. There are two forms of counseling records that can be kept by a therapist. They are generally referred to by three different titles (two common titles for one, and one for the other). All of the following titles may be used EXCEPT:
   a. The primary client record
   b. The clinical/medical record
   c. Journal notes
   d. Psychotherapy notes

148. A client has annual major depression events briefly accompanied by psychotic features. This has resulted in a misdiagnosis of bipolar disorder with psychotic features. The case manager notes that decompensation always occurs in the same month (the anniversary date of the death of her children in a car she was driving), and eventually discovers the misdiagnosis. In attempting to correct the problem, she is coached to leave it unchanged as the client's insurance will not cover the agency's services for a major depression diagnosis. The BEST social work response to this dilemma is to:
   a. Leave the diagnosis unchanged, as it was made by a psychiatrist
   b. Leave the diagnosis unchanged to preserve client services
   c. Seek supervision and/or consultation to explore the issue further
   d. Change the diagnosis to properly reflect the client's condition

149. A social worker has been working with a client for 18 months and the client's problem has been fully addressed and resolved. An appropriate process of termination has been concluded and all services have been discontinued. The state has no prevailing statute for a period of retention for social work records. The client's record should now NEXT be:
   a. Destroyed
   b. Thinned and only essential information retained
   c. Kept intact for another 3 years
   d. Retained in accordance with state medical record statutes

150. A social worker in a genetics clinic is employed to help families given difficult news about their own genetic makeup, or that of their children or unborn children. Part of the counseling process involves the discussion of abortion for fetuses that might otherwise be born with a variety of impairments, ranging from relatively mild to severe. The social worker at times feels distressed by offering the option of abortion in cases of only mild fetal defects. Her BEST response in such situations would be to:

a. Help the family explore their feelings about the defects, their family circumstances, and the meaning of available options

b. Present all options to the family in a dispassionate and officious manner

c. Discuss the sanctity of life and how essential it is to preserve it

d. Help the family understand how manageable it would be to raise a child with only mild defects

Answers and Explanations

1. D: Concrete operational thought. The client is demonstrating a very "concrete" and tangible-focused interpretation of the concept presented. Other key features of concrete operations include decentration (moving from an egocentric perspective to a view centered within a larger world view), reversibility, and manipulation of the steps of a process to achieve determined ends. Sensorimotor interpretation refers to the limited use of physical senses and movement to evaluate the world. Preoperational thought allows for the use of objects in representation (a stick as a sword, etc.), without the ability to logically reason or interpret with insight. Formal operations reflect the ability to reason through hypothetical and abstract concepts. Jean Piaget proposed four stages of cognitive development, noting specifically that some people do not develop past the concrete operational stage even in adulthood. Whether this client has regressed from formal operational thinking to concrete operational thinking, as a symptom of dementia, can be assessed by obtaining a history of his prior cognitive functioning. If so, such regression could represent an early symptom of cognitive impairment.

2. B: William James (1875) researched the function of consciousness as opposed to structure. Other early theorists, in order of theory construction, include the following: Wilhelm Wundt (1873): Structuralism (term coined by his student, Edward Titchener: examining the structure, not the function, of the conscious mind; Wundt is considered the "father of Experimental Psychology"); Sigmund Freud (1900) – Psychoanalytic Theory of Personality; Alfred Adler (1917) – Individual Psychology (birth order, personality development, self-image, etc.); John B. Watson (1920) – Behaviorism (conducted the "Little Albert" experiment, and focused on observable behavior as opposed to mental or emotional states); Ivan Pavlov (1927) – Classical or Respondent Conditioning (experimenting with dogs); Jean Piaget (1928) – Cognitive Development (producing a four-stage developmental model); Lev Vygotsky (1934) – Child Development and Social Development Theory (focused on language in learning processes); Kurt Lewin (1935) – Social Psychology (as well as applied psychology and organizational management); and Anna Freud (1936) – Ego Defense Mechanisms.

3. A: Lawrence Kohlberg (1958) researched the moral reasoning development and produced a six-stage moral judgment model. Other later theorists who focused on human development and behavior include Abraham Maslow (1943) – Hierarchy of Needs (producing a pyramid model of human needs, founded on those most basic and progressing to higher-order needs); Rene Spits (1945) – Ego Development (focused on maternal-child relationships, and identified a form of "hospitalism" called "anaclitic depression"); Erik Erikson (1950) – Ego Psychology (produced a psychosocial developmental model encompassing birth to death); Margaret Mahler (1950) – Separation-Individuation (studied maternal-infant interaction, and created a model of developmental stages from birth through 4 years); B.F. Skinner (1953) – Operant Conditioning (modifying behavior through consequences); John Bowlby and Mary Ainsworth (1969) – Attachment Theory (the psychological impact of losing important attachment figures—typically the mother); Elisabeth Kübler-Ross (1969) – Death and Dying (identified five grief stages when confronting death); Carol Gilligan (1982) – Feminist Social Psychology (studied gender

differences); and, James Karl and Karen Wandrei (1990s) – Person in Environment System (PIE) Theory.

4. A: James felt cognitive processing precedes emotions, while Wundt felt that emotions emerge prior to cognitive understanding. Wilhelm Wundt, *the father of experimental psychology*, posited a *structural* view of human consciousness. He focused on exploring the basic structures of the mind, and the subsequent elements of feeling and sensation that constitute consciousness. From this structural perspective, his research experiments in Liepzig, Germany, utilized a technique called *Introspection*, wherein research subjects were provided an experience and then asked to report their feelings and emotional responses. He did not foresee subconscious or unconscious elements in the mind, and thus his experiments were centered on exploration of the conscious mind. William James, *the American father of experimental psychology*, believed that the *functions* of consciousness were more significant and adaptive than the involved *structures*. Consequently, his work at Harvard University focused on how thoughts and behaviors (mental states) serve a functional role in individual adaptation to the environment.

5. D: Preconscious thoughts can be brought to awareness relatively easily, while unconscious thoughts are much more difficult to bring to awareness. Both forms of thought, feeling and ideas, however, actively influence emotions and behaviors and thus must be accounted for in exploring human thinking and behavioral dynamics. Distressing ideas and experiences (ie, that produce negative feelings and/or responses from others) may be *repressed* and pushed out of the conscious mind into the unconscious realm. Repressed experiences, thoughts, and ideas can exert considerable influence on human behavior. Substantial levels of distress from repression can produce psychological or even physiological dysfunction (e.g., emotional and somatic complaints). Treatment focuses on delving into and bringing repressed thoughts and ideas back to awareness, tracing the associated symptoms, and re-living the troubling experiences and situations in such a way as to produce constructive resolution. Freud's *Psychoanalytic Theory of Personality* addressed: structure of personality, psychosexual stages of child development, and levels of consciousness. Treatment techniques include *free association* and *dream analysis*.

6. C: The driving force is the Id, and the most effective intervention would be to cite the negative consequences of the behavior (arrest, punishment, etc.). Freud postulated three personality structures: 1) the *Id* (pleasure-seeking without regard to others needs or wants); 2) the *Ego* (reality-based, seeking needs in socially appropriate ways); and, 3) the *Superego* (morality based and conscience-driven, replacing the role of parents). This client is still living through the Id, and thus will respond most immediately to the threat or imposition of consequences. While most immediately effective, this has poor long-term influence. Next steps will involve teaching prosocial rules through logical cause-and-effect analysis and understanding (Ego development), ultimately followed by Superego development (teaching empathy and insight into the needs of others, the role of community solidarity and collective contributions to the shared social good, etc.). The Superego includes: a) the *conscience* (the "should nots" of behaviors) and b) the *ego ideal* (the "shoulds" that lead to rewards such as personal esteem and self-dignity and pride). *Life instinct* (Eros) refers to energy (libido) driving basic survival, pleasure, and reproductive needs.

7. D: Oral Stage. Freud suggested that fixation in the oral stage (the first year) might emerge in cases of infant neglect (inadequate feeding) or overprotection (excessive feeding). The

- 135 -

mother's breast (or a substitute) becomes an early object of cathexis (emotional attachment). Thus, a neglected child may become a manipulative adult, seeking to compensate for the neglect, and an overprotected child may regress to untoward dependence upon others. In theory, oral-stage fixations become evident in various oral stimulus needs (eating, chewing on things, garrulousness, alcoholism, smoking, etc.). The Anal Stage (2-3 years of age) is not relevant, as it manifests in preoccupation with bowel and bladder functions. The Phallic Stage (3-6 years of age) involves genital discovery and pleasure, as well as mastery of Oedipal or Electra Complexes, which are unrelated to this situation. The Latency Period (6-11 years of age) is not relevant as it focuses on work and play with same-sex friends, with fixation here resulting in later untoward discomfort with opposite-sex relationships. Finally, the Genital Stage (age 12 to adulthood) would not apply as it occurs with puberty, and a return to opposite sex interests.

8. C: *Birth order* and *guiding fiction*. While opposites may attract, mismatching can be complicated. Adler characterized the youngest as potentially dependent and spoiled, and potentially willing to manipulate others into caregiving and support. An oldest, by contrast, tends to be focused on responsibility and control. Both are evident in their conflicts. Further, the spouse's need for a superordinate work position suggests Adler's *guiding fiction* (an internally created self-image, never fully congruent with reality) is dysfunctionally present, where childhood feelings of inferiority compel him to find success beyond immediate experience or capacity and to shun any perceived menial work. *Needs hierarchy* is not Adlerian, as it was developed by Maslow, nor is it applicable here. Ego and superego are not relevant, as Adler did not accept these Freudian constructs. Inferiority and superiority issues are evident, but these concepts do not provide an optimal paradigm from which to pursue treatment.

9. D: John B. Watson. An American psychologist, Watson developed the concept of *Behaviorism*, which consisted of an objective method of analyzing the cause and effect of identified behaviors. In exploring behavior, he conducted the "Little Albert" experiment in which a child was taught to fear a white rabbit—not because of anything the rabbit did, but because of overprotective parental anxiety and chastisement. The initial target of Little Albert's fear was a white rat, but it was readily generalized to a white rabbit. In like manner, this child's fear of going outdoors and certain home situations gradually expanded to a great many other social situations. Both Skinner and Pavlov were behavioral theorists, but both also focused primarily on direct stimulus-response conditioning (action-consequence links), as opposed to the expanded generalized conditioning that was the focus of Watson's Behaviorism. Jean Piaget studied cognitive development as opposed to behavioral conditioning. Thus, Piaget could better describe the cognitive threshold required for such complex associations to be made, as opposed to the behavioral conditioning that could produce it.

10. D: A conditioned response. The word "Pavlovian" refers to the theoretical work of Ivan Pavlov. An unconditioned stimulus is one that evokes an innate unconditioned response (ie, a startle reflex at a loud noise). A conditioned stimulus is one that produces a learned response, because it has been paired with an unconditioned stimulus in the past (e.g., a rush of elation when your football team scores a touchdown—two experiences that would have no real meaning or response until they were paired and learned). The classic example is that of Ivan Pavlov's research with dogs. Presented with meat powder, the dogs would salivate. Eventually, a bell was added at the point of presentation of the meat powder. Ultimately the dogs would salivate at the sound of the bell alone, without any meat powder.

Thus, an unconditioned stimulus and response, when paired with another stimulus, eventually became a learned stimulus with a learned response.

11. B: Interactive scaffolding. The human development theorist Lev Vygotsky focused his research primarily on child development, and introduced a concept later known as *scaffolding*. His original concept, called the *Zone of Proximal Development* (ZPD), explains how a child functions at a lower limit if all help is withheld, and moves to a higher level with skilled assistance. *Scaffolding* is an extension of ZPD. It refers to a teaching pattern where an adult provides more intensive assistance to a child at the outset of learning a difficult task, and then tapers back as greater skill is acquired. A professional driving instructor uses a teaching vehicle with two steering wheels and two brake pedals, which allows for a measured transition between teaching and allowing the new driver to gradually assume full control. Scaffolding is not possible in a vehicle lacking these tools. Behavior modification may be helpful in extinguishing a persistent bad driving habit, but not in optimizing initial training. Defense mechanisms may explain the daughter's inability to learn from dad, but not the path to learning. Anaclitic depression is a concept from attachment theory with no bearing on this situation.

12. A: The *behavioral equation*. A German and American social psychologist, Lewin produced a heuristic formula by which to explain social behavior: $B=f(P, E)$, where B=behavior, P=person, and E=environment, illustrating how behavior is a function (f) of a person and his environment. Prior to this, efforts to explain individual behavior were largely limited to exploration of a person's past. Thus, the influence of peer pressure is best explained by exploration of a person's traits, past, immediate goals, and the social environment in which a behavior occurs. *Force field analysis*, which identifies both helping and blocking forces as related to a goal, is too limited a perspective for the concept of peer pressure. Lewin's concept of *sensitivity training* may help moderate peer pressure, but it fails to explain it. Finally, Lewin's work on *leadership climates* (authoritarian, democratic, and laissez-faire) also has only limited bearing when attempting to explain peer pressure and group dynamics.

13. C: Intellectualization. Specifically, *intellectualization* occurs when an individual attempts to use logic and reasoning to avoid facing difficult feelings. As with many other defense mechanisms, this coping effort is not necessarily problematic as it may offer the spouse a place of refuge until he is psychologically ready to encounter the devastating feelings that it is covering. Thus, this need should be recognized and accommodated unless it becomes unduly protracted and/or exclusive of gradual exploration of the underlying emotional concerns. *Projection* addresses the denial of one's own negative characteristics while attributing them to someone else (e.g., "I'm not a racist! You should see what my mom says about foreigners!"). *Compensation* refers to success seeking in one life area to substitute for barriers in another that cannot or have not been overcome. Rationalization involves hiding ones actual motivations under an appeal to more socially acceptable reasoning and logic (e.g., saying "I can't make the trip because the kids are sick," instead of admitting you don't enjoy the people or activity).

14. B: Fixation. The defense mechanism known as *fixation* refers to arrested personality development at a stage short of normative maturation. This client clearly identifies with individuals and activities that fall short of her age and maturity level. While enjoying youthful associations is not in itself problematic, seeking to live in those associations to the exclusion of normal relationships and activities is problematic. Identifying, addressing, and

overcoming the reasons behind this will likely be a major therapeutic endeavor. *Avoidance* is characterized by a refusal to become involved with objects, situations, and/or activities that are related to underlying impulses to avoid potential punishment (e.g., staying away from casinos to cope with a predilection for gambling instead of discovering and overcoming the underlying reasons for the compulsion). *Devaluation* involves the attribution of negative qualities to oneself or others to cope with stress or internal emotional conflicts (e.g., coping with being fired from a job by speaking negatively of the job and work colleagues). *Affiliation* involves seeking emotional support and advice from others instead of "going it alone," yet without trying to make others responsible to step in and fix the problem.

15. C: Permit some discussion on feelings of loss, but keep the focus on his immediate housing, transportation, and employment needs. Abraham Maslow's Needs Hierarchy posits that more essential and basic physiological needs must be met before higher order needs. Thus, needs regarding food, clothing, and shelter are more important than needs for safety (security, protection, predictability, and structure), belonging (friendships, affection, intimacy), esteem (recognition, respect, and appreciation), and self-actualization (meeting one's full potential). Thus, while it is important to acknowledge and make some room for the client's feelings of grief and loss, it is crucial that more basic survival needs be met first. Just "going where the client wants to be" is clinically irresponsible. Rejecting all talk about relationships and loss would be alienating, and referring him away would be abandoning him without the support that is available through the agency.

16. C: Stage 6: intimacy vs isolation. This stage is typically mastered during young adulthood (ages 19-30). Indicators of successful resolution include establishing a committed, intimate, nonexploitive sexual relationship, with meaningful tolerance for the burdens and risks that accompany the relationship. The client has not been able to establish a reciprocal, loving, intimate relationship with another individual. The sexual relationships that he has produced are transient, noncommittal, and often exploitive. Failure to negotiate this stage results in increasing isolation and narcissism. A, Stage 1 (trust vs mistrust), is not correct as the issue of failures in trust has not been identified. B, Stage 5 (identity vs identify diffusion), is not correct, as the client does not present with issues related to roles and self-identity. D, Stage 8 (integrity vs despair) is not correct, as this is an end-of-life construct dealing with self-assessment in retrospect and the client is not at this point in life.

17. D: Stage 3: Rapprochement. *Rapprochement* is one of four substages in Stage 3 of Mahler's child development model. During this substage, an infant (15-24 months of age) begins to strive for autonomy. Success requires maternal support, as the infant ventures away from immediate contact, and frequently returns for encouragement and assurances of security. Where these are not forthcoming, an infant can develop anxiety and fears of abandonment. This can evolve into a dysfunctional *mood predisposition* that, Mahler felt, could later produce Borderline and/or Narcissistic Personality traits or the full disorder. Answer A (normal autism phase) is not correct, as it refers to a natural obliviousness to the external world common from birth to 1 month. Answer B (symbiosis phase) refers to high levels of attachment between mother and infant from 1-4 months of age, with deprivation/disruption potentially resulting in later symbiotic psychosis and disconnection from reality. Answer C (differentiation [hatching] phase) refers to an infant's realization of being separate from its mother. As an awakening, rather than a process, it is does not produce psychological failure.

18. A: Positive reinforcement. The teenager's acting out led to a variety of responses and punishments. However, it is revealed that the teenager's underlying goal is time and attention from her father. As negative attention is better than no attention at all (ie, *positive reinforcement*), the teenager continued to act out to receive and extend attention from her father. Answer B (*negative reinforcement*) is incorrect, as it refers to the repetition of a desired behavior to avoid negative stimuli (consequences). The parents were supplying negative stimuli (stern lectures) to produce and strengthen positive (cooperative) behaviors. Answer C (*punishment*) was also being used to weaken the teen's use of negative behaviors. Answer D (*extinction*) refers to the weakening of a conditioned response in one of two ways: 1) in *classical (Pavlovian) conditioning*, it involves interrupting the pairing of a conditioned stimulus and an unconditioned stimulus; 2) in *operant conditioning*, it occurs when a trained behavior ceases to be reinforced (or when the reinforcement is no longer considered rewarding). Ignoring bad behavior is one (operant conditioning) way of bringing it to extinction.

19. B: Skinner's *operant conditioning* deals with the modification of voluntary behavior via consequences, while *Pavlovian conditioning* produces behavior under new antecedent conditions. Ivan Pavlov's classical (or respondent) conditioning utilized the identification of an unconditioned (natural) stimulus that evokes an unconditioned response (e.g., food inducing salivation). A conditioned stimulus is created when an unconditioned stimulus is repeatedly paired with a stimulus to be conditioned (e.g., ringing a bell with the presentation of food), which evokes the unconditioned response (salivation), which is gradually transitioned into a conditioned response (salivation at the sound of the bell). Skinner identified an antecedent (stimulus) that could be used to produce a response (behavior) that could be controlled or modified by means of a consequence (positive or negative). Positive and negative reinforcements strengthen targeted behaviors, while punishment and extinction weaken targeted behaviors.

20. B: Level 2: Stage 4. This stage embodies a law-and-order perspective, focused on adherence to concrete perceptions of correct behavior and duty. Clearly, the husband is intent on ensuring he does not fail in his role as husband and father. To increase marital satisfaction, however, the husband needs to progress beyond Levels 1 and 2, and past Level 3: Stage 5 (societal expectations and agreements) into Stage 6, which is conscience- and ethics-driven according to principles of goodness and morality. Answer A (Level 1: Stage 2) is incorrect as Level 1 (Pre-Conventional Morality) is focused first on a punishment avoidance orientation (Stage 1) and next on a reciprocity, instrumental orientation (Stage 2: "you scratch my back and I'll scratch yours). The husband is beyond these stages. He is also beyond Level 2 (Conventional Morality), which deals with approval seeking (Stage 3: being "good" for praise). Answer C (Level 3: Stage 5) is incorrect, as it refers to behavior that has been carefully examined via a social-contract perspective. Finally, answer D (Level 3: Stage 6, ethics and morality driven) is the desired goal, which has yet to be pursued.

21. C: Disrupted attachment, which may result in subsequent oppositional defiant disorder as seen in this child, suggested by loss of the father and the mother's significant absences during formative infancy and beyond. Bowlby's work identified separation anxiety (evident at 6-8 months of age), stranger anxiety (at around 8 months of age), and phases of separation distress (protest, despair/depression, detachment, and anaclitic depression). Bowlby also clarified four key characteristics of proper attachment development: proximity maintenance (needing to be close to attachment figures); safe haven (knowing the attachment figure will be available as needed); secure base (a point of security available to

- 139 -

return to when learning to venture out); and separation distress (anxiety in the absence of the attachment figure). Ainsworth then identified three styles of attachment that resulted from variances in attachment availability, with Solomon and Main later adding a fourth: 1) secure (with undisrupted attachment development); 2) ambivalent-insecure (from an undependable attachment figure); 3) avoidant (preferring strangers, due to past abuse/neglect); 4) disorganized-insecure (inconsistent attachment experiences). Poor attachment often underlies symptoms of oppositional defiant disorder (bad, but not criminal disobedience), conduct disorder (with overtures of violence and criminality), or posttraumatic stress disorder.

22. A: It diagnostically identifies cause and effect relationships. The PIE system is not a diagnostic tool, as it does not explore cause and effect relationships. It was developed in the 1990s by James Karl and Karin Wandrei, specifically for use in social work. The goal of the PIE system is to identify and balance a review of all client problems and strengths. The four domains addressed (called "factors") are as follows: Factor I: social functioning (social roles, relationship types, severity, duration, and coping). Factor II: environmental problems (social environment, institutions and resources, severity, and duration). Factor III: mental health problems (*DSM-5* information and coding). Factor IV: physical health problems (medical conditions, and possible ICD-10 information and coding). Factors I and II have professional coding available. The codes consist of two-part number groupings, separated by a dot. The initial two numbers identify the role group (eg, family) and a role (e.g., parent). The next two numbers identify the relationship type and its issue (e.g., parenting, ambivalence). The final 3 numbers code: severity (1 [no problem] to 6 [catastrophic]), duration (1 = more than 5 years to 6 = less than 2 weeks), and coping dimensions (1 = excellent to 6 = no coping skills).

23. D: Language development. This developmental period requires mastery of *phonology* (making sounds correctly); *semantics* (the encoding of messages); *syntax* (proper combining of words); and *pragmatics* (proper use of word context). Because of the complexity of language development, some forms of psychopathology (e.g., autism) are more readily apparent in this developmental phase. Irregularities in physical developmental milestones are more likely to identify congenital defects, while poor cognitive development may more readily reveal genetic and drug exposure issues. Sexual development requires careful parenting, to ensure sexual curiosities are properly directed in socially appropriate manners, while also ensuring that emerging sexuality is not "shamed" or otherwise impaired or distorted.

24. C: 12 months. On average, from birth to 2 months infants respond to faces and bright objects; by 2 months, most visually track moving objects and exhibit social smiling; by 4 months, cooing sounds are evident as well as enjoyment of important people and familiar objects; by 5 months, grasping and holding skills are observed; by 6 months, babies can turn over and teething begins; around 7 months objects can be picked up; by 8 months sitting independently occurs, and stranger anxiety begins; at 9 months crawling is usually seen; at 10 months active play and paying attention are evident; at 11 months standing can be achieved with help; at 12 months a baby can turn pages to see pictures; from 10-12 months the range of emotional expression broadens, and walking with help begins; by 15 months independent walking starts and naming of familiar objects is evident; by 18 months running is observed; at 24 months speech in short sentences is possible; and by age 6 years speech and imagination are both well demonstrated.

25. D: Reassure the parents that this is not itself a symptom of sexual abuse. Approximately 10% of
girls will experience menarche before age 11, most at 12.5 years of age, and 90% by 13.75 years of age. Adolescence is typically identified as the period from 12 to 18 years of age. Sexual maturation may begin as young as age 10. Interest in the opposite gender becomes increasingly prominent as maturation progresses. Adolescent development broadens into areas such as emotional and spiritual awareness and capacity. The period is markedly influenced by factors such as gender, socioeconomic status, culture, genetics, and disabilities. Friends and institutional influences become more significant, and adolescents experiment with a variety of "personality styles" as their self-image is formed. Gender identity and potential confusion may occur and require careful response to avoid psychological distress and accompanying increases in depression, abuse, and suicide. Of all developmental periods, this transitional time is typically the most turbulent and traumatic.

26. C: The pressure of couples still rearing children while being required to care for aging parents. Other significant pressures in adulthood include: 1) caring for disabled children (whether due to health, substance abuse, or other disability); 2) rearing grandchildren for divorced or otherwise unavailable children; 3) economic challenges and poverty, including difficulties accompanying retirement; and 4) personal health changes related to aging. Early to-mid-adulthood is characterized by a focus on dating, marriage, home establishment, and childbearing and rearing. Early family structure can be particularly compromised by physical and/or mental illness, divorce or widowhood (with the accompanying financial, emotional, and social changes), and poor parenting skills (often derived from family of origin). The availability of social work resources can help mitigate the impact of these stressors and challenges. Late-life stressors also include mobility and cognitive changes (e.g., inevitable declines in short-term memory, and the possibility of dementia due to Alzheimer disease, Parkinson disease, stroke).

27. B: The mother. While sexual abuse and/or physical abuse in a child older than 14 years is more likely to be perpetrated by a father or other male father figure in the home, for nonsexual abuse of a child younger than 14 years, the most common perpetrator is the female parent. Common signs of physical abuse include bruising, welts, burns, fractures, and internal injuries. Routine signs of sexual abuse include trouble sitting or walking, inordinate shyness in changing clothes around others, sexual acting out, running away from home, and sexually transmitted diseases. Emotional abuse signs include delays in language skills, distrust, overeagerness to please, insecurity, anxiousness, poor self-esteem, relationship issues, substance abuse, and criminal behavior. Signs of abusive neglect include emotional problems (particularly depression), malnourishment (seen in inhibited development), cognitive delays (due to inadequate stimulation), medical problems and illnesses (especially when left untreated), poor social skills, impaired school performance, poor parental supervision, chronic tardiness or truancy, poor hygiene, and inappropriate clothing.

28. D: Contact the local Adult Protective Services (APS) to report suspected abuse. With continued nursing visits, it might be possible to defer a referral if the sole issue is marginal care, while an extended family conference is arranged (option C). However, the withholding of financial resources (the house), as well as isolating and neglecting the client's emotional and nutritional needs, meets clear standards of abuse. Most states have mandatory reporting guidelines when abuse is clear, and the social worker could not ethically or legally withhold the APS referral. Option A is clearly incorrect as it allows the abuse to continue. Option B is not acceptable as it defers any change in the ongoing abuse for at least 2

additional months. Elder abuse includes physical abuse, financial exploitation, and neglect, as well as verbal and emotional abuse, with family being the most common perpetrators. Neglect is the most commonly reported abuse. Living on the client's income and in the client's home are particular risk factors, as are: 1) a difficult to manage client (violent, demented, argumentative, etc.); 2) compromised caregivers (finances, substance abuse, mental illness, etc.); and 3) poor housing (crowded, inadequate, etc.).

29. A: Threats of further abuse. During the reconciliation phase the perpetrator is seeking to reestablish stability in the relationship. Added threats would not accomplish this. Thus, expressions tend to center on apologizing for the abuse and giving excuses for the abuse (e.g., "I was drunk" or "upset by something else"). More aggressive reconciliation tends to be limited to a) blaming the victim for the abuse; b) minimizing the level of the abuse; or c) denying that the actions were at all truly abusive. The four phases of the Cycle of Abuse are: *Phase I: Tension building* (communication breakdown, causing the victim to become fearful and to try to calm the abuser). *Phase II: Incident* (the abuse occurs, whether physical, verbal, or emotional, infused with great anger, blaming, and/or intimidation). *Phase III: Reconciliation* (apologies, blaming the victim, minimizing, excusing, etc.). *Phase IV: Calm* (the Honeymoon Phase: gifts, charm, and expressions of love leading to forgiving and feeling that the abuse is forgotten and past).

30. B: Codependent. Addiction is frequently a family disorder, as it affects all members in the household. Codependent behavior can include making excuses for the addiction, minimizing the extension of the addiction, covering for (or hiding) the addict's behavior, providing access to the substance to keep peace and minimize discord, and bypassing important obligations and responsibilities to compensate for the addict's behaviors and to ensure the safety of the addict or others. Addictions tend to persist because they engage the brain's pleasure center, releasing neurotransmitters that reinforce the addiction. While many addictions involve the use of psychoactive substances, other areas of addiction include eating, shopping, gambling, hoarding, pornography, and the excessive use of electronic devices (computer games, etc.). While most treatment tends to be cognitive behavioral in nature, there are numerous treatment approaches; no one treatment will meet the personality and needs of all addicted individuals.

31. C: Grief bargaining. Drawing upon the work of Kübler-Ross, the therapist recognizes the symptoms of the *bargaining* stage of coping with profound loss. The stages of anticipatory dying were first outlined by the psychiatrist Elisabeth Kübler-Ross. She identified five stages associated with anticipatory grief: *Stage 1: Denial* (rejection of the diagnosis; often a feature of emotional shock). *Stage 2: Anger* (rage, resentment, and frustration with God and others). *Stage 3: Bargaining* (attempting to make a deal with God or others). *Stage 4: Depression* (profound sadness as reality sinks in). *Stage 5: Acceptance* (ceasing to struggle against impending death). Answer A (psychotic break) is not correct, as a psychotic break is symptomatic of a complete detachment from reality, rather than just one deeply distressing element of life. Answer B (chemotherapy toxicity) is inaccurate, as it suggests a chemically driven psychological stage that would be very poorly integrated and lack goal-directed intent. Answer D (acute denial) is not correct, as it would manifest more as a total rejection of the diagnosis, rather than an effort to bargain around it.

32. B: Employment class. While employment and employment class (while collar, blue collar, trades, professions, etc.) may be relevant to a number of important social work endeavors with any given client or family, it is not generally considered an issue of cultural

diversity. Primary areas of cultural diversity are: 1) age (particularly as related to elderly persons); 2) sex (particularly as related to issues of feminism); 3) gender identity and expression (specifically involving lesbian, gay, bisexual, and transsexual [LGBT] issues); 4) ethnicity (common cultural and sometimes physical characteristics); 5) race (biologically determined common traits); 6) skin color (often not actually race based); 7) religious beliefs and affiliations (to include spirituality and not just religion); 8) national origin (country of birth); and 9) disability (per the ADA: a physical or mental impairment that significantly impairs life activity). Social diversity can be expanded to include marital status, political beliefs, social organization membership, educational status, and socioeconomic class, etc. Social workers must be sensitive to cultural and social diversity to work well with a wide variety of clients, and have special awareness of their limitations in these areas.

33. D: Group affiliations. Cultural competence does not require specific group affiliations relevant to engaged cultures, though this may be helpful. Knowledge of cultural diversity refers to: 1) information gleaned from appropriate literature, 2) direct involvement with other cultures; 3) familiarity with traditions and language, as well as 3) an awareness of potential unique regional and other differences. Attitude refers to 1) awareness and acknowledgement of any personal beliefs, values, biases, and countertransference issues likely to affect the social work process; 2) a willingness to avoid assumptions; 3) an openness to unique strengths and drawbacks of cultural perspectives, as identified and defined with the client; 4) the need for time to build trust; 5) sensitivity to discrimination and oppression; 6) cultural variations regarding privacy and confidentiality; 7) openness to referring clients to more appropriate services where adequate accommodation cannot be achieved for any reason (personal or otherwise).

34. C: Ethnographic interviewing. This form of interviewing allows for deeper cultural insights to be winnowed out of a client's narratives. Attending to both feelings and cultural meanings, the interviewer is better able to delve into and understand narratives and circumstances from the client's unique perspective. Common listening techniques such as *reframing* and *paraphrasing* are avoided, as they tend to suffuse the narrative with meanings and understandings that reflect the culture and history of the interviewer rather than that of the interviewee. Instead, *restating* and *incorporating* are used to retain the client's unique meanings. The use of an interpreter is important to ensure that unique expressions, such as idioms, or borrowed native-language terms, are not misunderstood or overlooked. Other culturally responsive assessment tools may be helpful. For example, 1) A *Culturagram* can be used to examine family relationships, cultural ties, and offer some perspective about the role and depth of culture in the client's life. 2) A *Cultural Evaluation* may also be used, as it explores a variety of cultural beliefs, values, behaviors, and support systems during the assessment process.

35. A: The *nurturing system* refers to family and intimate supports, while the *sustaining system* refers to institutional supports and society as a whole. As theorists such as Leon Chestang posit, everyone is a part of and in need of both systems of support. Thus, it is essential to understand the roles that culture and diversity play in either furthering or hindering the efficacy and balance of both of these systems in the lives of individuals. In particular is a "dual perspective," which may arise in the lives of culturally diverse clients, wherein they must constantly reposition themselves between nurturing family supports and a broader social construct that may not be in support of the nurturing family's culturally unique ways of living and supporting family members. Discrimination and

cultural norms that are incongruent with the broader sustaining system may significantly impede the utilization of important social services in particular.

36. C: Assimilation. In developing a bicultural identity, *assimilation* occurs when the norms and values of the sustaining system (institutions and society) are learned and followed to the exclusion of the norms and values of the nurturing system (family and cultural roots). This division can be particularly problematic among new immigrants and their young offspring. The parents, especially those from highly divergent cultures with markedly different languages and traditions, often find themselves unable to function well in mainstream society. Consequently, they become significantly dysfunctional in the eyes of the children, who far more quickly learn the dominant language and ways. As the parents turn to their young children for help in interpreting and guiding them through systems and technologies, traditional values of respect and reverence for adults can be significantly diminished. *Traditional adaptation* exists where adherence to the nurturing system (family and culture) remains dominant. *Marginal adaptation* occurs when neither the nurturing nor the sustaining systems' values and norms are followed. *Bicultural adaptation* exists when the norms and values of both systems become functionally integrated.

37. B: Individual independence is diligently fostered. In general, this is not true. Rather, mutual interdependence is more typically fostered among African American family members. Church membership and spirituality are both important, and religion and religious teachings are often taught and shared in the home. Family members usually feel deeply responsible for each other. Where hardship is encountered, family members feel a high degree of obligation to assist and support each other. Extended kinship relationships are also significant. Aunts, uncles, and grandparents often have significant roles in raising, teaching, and guiding the younger generations. Due to a history of disenfranchisement and prejudice, mainstream cultural assimilation and adaptation has been difficult for some. Especially problematic has been a subculture of violence and substance abuse that has greatly impaired the strong traditional cultural values common to most families. This has resulted in homicide being the leading cause of death for African American males ages 10-24.

38. D: Religion has no major role in family life. In fact, religion is in many ways central to family life, with many traditions and values centered in religious observance and celebration. Patriarchal family leadership is emphasized, with parents making most significant decisions. Children are expected to respect and follow these decisions. The family is more important than the individual, and individual sacrifices are expected when the needs of the family become acute. Working and giving funds to parents and other families is not uncommon when hardship exists. Personal problems are expected to be kept within the family. This can be problematic when issues of abuse, addiction, criminality, or other troubles are encountered. Social service systems must account for such cultural barriers and manage the engagement of private issues with particular sensitivity and care. Modeling self-disclosure and verbal expression may at times be an important social work contribution to addressing and resolving problems.

39. C: Stage 7: Pride in Identity. The client is still lingering in Stage 6 (withdrawal from the heterosexual world) and Stage 7, as pride and assertiveness about her sexual orientation is still only in its formative processes. The *Coming Out Process* involves 10 Stages: Stage 1: Confusion over sexual identity. Stage 2: Recognition of sexual identity. Stage 3: Exploration relative to sexuality identity (seeking to understand, define, and express sexual identity

internally and with others). Stage 4: Disclosure to others. Stage 5: Acceptance of sexual identity. Stage 6: Avoidance of the heterosexual world. Stage 7: Pride in sexual identity. Stage 8: Extending disclosure (to all others). Stage 9: Re-entering the heterosexual world. Stage 10: Moving past sexual orientation (in identity and life focus).

40. A: Ambiguous sexual anatomy (hermaphrodite). Heterosexual orientation is most commonly referred to as being *straight*. There is no specific term for sexual encounters outside of orientation preference. Sexual attraction to both men and women is known as *bisexuality*. Homosexual men are most often referred to as *gay*, while homosexual women are referred to by the term *lesbian*. *Pansexuality* refers to an attraction to and association with any partner regardless of sexual identity. *Transgender* (also called bi-gender) refers to an identity different from birth sex type, with a focus on gender. Transgender individuals may live a heterosexual, homosexual, bisexual, or asexual lifestyle. *Transsexual* individuals have identified themselves as transgender with a focus on sexual orientation. Further, they have an added desire to live an opposite sex lifestyle and desire hormonal and/or sexual surgery to achieve physiological congruence. *Genderqueer* and *Intergender* are catch-all terms for those who feel they are both male and female, neither male nor female, or entirely all binary gender identity.

41. D: Refer the client to a primary care physician for a health evaluation. Women are far more likely than men to be diagnosed with a psychiatric disorder, especially a psychogenic disorder of mood, when an underlying medical condition (such as hormone imbalance) is the cause. Seeking parity with men in many areas, including psychiatry, remains a challenge. Culturally, women continue in subordinate positions in society, specifically in medical, legal, and institutional arenas. Problems include 1) psychiatric and medical studies run by men and for men, with findings normed to men (especially in pharmaceutical findings where doses are normed to men's larger size and faster metabolic patterns, and in psychiatric studies that tend to either ignore or pathologize women's unique nature); 2) being uninsured or underinsured (double the rate of men); 3) lower pay for similar work (even worse for female minorities); and 4) poverty (women represent 66% of all Medicaid recipients). Women also fare poorly in intimacy, being far more often abused and more prone to sexual infections (such as HIV). All are also contributors to depression, beyond simple endogenous factors.

42. D: Key in on the phrase and inquire directly about suicidal thoughts. Elderly people face many challenges, among which is Erikson's *Integrity vs Despair* resolution process becoming profoundly acute in older years. Among elderly people, losses accumulate, health is fading, children have left, options are narrowing greatly, and the future can easily seem dim. Health and medication problems can further complicate the scenario. Of particular note, while the highest rate of completed suicide is among middle-aged Caucasian men (45 to 64 years old), the second highest rate is among elderly Caucasian men. While women attempt suicide three times as often as men, men are four times more likely to succeed, primarily because they often use more lethal means (firearms, suffocation, etc.). Of all completed suicides, 78.5% are male and 21.5% female. On average, 12 people attempt to harm themselves for every reported death by suicide. Many of these represent gestures rather than real attempts. Elderly persons, however, are decidedly lethal. While the ratio of attempts to completed suicides is 25:1 among youth, it is 4:1 among the elderly. Certainly it is always important to ask if concerning words are used.

43. A: HIV is a virus and AIDS is an illness. HIV refers to the *Human Immunodeficiency Virus*, which is the infective agent. One can contract HIV, and even transmit it, many years before symptoms of the virus become apparent. AIDS refers to *Acquired Immunodeficiency Syndrome*, which is characterized by a severely compromised immune system that is unable to fight off infections, which can then become deadly. Answer B is not true, as the virus is not caused by its condition. Answer C, HIV is a precursor to AIDS, is true. However, it doesn't describe the difference, but rather the pathway. Answer D is obviously false, as there is a distinct difference. Clients with HIV typically engage the anticipatory grieving stages outlined by Kübler-Ross (denial, anger, bargaining, depression, and acceptance). When first learning of the diagnosis, clients are at risk for depression, anxiety, adjustment disorder, and even suicide. Cognitive Behavioral Therapy (CBT), lifestyle changes (especially safe sex practices), support groups, and psychotherapy are among the more common social work interventions provided.

44. B: Disciplinary issues. Military discipline (assignment changes, rank changes, sanctions, etc.) would not normally contribute to a diagnosis of *Posttraumatic Stress Disorder* (PTSD). Combat stress (battle fatigue) is a primary contributor to PTSD. It includes exposure to experiences of violence and mayhem, and the psychological trauma associated with killing and living under the constant stress of being killed. *Military Sexual Trauma* (MST) is often overlooked in recovering veterans (rates of MST are 22% and 1.2%, respectively), especially if the veteran is male. *Mild traumatic brain injury* (MTBI) is also an often overlooked contributor. Of note, MTBI does not require loss of consciousness or even a diagnosable concussion to be an issue. Any substantial blow to the head or even close proximity to certain kinds of explosive blasts can bring it on, sometimes immediately and sometimes in a delayed form. They key symptoms are unexplained episodes of confusion, disorientation, loss of concentration, feeling dazed, etc. Neuropsychiatric consultation is important in such situations.

45. B: Transitioning undocumented immigrants back to their homeland. The NASW position on undocumented immigrants, established in 2008, is to assist these individuals and families in obtaining rights, services, benefits, education, health care, mental health, and other services whenever possible. Not only does the NASW Code of Ethics direct members to oppose any mandatory reporting by social workers, but to also oppose such requirements by members in other professions such as health, education, mental health, policy makers, and among public service providers. Further, undocumented immigrants are to be recognized as particularly vulnerable to exploitation and abuse, and thus they are to receive advocacy services and all available protections from violence (especially as perpetrated upon women) and other forms of abuse and exploitation. All these services are to be provided in a culturally competent manner.

46. C: Insurance and ability to pay. This information is obviously important, but it is not part of an *Intake Interview*. Rather it is a part of screening for services. Key areas of an intake interview include the following: 1) Problem areas (presenting problem, or chief complaint); common areas include relationships, finances, and psychosocial functioning. 2) Strengths: coping skills, resources, capacities, etc. 3) Support systems: significant others, family, friends, organizations, and affiliations, and their scope of involvement and availability. 3) Attitude: positive and progressive versus defeatist and negative, which may influence treatment. 4) Motivation: direct and clear, or for secondary gain or manipulation (e.g., to placate others, meet legal or employment requirements). 5) Relationships: nature, significance and role in life. 6) Resources: those used previously and others currently

available, as well as personal resources (faith, values, cognitive capacity, problem-solving skills, etc.). 7) Danger to self or others: suicidality and homicidality must always be explored if there is any indication of relevance. Important risk factors that might contribute to dangerousness should also be noted.

47. A: Psychiatric status. A client's psychiatric status is obtained via a mental status screening (brief) or mental status examination (in depth). It cannot be ascertained visually. Observational Assessment involves: 1) Physical appearance: appropriateness of attire (if properly worn, fastened, cleaned, and used, and if congruent with weather, activity, and occasion); grooming (hair combed, teeth brushed, face and hands clean, etc.); facial affect (if stable or labile, and if congruent with mood, context, and circumstance). 2) Health signs: self-care, social skills, emotional functioning, and cognitive context of behaviors. 3) Life skills: mobility (balance, strength, and positional use of the body), self and environment management, social skills, communication abilities, organizational skills, work skills, problem-solving skills, money management (making change, paying bills). Careful observation can reveal things to the observer well beyond what the client's verbal responses may otherwise indicate.

48. B: Medical model. The *medical model* in health care is focused on the *presenting problem* or *chief complaint*. Thus, when used in mental health, it is focused on clients' complaints, deficits, and identified problems. However, this assessment approach tends to miss identification of a client's positive life features, strengths, resiliency, and motivation. The *strengths perspective* views a client's capacities, internal motivations, and dedication to be essential elements of successful problem resolution, healing, and overcoming. A focus on problems can often disempower a client, leaving them feeling mired and overwhelmed in their challenges. In contrast, the strengths perspective focuses on competencies, capacities, resources, confidence, and alternatives—all of which are empowering, positive, and success focused. The *biopsychosocial model* explores the biological (physical), psychological, and social features that may be contributing to a client's concerns and challenges. It readily accounts for issues of environment, culture, poverty, social status, and health as a relevant constellation in which problems and challenges are embedded. Each model has something valuable to offer, and one or another may be preferable depending upon the clinical purpose, therapeutic goals, and environment (crisis vs long-term contacts, etc.).

49. B: Social history. A *social history* endeavors to reveal the quality and extent of a client's family, interpersonal, relational, and community interactions. It covers: 1) *Personal history*: place of birth, where raised, socioeconomic transitions/moves, primary language(s), and associated race/ethnic/cultural features. 2) *Family of origin*: parents, siblings, and extended family relationships. 3) *Educational history*: trajectory of education, diplomas, degrees, certifications, etc., as well as social, community, and/or professional associations. 4) *Marital*: marriages and divorces, children from each, current status, etc. 5) Significant relationships: current living relationships in the home and/or actively involved in life. 6) Legal history: any criminality, domestic violence and restraining orders, arrests, convictions, jail or prison terms, probation or parole, and any residual issues (e.g., felony convictions affecting employment). 7) Substance abuse history: past drug use, drug(s) of choice, frequency of use, social aspects of substance abuse, current substances used, and when/if treatment was sought, attempted, and/or completed. 8) Sexual history: orientation, numbers of partners, resulting offspring, sexually transmitted infections and treatment history. 9) Religious/spiritual history: any organized religious affiliation, transitions, current practices, and current level of personal spirituality.

50. B: Discuss his concerns and support him, but require the collateral contact. It is important to create a therapeutic bond with the client, but not to the exclusion of collateral contacts that are reasonable. The client should be given every opportunity to discuss his concerns, particularly if the therapy ended badly, and he should feel well heard and supported. Further, some collateral contacts (such as with a bitter ex-spouse) can very understandably be refused, but an extended therapeutic relationship should not be circumscribed by a client, as crucial information could be lost and the therapeutic work be thwarted.

51. C: Complete a suicide risk evaluation, and then arrange voluntary hospitalization if the client will accept it. As the client's therapist, it is important to complete a suicide risk evaluation, recognizing that it may be more complete, candid, and factual than what the client might reveal during assessment by an unfamiliar clinician. Given the client's emotional state (deliberate calm), detailed plans, and summary rationale, the client is at very high risk for acting on her suicidal thoughts. Further, she has not only motivation and rationale, but the means and anticipated timing for carrying out her plans. Therefore, even if the client were to recant, hospitalization would still be essential to ensure client safety. Calling 911 immediately would be premature and overly reactive. Calling local law enforcement is also overly reactive, and prevents the client from accepting voluntary hospitalization (as involuntary confinement is traumatic, and may produce unintended legal, social, and emotional consequences). Finally, research suggests that suicide prevention contracting alone tends to be ineffective, though potentially meaningful in early suicidal ideation situations.

52. D: Know your state laws. In some states (where physicians are designated reporters), B is correct, while C is correct in others. A client may be deemed a threat to others if: 1) a serious threat of physical violence is made; and 2) if the threat is made against a specifically named individual. Keys here are as follows: a) the potential victim is known; b) the marriage leaves the partner without reason to suspect or inquire; and c) the threat of lethal harm is high. This creates a "Duty to Protect" and "Duty to Warn."

53. A: Addictions and Compulsions. The domains examined in a Mental Status Examination (MSE) are: alertness (attending) and orientation (to person, place, and time = A&Ox3) appearance (physical presentation, dress, hygiene, grooming, etc.), attitude (e.g., cooperative, hostile, guarded, suspicious), behavior (activity, eye contact, movements, gait, mannerisms, psychomotor agitation or retardation, etc.), mood and affect (euphoric, euthymic, dysphoric, anxious, apathetic, anhedonic, etc.), thought processes (rate, quantity, and form [logical or illogical, rapid, or pressured "flights of ideas," perseveration], etc.), thought content (delusions [with or without ideas of reference], grandiosity, paranoia, erotomanic, insertions, broadcasting, etc.), speech (rate and rhythm, poverty or loquacious, pitch, articulation, etc.), perception (hallucinations [visual, auditory, tactile, gustatory, or olfactory], depersonalization, derealization, time distortion [déjà vu], etc.), cognition (alertness, orientation, attention, fund of information, short- and long-term memory and recall, language, executive functions [tested via interpretations], etc.), insight (understanding of problems and options) and judgment (logically reasoned decisions).

54. C: Behavior, intervention, response, and plan. Behavior (of the client), intervention (from the behavior), response (to the intervention), and plan (next steps in light of the behavior-intervention outcome). Other charting methods include narrative (progressive

story of the problem unfolding and being addressed); problem-oriented (focused on the client's view of issues and intervention outcomes); and SOAP (subjective = client's states; objective = what followed factually; assessment = interpretation of the new situation; plan = the new intervention or response). Various recordkeeping formats may be individually advantageous, depending upon the setting, the clientele, goals, and outcome monitoring.

55. B: Delineate subtypes and severity. Diagnostic *specifiers* in the *Diagnostic and Statistical Manual of Mental Disorders* (*DSM*), currently in its fifth edition, are used almost exclusively to indicate a diagnostic subtype or to rank the status or severity of a diagnostic condition. Many old specifiers and numerous new specifiers are now in use. Common specifiers include "generalized," "with mixed features," "with (or without) insight," "in controlled environment," "on maintenance therapy," "in partial remission," "in full remission," and "by prior history." Other specifiers are used to rank symptom severity (e.g., mild, moderate, and severe). While the NOS (not otherwise specified) acronym has been omitted, the NEC (not elsewhere classified) option has been continue or updated in some diagnostic categories, allowing for idiosyncratic presentations and/or early diagnostic ambiguity.

56. D: Mild. Intelligence quotient (IQ) scores include a margin for measurement error of five points. Generally, IQ scores of 50-55 to approximately 70 indicate mild intellectual disability, moderate scores are 35-40 to 50-55, severe scores are 20-25 to 35-40, and profound scores fall below 20 or 25. In the *DSM-5*, the term *Intellectual disability* has been replaced with *Intellectual Disability (intellectual developmental disorder)* or ID, to better conform to terms in medical and educational fields. While IQ scores have been removed from the diagnostic criteria, placing greater emphasis on *adaptive functioning*, testing is still necessary. Deficits must now exist in three domains: 1) intellectual functioning (e.g., reasoning, judgment, abstract thinking, and academic and experiential learning); 2) in personal independence and social responsibility (e.g., communication, self-care, home living, social/interpersonal skills, use of community resources, self-direction, functional academic skills, work, leisure, health, and safety); and 3) with onset during the "developmental period" (less rigid than "before age 18"). Supporting associated features include poor social judgment, gullibility, an inability to assess risk, etc.

57. D: *Expressive Language Disorder*. This diagnosis is characterized by substantial impairment in speaking, as seen in lower scores on standardized tests of language use in the presence of otherwise normal cognitive capacity. *Phonological Disorder* presents as substantial impairment in making appropriate speech sounds, sufficient to impede success in academic, occupational, or interpersonal communication. *Stuttering* involves a disturbance in the timing and fluency of speech, unrelated to age and normal development. *Mixed Receptive-Expressive Language Disorder* is characterized by substantial impairment in both expressive (spoken) language and receptive (heard) language comprehension. These diagnoses are most commonly encountered in infancy, childhood, or adolescence.

58. C: Autistic Disorder. The presentation as outlined includes virtually all classic symptoms. *Asperger Syndrome* (AS, or Asperger disease) is on the *Autism Spectrum Disorders* (ASD) continuum, but is less severe. This has led some to refer to AD as High-Functioning Autism (HFA). Those with autism tend to experience delays in language development and have below average IQ, while those with AD tend to have an average or above average IQ and speak at their expected age range. Children with AD become obsessed with a single object or topic, and tend to talk about it nonstop. Social skills are significantly impaired, and they are frequently uncoordinated and awkward. *Rett Syndrome* has clear

physiological and behavioral components, including a slowing in head growth, severe psychomotor retardation, regression in previous manual dexterity, as well as gait and trunk movement impairments, and severe expressive and receptive language and social skill impairments. *Childhood Disintegrative Disorder* follows a 2-year period or more of normal development, after which there is a profound loss in language, social skills, play and motor skills, and bowel and bladder control.

59. A: Oppositional Defiant Disorder (ODD). The argumentative, temper, and hostility-driven nature of the teen's interaction with his parents is characteristic of ODD. It has gone on longer than 6 months, and bears nearly all diagnostic features. Conduct Disorder (CD) would not be diagnosed because the behavior has not risen to the level of consistently violating basic rights of others, or breaking major societal rules and values, such as property destruction (vandalism, fire-setting, etc.), bullying (intimidating or threatening others), fighting (particularly with a weapon), physical cruelty to people or animals, stealing, truancy, or running away from home. Bipolar disorder would not be diagnosed as there is no evidence of mood swings, particular mania. Attention Deficit Hyperactivity Disorder (ADHD) would not be diagnosed as the requisite signs of distractibility, inattentiveness, poor school work, disorganization, forgetfulness, and agitation are not present.

60. C: Anorexia Nervosa. The classic symptoms of *Anorexia* center around a poor body image (e.g., seeing oneself as fat) and the avoidance of food to control weight. This may be accompanied by the use of laxatives and exercise to further manage body weight. The persistent ingestion of nonfood items and materials is known as *Pica*. Key features include compulsive craving for nonfood material (for some, ice; rarely, caused by mineral deficiency), and an otherwise normal use of normal foods. *Bulimia Nervosa* involves binging followed by purging (e.g., vomiting and/or laxative use). *Rumination Disorder* involves regurgitating food and re-chewing it. In deriving a tentative diagnosis, note that this adolescent is losing weight, avoiding regular food, and consuming a nonfood item that can induce a feeling of fullness. Other signs include consumption of mineral oil (a laxative) and ice chips—both non-nutritive and calorie free. There is no binge-purge cycle, no apparent compulsion for nonfood items, a normal desire for food items, and no re-chewing of swallowed and regurgitated food. While a diagnosis of Pica may develop, absent more information this does not appear to be the case.

61. D: All of the above. *Encopresis* refers to incontinence of bowel in an individual who is at least 4 years of age, chronologically or mentally. It may occur due to stress, anxiety, or constipation, as oppositional or retaliatory behavior, and it may be either voluntary or involuntary. It must occur at least monthly for 3 consecutive months. It must not, however, be due to a neurological, medical, chemical-, or substance-induced disorder or stimulant. The term for similar problems with bladder incontinence is *enuresis*, which has similar diagnostic features, with the exception that bladder incontinence must occur at least twice a week over 3 consecutive months.

62. B: Separation Anxiety Disorder. *Separation Anxiety Disorder* involves profound distress when an individual separated from the presence of a primary attachment figure. Onset must be before the age of 18, and the symptoms must be present for at least 4 weeks prior to diagnosis. Symptoms frequently include undue anxiety, irrational fears or worries about safety, inability to fall asleep alone, nightmares, and exaggerated homesickness. These symptoms may also be accompanied by somatic symptoms such as stomachache, dizziness, palpitations, or vomiting, which may lead to medical evaluation when the underlying

disorder is psychological in nature. Symptoms during attachment figure separation are developmentally expected until a child reaches 3 to 5 years of age. Clinicians must first rule out agoraphobia before making this diagnosis, especially in older children. *Oppositional Defiant Disorder* requires rebelliousness; *Panic Disorder* involves intense generalized fear that something bad is about to happen; *Agoraphobia* (a type of Panic Disorder) involves severe anxiety in situations deemed uncomfortable, dangerous, or remote from help. None of these are relevant in this situation.

63. D: None of the above. Both delirium (ICD-9 code of 293.0) and encephalopathy, whether metabolic (348.31) or toxic (349.82), are clinically virtually the same condition. Toxic encephalopathy/delirium occurs secondary to drugs (including alcohol), while metabolic refers to all other inducing mechanisms (sepsis, renal or hepatic failure, etc.). The term delirium tends to be used in psychiatry, while encephalopathy tends to be used in medicine, especially by neurologists. Of note, delirium is a nonspecific ICD (International Classification of Disease) code by Medicare (and thus, by most other payers). Some medical insurers will not reimburse for 293.0 (see ICD-9), as it falls into a "mental disorder" definition (within the 290-319 ICD code range). However, both terms refer to sudden-onset altered mental status conditions, most of which are reversible if the underlying cause is resolved. In elderly persons, medication toxicity and underlying infections with fever are typical causes of delirium/encephalopathy.

64. D: Advocate for the patient to be admitted for further medical evaluation. There is too much unknown about this seriously compromised elderly patient. He may be malnourished, toxic from overmedication, mildly septic without pyrexia (fever) or elevated WBC, particularly if a urinary tract infection is involved. Sending him back home, from where he apparently wandered away, would be unethical and inhumane. Placing him outside his home, even on a short-term basis, could further compromise his mental status and traumatize him. Delaying discharge until collateral contacts can be made is an option, but family cannot provide an adequate medical explanation for his condition and his safety is clearly at risk. Living alone and wandering suggests delirium (a sudden onset, likely reversible condition) rather than insidious dementia (slow onset, with irreversible impairment) With hospitalization, it can be seen if his condition clears or worsens, collateral contacts can be ensured, and underlying health problems can be explored and potentially resolved. Advocacy in such a situation is a key social work role.

65. A: Alzheimer disease. *Alzheimer disease* (AD) accounts for 60% to 80% of all dementia diagnoses. AD is characterized by an overabundance of neurofibrillary tangles and beta-amyloid plaques that interrupt normal brain cell processes and cause the cells to die. The result is memory loss, personality changes, and other cognitive problems. Early symptoms include short-term memory impairment, apathy, and depression. Later symptoms include communication problems, confusion, disorientation, poor judgment, and unpredictable behaviors. End-stage symptoms include difficulty speaking, swallowing, and walking. AD is a fatal disease, if no other lethal illness intervenes (e.g., heart attack, cancer). The second most common form of dementia is called *Vascular Dementia*, caused by blood-flow problems in the brain—ruptured blood vessels (hemorrhagic stroke), or blood vessels blockage (ischemic stroke) caused by blood clots or cholesterol deposits, with both preventing oxygen delivery to an area of the brain. Senility is not itself a dementia. The term *senile* simply means "old-age related." Thus, the phrase "senile dementia" says nothing about its cause, but rather only that the onset was in old age (usually defined as 65 years and older).

66. B: Alcohol abuse. The determination to categorize his use as abuse is due to the level of problems it has produced in his life (missing work and legal issues). Alcohol dependence (alcoholism) refers to symptoms of withdrawal (delirium tremens, etc.) that arise with the cessation of drinking. It is also typically characterized by continued use in the face of serious consequences. Recreational use involves sporadic ingestion at such times and in such a way as to avoid negative family, employment, and social consequences, but used heavily enough to produce a pleasurable (recreational) effect. Casual alcohol use might best be described as the occasional glass of wine at a special meal or on a special occasion. It, too, has no immediate negative consequences.

67. C: Schizophrenia. The client is clearly displaying both hallucinations (seeing things not there, objects floating) and delusions (believing things that are not true, thought control), as well as the rambling and disorganized speech characteristic of *Schizophrenia*. The condition has existed longer than 6 months, though it is currently in an acute phase. No subtype specifier is required, as the *DSM-5* no longer uses the prior specifiers (paranoid, disorganized, undifferentiated, etc.), with the exception of catatonic type. A diagnosis of *Bipolar Disorder* would not be correct, as there is no evidence of mood cycling and this is not an exacerbated manic phase with psychotic features. *Schizoaffective Disorder* would not be correct, as it requires the presence of a clear affective component (mania or depression), which is not in evidence either by history or presentation. *Substance-Induced Psychosis* requires the proximate use of a mind-altering substance (such as methamphetamine), which is also not in evidence. While there is a remote history (and one cannot entirely rule out more recent ingestion), the parents indicate the symptoms have been consistently present for the greater part of a year, which precludes the episodic presentation of Substance-Induced Psychosis.

68. D: Erotomanic type. The client openly indicates that this famous person has loving feelings for him, in spite of the fact they've never met or directly communicated in any way. Classic features of *erotomania* (sometimes also called de Clérambault syndrome) include identification with someone in higher status (famous, wealthy, etc.), and is more common among women than men. The symptoms are not infrequently manifest in either schizophrenia or bipolar mania, at which point either would be the proper primary diagnosis (e.g., bipolar, acute manic phase, with erotomanic features). *Grandiose type* is not correct as it focuses on a client's belief that he or she has special talents, unique understandings, or an unrecognized or unreported extraordinary accomplishment. *Jealous type* is not correct, as the inordinate jealousy must be centered in faulty perceptions of infidelity in a real relationship. *Persecutory type* is not correct, as it focuses on a fear of a conspiracy by others to do him harm.

69. B: Brief Psychotic Disorder. The diagnosis of *Brief Psychotic Disorder* requires schizophrenic-like symptoms for at least 1 day and no longer than 1 month (e.g., such as hallucinations and/or delusions, both of which this client claimed). It cannot be due to drug-induced psychosis (illicit or licit drugs), or another medical condition. *Posttraumatic Stress Disorder* would not be appropriate as it is not characterized by schizophrenic-like symptoms, but rather flashbacks and trauma-linked stressors that are not indicated here. *Drug-induced psychosis* would not be appropriate, as the vignette specifically disclaims drug use. *Bipolar disorder* would not be correct, as there is no evidence of cycling (manic depression). Thus, Brief Psychotic Disorder is the diagnosis that best fits the available information.

70. C: Cyclothymia. The moodiness must have been present for at least 2 years (at least 1 year in children and adolescents) and there must have been multiple periods with hypomanic symptoms that do not meet criteria for a manic episode and numerous periods with depressive symptoms that fall short of a major depressive episode. Finally, the hypomanic and depressive periods must have been present at least half the time and never without the symptoms for more than 2 months at a time. Bipolar disorder involves more dramatic mood swings, with extreme mania and depression. Dysthymia is a form of depression that does not meet Major Depression criteria and does not have hypomanic or manic features. Mood Disorder NOS is a possibility, but there is sufficient information to move further diagnostically.

71. D: Persistent complex bereavement disorder. This disorder is diagnosed when intense and compromising grief extends at least beyond the first year. Key features with the client is her sense of meaninglessness without her spouse, estrangement from others, emotional numbness, and preoccupying thoughts about dying to be with him again. The diagnosis of Major Depression would not be correct due to the fact that the focus is on the loss, rather than a generalized meaninglessness, hopelessness, and helplessness. Posttraumatic stress would not be correct because it centers on key features associated with experiencing an overwhelming and traumatic event (such as combat), with flashbacks and other emotions tied directly to the event itself, rather than to a loss. Uncomplicated bereavement would not be correct, as the intensity and compromising features of the loss are not resolving over time, but rather becoming overly protracted. Of note, *DSM-5* has removed the "bereavement exclusion." It is possible to be diagnosed both with bereavement and major depression, if the circumstances warrant.

72. A: Bipolar I involves mania and Bipolar II involves primarily depression. Bipolar I Disorder requires a minimum of one manic episode (or mixed episode), as well as episodes with features typical of Major Depression. In contrast to this, Bipolar II requires at least one Major Depression episode, and a minimum of at least one Hypomanic episode. Adequate control requires medications. Preferred treatment medications more commonly focus on atypical antipsychotics (Abilify, Geodon, Risperdal, Seroquel, or Zyprexa), which provide greater symptom relief than the older mood stabilizing medications such as lithium, Depakote, or Tegretol. These are now more commonly used only as adjuncts. An extended depressive episode may also be treated with antidepressants. Education about the condition, as well as therapy (e.g., cognitive-behavior, interpersonal, social rhythm, family therapy), greatly enhances successful management.

73. D: Panic disorder without agoraphobia. The symptoms of a panic attack appear very quickly and generally peak within 10 minutes. Typical symptoms include rapid heart rate, shortness of breath, light-headedness, trembling, derealization and depersonalization (feeling surreal and detached from self), nausea, dizziness, numb and tingling feelings, etc. These are typically accompanied by feelings of impending doom and/or death. Many of the symptoms are a direct result of hyperventilation during the acute panic phase. Anxiety disorder due to a medical condition is not correct, as there is no underlying medical condition. Generalized anxiety disorder is not correct, as it does not have sudden onset but rather is an accumulation of worry and anxiety that persists for 6 or more months (without an underlying medical condition or substance use precipitant). Acute stress disorder is not correct, as it involves a precipitating PTSD-like traumatic event that induces the symptoms of stress.

74. C: Illness Anxiety Disorder (care-seeking type). Key features of this disorder include an intense preoccupation with the acquisition of a serious health problem, an absence of actual somatic symptoms (or only very mild symptoms), an honest belief and fear of an illness (e.g., not manipulative in any way), a high level of health anxiety, and excessive health-preoccupied behaviors that have continued for more than 6 months. Care-seeking type can be specified, as the client continues to seek help and support from a medical provider on a regular basis, even after adequate reassurances have been provided. Malingering Disorder is not correct, as it involves exaggerating or falsely claiming symptoms for secondary gain (e.g., insurance claims, to be relieved of unpleasant work). Factitious Disorder is not correct, as it involves the deliberate fabrication of symptoms without the intent to receive tangible or concrete rewards, but rather for the nurturance or attention thereby derived. Somatic Symptom Disorder is not correct, as it requires the presence of actual somatic (physical) symptoms. Note: Somatization Disorder, Hypochondriasis, Pain Disorder, and Undifferentiated Somatoform Disorder have been removed from *DSM-5* and replaced with Somatic Symptom Disorder.

75. C: Dissociative Fugue. Key features of this diagnosis are localized or selective amnesia surrounding certain events, or generalized amnesia involving identity and life history, along with some sort of purposeful travel or simply aimless wandering. The amnesia must produce significant distress, and/or impairment in social, occupational, or other significant areas of personal function. It must not be a result of substance ingestion or a medical (especially neurological) condition. In the *DSM-5*, this diagnosis is now specified under the more general diagnosis of Dissociative Amnesia, which itself is not correct as it does not involve traveling or wandering. Dissociative Identity Disorder (in the past known as Multiple Personality Disorder) would not be correct as it involves the development to one or more separate identities.

76. B: Dyspareunia. This term refers to any form of pain during sexual intercourse that persistently recurs. Causes can include involuntary contractions of the outer third of the vagina (involving the pubococcygeus muscles), vaginal dryness, inflammation, infection, skin conditions, sexually transmitted infections (STIs), or any other underlying medical condition. The vignette specifically excluded involuntary contractions of the vagina, so vaginismus would not be correct. Sexual Aversion Disorder would not be correct because it involves a psychological aversion to or avoidance of sexual activity, rather than physical pain. Female Orgasmic Disorder is incorrect because it involves a failure to reach orgasm, even with appropriate stimulation, excluding an underlying medical condition.

77. D: Other specified paraphilia. Exhibitionism involves a minimum of 6 months of recurrent urges, fantasies, and/or behaviors involving the exposure of one's genitals to an unsuspecting person, or where clinically significant distress or impairment in social, occupational, or other meaningful areas of functioning occurs. In this case, however, the recipient of the client's disrobing behaviors is not an unsuspecting stranger, nor does the vignette specify that she exposes her genitals or if she fully or only partially disrobes. Thus, this is more an act of consensual sex-play, rather than exhibitionism. Voyeurism is not correct, as it involves watching an unsuspecting person disrobing. Frotteurism is inaccurate as it involves intense sexual arousal from the urge, fantasy, or act of touching or rubbing against a nonconsenting person.

78. A: Narcolepsy. In particular, the diagnosis must involve sudden onset, intense sleep need, refreshment from the sleep, the presence of REM (rapid eye movement) sleep

features, and concurrent cataplexy. Helpful lifestyle changes include exercise, short planned naps, and avoiding stimulant substances. Primary insomnia is incorrect as it involves difficulty falling asleep or staying asleep. Primary hypersomnia is inaccurate as it involves excessive sleep needs not due to a clear physical need or substance. Circadian sleep disorder is not correct, as it deals with external impediments to a normal sleep cycle (e.g., jet lag, work shift changes).

79. C: Borderline Personality Disorder. This disorder is characterized by, among other features, a pervasive pattern of unstable relationships, chronic feelings of emptiness, poorly controlled chronic anger, and alternating devaluing and overvaluing relationships, followed by frantic efforts to avoid abandonment. Histrionic Personality Disorder would not be appropriate, as the client's high emotions and attention-seeking behaviors are just a subset of other problematic issues, beliefs, and behaviors. Narcissistic Personality Disorder is also not correct, as the client's problems are not centered on grandiosity, absence of empathy, arrogance, or entitlement, etc. Antisocial Personality Disorder would be incorrect, as features of aggression, violations of the law, or absence of remorse are not central to the client's presentation. The presence of a personality disorder, however, is clear, as the issues involve a pattern of interacting with the world that guides her life and shapes her experiences.

80. D: All of the above. The listed terms are all used interchangeably. Common guidelines for direct practice include: 1) Start with client-identified issues. 2) Use positive goal setting. 3) Overcome difficulties by modeling honest and direct communication. 4) Ensure culturally competent service by careful assessment. 5) Use a client's native language, if possible, or obtain an interpreter. 6) Avoid reality testing a delusional client's thoughts, and instead seek to calm and support pending further assessment and/or medications. 7) Carefully watch for transference and countertransference processes. If a client requires hospitalization, seek a voluntary placement where possible, and carefully follow involuntary hospitalization and evaluation guidelines when necessary.

81. B: Systems theory. Systems theorists recognize the interconnectedness of all relational groups—families, communities, society, etc. They also understand that systems are composed of individual participants, boundaries, alliances, and networks, and that superordinate change requires change at all levels and aspects of a system. They also understand that change in any one area will induce unavoidable changes in many if not all other parts of the system. The concept of homeostasis (resistance to change) is seen as both an obstacle and tool, depending upon which end of the change process is being encountered. By better identifying and understanding roles, relationships, and interactive dynamics, social workers are better enabled to understand deleterious problems and optimal pathways to change and improvement. Conflict theory focuses on the role of conflict and dissent in relationships. Freudian theory focuses on past history and unconscious motivations and defenses. Individual theory is not a recognized theoretical body of knowledge.

82. B: Transitional. While life transitions can be stressful, these transitions tend to be gradual and thus lack the short-term and overwhelming qualities that properly define a crisis. Cultural-Societal crises are those where fundamental worldviews collide in traumatic ways, for example, immigrating to a foreign country, or revealing homosexuality in a heterosexual community. Maturational crises involve developmental events, such as beginning school, leaving home, or marriage. Situational crises involve a sudden traumatic

- 155 -

event, such as a car accident, witnessing violence, or being assaulted. To help individuals re-establish their coping skills and equilibrium, Crisis Intervention has three primary goals: 1) reducing the impact and symptoms that accompany a crisis (e.g., normalizing, calming, empowering); 2) mobilizing resources, both internal (psychological) and external (e.g., social, financial); and 3) restoring the precrisis level of function.

83. C: 7 Stages. Roberts (1991) proposed a seven-stage model for working through a crisis: Stage 1) Safety and lethality assessment: accomplished thorough a biopsychosocial assessment, including supports, stressors, medical issues, medications, substance abuse, coping skills and resources, as well as suicidality with or without real intent and a plan, history of past attempts, and related risk factors (substance use, isolation, and recent losses). Stage 2) Establishing rapport, ideally through the assessment, facilitated by warmth, genuineness, and empathy. Stage 3) Problem identification: current issues and any so-called "last straw," in order of working priority. Stage 4) Address feelings: validate via listening skills (paraphrasing, reflective listening, and probing questions) and challenge maladaptive beliefs. Stage 5) Generate alternatives: explore options and include client input on what has previously been helpful. Stage 6) Develop an action plan: shifting from crisis to resolution processes, using steps identified in the prior stage, and helping the client to find meaning in the crisis event. Stage 7) Follow-up: a post-crisis evaluation of client functioning and progress, via phone or in-person visits at specific intervals.

84. D: A method for increasing desired behaviors. The *Premack Principle* is applied by pairing a low-probability behavior with a high-probability behavior in order to increase the frequency that the low-probability behavior will be engaged. For example, a child will be permitted to play sports, watch television, or play video games only after he or she has completed all daily assigned homework. In this way, the motivation and desire to complete assigned homework is increased. This is a form of *Operant Conditioning*. Other Operant Conditioning tools include: 1) The use of *Reinforcers* (positive consequences following a desired behavior). Reinforcers may be *primary* (naturally reinforcing, such as needs for food, water, and sleep), or *secondary* (a stimulus that an organism learns to value). *Positive reinforcement* involves a stimulus reward following a desired behavior, and *negative reinforcement* involves the withdrawal of an unpleasant consequence when desired behavior occurs.

85. D: All of the above. A *Contingency Contract* is used in treatment to specify a particular consequence, either positive or negative, contingent upon whether or not a specific behavior or behaviors occur as agreed upon. It is a meaningful tool for modifying individual behavior. Another commonly used *Operant Conditioning* tool to reinforce desirable behavior is called the *Token Economy*. It involves the delivery of representative tokens that can be redeemed for desirable reinforcers by the individual. It is most commonly used with children to modify behavior. Other concurrently used strategies include the use of *verbal prompts* and *clarifications*. As reminders (prompts) are provided and clarifications are supplied to increase understanding and focus, behaviors can be more rapidly modified and solidified.

86. A: *Cognitive-behavioral therapy* (CBT). Three forms of CBT predominate: 1) Aaron Beck's *Cognitive Therapy* views depression and mental illness as a bias toward negative thinking via thinking errors (all-or-nothing and black-and-white/dichotomous thinking, emotional reasoning, overgeneralization, magnification and minimization, catastrophizing, and mind reading). Relief is found through collaborative empiricism, Socratic dialogue, guided

discovery, decatastrophizing, reattribution training, and decentering. 2) Albert Ellis' *Rational Emotive Therapy* identifies common irrational beliefs (demands and absolutes), which are rationally challenged, evaluated, clarified, and resolved. 3) Donald Meichenbaum's *Self-Instruction Training* focuses on maladaptive self-statements that frequently underlie negative thinking patterns, negativity, and self-defeating thoughts and behaviors. Therapy involves thought assessments, situational self-statement exploration, and developing new self-statements that better reflect truth and mental health.

87. C: Solution-Focused Therapy. The key components of *Solution-Focused Therapy* include the following: 1) problem description; 2) formulating goals; 3) collaboratively identifying solutions; 4) feedback at close of session; and 5) evaluation of progress. *Dialectical Behavioral Therapy* is most often used in the treatment of Borderline Personality Disorder, and consists of four modules: 1) mindfulness (observe, describe, and then participate); 2) interpersonal effectiveness (learning to assertively ask for change and say no when needed); 3) distress tolerance (identifying and tolerating things that cannot be changed); and 4) emotion regulation (becoming emotionally aware and able to direct emotions). *Reality Therapy* focuses on meeting four psychological needs (belonging, freedom, fun, and power) through internally oriented, purposeful behaviors. It rejects the medical model of mental illness, and side-steps past attitudes, behaviors, and feelings in favor of current perspectives on whether any given behavior can responsibly meet one's needs without damaging others. Reality testing is used to reject unsuccessful behaviors and identify those that will truly succeed.

88. B: *Karen Horney*. Horney concurred with Freud that anxiety underlies most neuroses. However, she disagreed that conflicts between instinctual drives and the superego produced this anxiety. Rather, anxiety arises through problematic parental behaviors: rejection, over-protectiveness, and/or indifference. Children cope by: 1) over-compliance (moving toward people), 2) detachment (moving away from people), or 3) aggression (moving against people). Resolution requires: 1) meeting biological needs, and 2) protection from danger, fear, and pain. *Erich Fromm* also moved past Freud and Marx, believing that individuals can transcend biological and societal barriers through pursuit of internal freedom. Efforts to escape freedom (responsibility) produce self-alienation and "unproductive" families that favor symbiosis (enmeshment) or withdrawal (indifference). He identified four problematic personality orientations: 1) receptive, 2) exploitative, 3) hoarding, and 4) marketing, and one healthy orientation, 5) productive (rational responsibility). Harry Stack Sullivan emphasized relationships over lifespan issues, focusing on three modes of cognitive experience in personality development: 1) Prototaxic (momentary perceptions in early life); 2) Parataxic (misperceptions or distortions of early important events); and 3) Syntaxic (the emergence of logical, sequential, modifiable, and internally consistent thinking).

89. D: Abreaction. Carl Jung developed the concept of *abreaction*, which involves relieving, retelling, and reorienting an experience to discharge the negative psychological burdens that accompany the experience. Abreaction is a form of *catharsis*, where abreaction involves dealing with specific biographical experiences and catharsis involves the release of more generalized emotional and physical tension. Jung felt that behavior is derived from past experiences in the context of future goals and aspirations. Personality is two-fold: the *conscious*, oriented toward the external world, and the *unconscious*. The unconscious is composed of personal and collective elements. *Personal unconscious* consists of repressed or forgotten experiences, and the *collective unconscious* consists of inherited memory traces

- 157 -

and primordial images (*archetypes*) that produce commonly shared understandings in societies. Key archetypes include the *self* (producing unity in the personality), the *persona* (a public mask), the *shadow* (or dark side) of personality, and the *anima* (feminine) or *animus* (masculine). Personality consists of attitudes (introversion and extroversion) and four basic functions (feeling, intuiting, sensing, and thinking).

90. D: Gradually defining oneself by thoughtful rejection or integration of outside ideas. Gestalt Therapy differs from Freudian Psychoanalysis on introjection primarily in its definition of a gradual rather than immediate construct. Psychoanalysis posits a prompt and full acceptance by the client of the analyst's conclusions, whereas Gestalt suggests a gradual integration of only that information that the client deems accurate following due reflection. Four key boundary disturbances defined in Gestalt Therapy are: 1) introjection: differentiating between "me, and not me," lacking which a client is overly compliant and attempts to please others at the loss of true self; 2) projection: assigning uncomfortable aspects of the self to others (e.g., "he never liked me," when it is you who dislikes him); 3) retroflection: directing inward the feelings one has for another (seen as expressions of self-blame when addressing such feelings with another); and 4) confluence: an absence of boundaries between self and others, resulting in feelings of both guilt and resentment over actual differences. The therapeutic goal is to create healthy boundaries and self-integration (integrity).

91. D: An ongoing growth group. Generally, groups are defined as either task or treatment oriented. Open-ended groups have no termination date. Task groups are formed solely to accomplish a specific goal (preparing a New Year's dance, etc.). Treatment groups serve to enhance members' social and/or emotional needs and/or skills. Types of treatment groups include: 1) educational groups: formed to enhance learning about specific issues or problems, providing needed information and skills; 2) growth groups: focus on personal enrichment and progress, as opposed to remediating past problems and concerns; 3) socialization groups: aid members in accommodating role and environmental challenges (e.g., a new immigrants group); 4) support groups: bring together people with common issues or circumstances to help them in coping with their shared concerns (e.g., a bereavement group); and 5) therapy groups: serve to offer remediation and/or rehabilitation of a specific concern or problem (e.g., a gambling problem group).

92. A: Transference to quiet members (self-figures). Transference does not occur in a context of figures representing the self. Rather, it is characterized by unconscious redirection of feelings from one person toward another representing a meaningful figure in the individual's life. Typically, it is the appearance of a childhood relationship in a present relationship, often manifest as feelings and desires unconsciously retained now redirected toward a new object. It often constitutes the emotions of repressed experiences, projected onto an individual serving in substitution for the original target of these repressed impulses. First described by Sigmund Freud, it is an important concept by which to better understand feelings and behaviors. While often considered inappropriate, in truth transference is normal and often unavoidable. It does not represent an underlying pathology unless the patterns of transference result in thoughts, feelings, or behaviors that are maladaptive.

93. B: Triangulation. Triangulation is the introduction of a third party into a conflict between two individuals. The goal is to produce a power asymmetry in order to turn events to one's favor. Family problems typically involve triangulation. Therapeutic triangulation

occurs when a therapist is drawn into taking sides. The eight interlocking concepts of Family Systems Theory include: 1) *Self-Differentiation* (vs fused identities); 2) *Nuclear Family Emotional System* (formerly the *Undifferentiated Family Ego Mass*) of fused identity; 3) *Triangles* (drawing a third party into conflicts); 4) *Societal Emotional Process* (emotional processes in societal interactions, similar to family); 5) *Emotional Cutoff* (severing intergenerational ties); 6) *Sibling Position* (drives some personality characteristics); 7) *Family Projection Process* (parents transmitting patterns to offspring); and 8) *Multigenerational Transmission Process* (patterns transmitted intergenerationally).

94. C: Equifinality. Many interpersonal goals can be achieved in a variety of ways. The *Circular Model of Causality*, however, notes that the behaviors of different subsystems can nevertheless reciprocally influence each other. Responses B and D are not formal Communications/Experimental Therapy terms. Other forms of dysfunctional communication include criticizing, blaming, mind-reading, implying events that can be modified or improved are unalterable, overgeneralizations, double-bind expressions (contradictory demands that functionally allow only one of two required consequences to be achieved), denying that one is communicating (which can never be true), and disqualifying other's communications.

95. C: Congruent communicator. Virginia Satir identified five forms of communication within families, only one of which was functional: the congruent communicator (1). This communication style involves straightforward, open, genuine, and clear messages between the participants. The other dysfunctional styles are: 2) the placater style involves a bias toward agreement, over-apologizing, and other communication efforts to please; 3) the super-reasonable style presents as calm, cool, and reasonable, but actually emotionally detached; 4) the irrelevant style is disconnected from what is actually transpiring, and seeks to distract others from the issues; and 5) the blamer style uses criticism and accusation to disarm and dominate others.

96. A: Complementarity. The concept of *complementarity* addresses the harmony and disharmony that arises when family roles cannot be reconciled. *Alignments* are coalitions that are produced between various family subsystems to achieve specific goals, the nature of which may or may not be dysfunctional. *Power hierarchies* reveal the distribution of power within the family as a whole. *Disengagement* occurs when family members and subsystems become emotionally and/or interactively isolated. Of further note: *subsystems* are separate functional family units (e.g., parents) that operate within the larger family structure. *Enmeshment* results from over-involvement or concern with family members to the point that individual recognition and autonomy are lost. *Inflexibility* addresses situations in which the family structure becomes so rigid that adaptation cannot occur when required.

97. D: Circular questioning. *Circular questions* are used to enhance relational perspectives by helping family members to take the standpoint of another, particularly with a family member who may otherwise be misunderstood. *Hypothesizing* is something done by the therapy team, wherein they attempt to understand the presenting problem and formulate a successful intervention, refining throughout the therapeutic process. *Counter-paradox* is an extension of *paradoxical prescription* (wherein problem behaviors are actually prescribed) by which a problem behavior and all related interactions around it are prescribed. *Positive connotation* reframes problematic symptoms as efforts to preserve the family and promote solidarity. Other techniques include *neutrality* (in which therapist-family member alliances

are avoided to prevent triangulation}, and *rituals* (repetitive behaviors used to counter dysfunctional family rules).

98. C: The community itself. Community organization involves work with larger entities, citizen groups, and organization directors for the purpose of: 1) solving social problems; 2) developing collaborative and proactive qualities in community members; and 3) redistributing decision-making power through community relationships. Community organizers assist communities to learn how to meet their needs, eradicate social problems, and enrich lives, as well as balancing resources and social welfare needs. To accomplish this, the community must first be accepted as it is, and then learn of the interdependence of its constituent members and intra-community entities.

99. B: Whistleblower. Social workers often serve as community organizers, and may readily be approached with problems in the community. In this situation, the first and best step for the citizen to take is as a whistleblower. This step draws attention to the problem, activates oversight agencies, and begins to bring a problem out into the open. Next steps may include: 2) negotiation with the factory leadership; 3) community education, to help others understand the problem; 4) social protesting (picketing, demonstrations, boycotting); 5) lobbying entities responsible to intervene; 6) conducting action research to further explore the problems; 7) forming self-help groups to assist the oppressed to better understand resources and their rights; and 8) legal efforts such as mediation and/or lawsuits to compel change.

100. B: Legal advisor. Only an attorney can offer legal counsel and advice. A social worker can, however, point out options and refer a client or community to appropriate resources for legal counsel and advice. Other intervention roles that may be assumed by a social worker include: 1) broker: identifying and referring clients to needed resources within a community; 2) case manager: assisting clients lacking the capacity to take independent action and/or follow through with resource referrals; 3) client advocate: working on behalf or in conjunction with clients seeking access to needed resources; and 4) mediator: collaborating with both the client and resource provider(s) to overcome conflicts and obstacles in identifying a path to receive needed services and resources.

101. C: Humor. Involuntary clients may utilize humor in their interactions, but not as a primary mechanism for resisting the treatment process. More commonly, resistance comes in the forms of: 1) aggression: becoming either verbally or even physically assaultive, or producing a pseudo-cooperative passive-aggressive response that needs to be mitigated before meaningful progress can be made; 2) diversion: commonly seen through blaming ("someone else made this happen"), seeking to turn attention to others ("he did something way worse"), shifting the focus back to the social worker ("you think you're better than the rest of us"), or simply guiding the discussion in another direction; and 3) withdrawal: seen as a refusal to talk, avoiding discussions about feelings, or minimizing relevant issues, etc. Each of these forms of resistance must be overcome before treatment can properly proceed.

102. B: Meeting the clients' individual needs. It is important to recognize the difference in purpose between supervision and supervising tasks. The primary purpose of supervision is to ensure that clients' needs are fully, ethically, and competently addressed and met. To accomplish this, the supervisor must also ensure that staff have adequate training and necessary access to resources and services. The supervisor must also establish and conduct quality control reviews to regularly monitor the work of agency staff and outside providers.

The primary task of the supervisor is to ensure that essential work is completed. This is necessary to keep the agency functioning and to ensure that an appropriate number of clients can be served. This requires both administrative and clinical expertise on the part of the supervisor and his or her designated leaders within the agency.

103. A: Share expertise. The purpose of consultation is to share expertise, seek options, consider recommendations, and otherwise collaborate and explore clinical and/or operational needs and resources and optimal options. Consultation is not designed to serve as alternate leadership, to be directive or determinative, or to serve as a deferral opportunity such that leaders or staff relinquish their obligation to continue to carry out their professional responsibilities. Consultation may be considered in six stages: 1) entry (early contracting, orientation, and overcoming resistance; 2) identifying consultation goals (which requires adequate problem exploration and understanding); 3) defining goals (which must be a collaborative venture); 4) providing intervention(s) (supported by brainstorming and Delphi methods to obtain participation from all); 5) assessment (of progress and continuing or new problems); 6) concluding the relationship (involves fostering independence, determining continuing availability, etc.).

104. D: Structuralist. This management style views organizations as deeply impacted by environmental factors, with conflict as inevitable but not necessarily negative if handled properly. Bureaucratic theories (Max Weber) espouse vertical hierarchy, policy-driven, merit rewards, and a careful division of labor that maximizes efficiency and control. Scientific theories utilize an economic and rational perspective to maximize productivity. Contingency theories focus on flexibility and responsiveness. Participative theories conclude that democratic leadership and participant buy-in make for greater loyalty and productivity. Quality Circles are based on self-governance and evaluation. Total Quality Management (TQM) focuses on service delivery processes and a broader view than Quality Assurance models. Maslow's Hierarchy of Needs theory allows management to ensure greater participant fulfilment and thus job satisfaction and productivity. Job Enrichment theory (Herzberg) posits that good job "hygiene" (benefits, conditions, salary, etc.) plus motivators (freedom, challenges, growth, etc.) optimized management outcomes. Needs Theory (McClelland) views the paramount needs as power, affiliation, and achievement as the path to optimal management and staff success.

105. C: Summative Program Evaluation. *Summative Program Evaluation* examines the degree to which goals and objectives are realized, as well as how generalizable the outcomes may be to other settings and populations, in determining program efficacy and value. *Cost-Benefit Analysis* produces a ratio of direct costs to outcome benefits in determining program effectiveness. *Cost Effectiveness* evaluation focuses on a program's operational costs as compared with final output (unit) costs, requiring a favorable ratio to deem a program effective. *Formative Program Evaluation* is conducted longitudinally (from program inception through implementation) to determine its final efficacy and value. *Peer Review* involves collegial evaluations using professional standards to determine the quality of work and the resultant outcomes.

106. D: All of the above. The Americans with Disabilities Act (ADA) of 1990 was passed to ensure that all Americans with disabilities would not be discriminated against in areas of employment, public services access, or access to public or private transportation, and would have adequate access to important telecommunication services in spite of disability (particularly braille lettering for blind persons and TTY services for deaf persons). Other

significant legislation includes: 1) TANF (Temporary Assistance for Needy Families, 1996), which replaced AFDC (Aid for Families with Dependent Children), revised primarily to place time limits on public assistance as well as requiring eventual employment. 2) IDEA (Individuals with Disabilities Education Act of 2004) passed to extend children's rights to educational services and to enhance the role of parents in planning for their children's education. 3) The Elder Justice Act of 2009 was designed to better monitor and prevent elder abuse, neglect, and exploitation.

107. B: Domestic Violence Shelters. A given state's Division of Child and Family Services (DCFS, though sometimes called by other titles in various states) would not typically provide safe shelters for victims of domestic violence. They would, however, provide referrals and linkages for services of this nature to ensure the safety of individuals who are in an unsafe home environment. Services commonly provided directly include therapy services, educational referrals, employment training, family counseling and intervention, and other services designed to mitigate family problems and restore successful family functioning. Within most DCFS programs are Child Protective Services (CPS) programs that offer services such as investigations of abuse, shelter care, family therapy, juvenile court linkages, foster care, and other services and resources to help stabilize difficult home situations.

108. D: Promptly refer the asthmatic boy to a medical doctor. Asthma can be life-threatening, and the child is also described as congested and unwell. Given that "all" possessions were lost, it is reasonable to conclude that the child has little or no remaining inhaler medicines for an asthma crisis. While all may attend the medical visit, the boy needs to be seen urgently. Following or concurrently, a complete psychosocial evaluation needs to be completed. After further evaluation, the key elements of a case presentation for the director should include: 1) psychosocial history: mental health issues and social history such as living situation, finances, education, etc.; 2) individual issues: substance abuse history, legal history, physical abuse and neglect history, as well as resources, strengths, and resiliency, etc.; 3) family history, family dynamics, and extended family resources; 4) potential community resources and supports; 5) diversity issues: culture, language, race/ethnicity, orientation, etc.; 6) potential ethical issues and presenting issues in self-determination; and 7) intervention recommendations, including requisite resources.

109. C: Subjective, Objective, Assessment, Plan (SOAP). This method of documentation or charting is frequently used by health care providers to structure their clinical notes. An entry typically includes some or all of the following information: 1) Subjective information: information reported by the client and others closely involved. 2) Objective information: such as laboratory results, test scores, examination data, and scores from screenings. 3) Assessment: the summary review and ultimate conclusions derived from the subjective reports and objective tests, evaluations, examinations, screenings, etc., concluding in an overall impression of the presenting problem(s). 4) Plan: the steps that need to be taken to resolve the presenting problem(s), as derived from all prior information and conclusions drawn.

110. D: All of the above. Case management includes: 1) information gathering; 2) assessment of problems, goals, strengths and needs; 3) the assembly of multiple services sufficient to address the relevant problems, needs and goals; 4) coordination of services involved to streamline efficiency and optimize effectiveness and outcomes; 5) monitoring of services to ensure quality service and continuous client progress; 6) service effectiveness

evaluation to ensure the optimal application of all available resources; and 7) advocacy for the client to continuously ensure the retention of services and expansion and addition of further services as/if required for the best outcomes possible.

111. A: 10 standards. In brief, the standards are as follows: 1) possession of an accredited baccalaureate or graduate social work degree, and requisite case management (CM) skills; 2) professional skills focus on the client's best interests; 3) clients are involved in CM as much as possible; 4) privacy and confidentiality must be maintained; 5) the focus of CM shall remain at the direct level to clients and their families; 6) intervention at the service systems level shall be pursued to support CM as necessary; 7) the case manager shall be knowledgeable about resources and fiscally responsible; 8) service systems and CM shall be continuously evaluated for efficacy and quality; 9) a case manager shall have a reasonable caseload to ensure effective services; and 10) work with colleagues and intra- and inter-professional and inter-agency interactions shall foster cooperation and be in the best interests of the client.

112. B: Causal Comparative Research. Explanatory, or Causal Comparative Research requires data analysis in search of the causal factors behind observed consequences. Other kinds of research include: 1) Action Research develops new approaches to solve problems; 2) Case Study (or Field) Research is an in-depth study of a single case or research unit; 3) Correlational Research attempts to identify the extent to which changes in one variable are related to changes in another variable, using correlation coefficients; 4) Descriptive Research (surveys) describes target areas to formulate relevant future research questions; 5) Evaluative Research seeks measures off efficacy and success; 6) Experimental Research uses experimental and control group comparisons to identify causal relationships; 7) Exploratory Research (Formulative) generates preliminary data for later research; 8) Historical Research draws upon the past to guide present study; 9) Pretest/Post-test evaluates interventions; 10) Qualitative Research describes study targets without data collection (ethnographic, in context of the individual [emic] and group [etic] perspective).

113. C: Conduct standards based on values. A belief system is defined by core values, and ethics operationalize the values-defined belief system into standard of conduct. The core values of the social work profession are as follows (NASW, 2008): 1) dignity and worth of the individual; 2) the importance of human relationships; 3) the pursuit of social justice; 4) competence in professional knowledge and practice; 5) personal and professional integrity; and 6) service. The NASW Code of Social Work Ethics applies to all who practice social work, whether or not they belong to the NASW. There are six ethical areas: 1) responsibilities to clients; 2) responsibilities to colleagues; 3) responsibilities in practice settings; 4) responsibilities as professionals; 5) responsibilities to the profession; and 6) responsibilities to society.

114. D: The right to personal autonomy and decision making. Social workers are charged with helping their clients choose their own life's direction and destiny. An exception is when a client's choices are suicidal, homicidal, or abusive of others' rights. True self-determination requires: 1) the internal capacity for autonomy, 2) freedom from external constraints, and 3) information to make well-informed choices. Social workers should primarily assist clients in identifying and clarifying their own goals, rather than goals others might choose for them. Involuntary hospitalization or other mandated limits placed on self-determination do not allow professionals to fully ignore this ethical principle. Thus, the concepts of "least restrictive" and "least intrusive" come into play. Involuntary or mandated

courses of action should be used only as a last result as is possible, without unduly risking the client's life or intruding upon or abusing other individuals.

115. A: The lack of signage on a substance abuse treatment facility. *Confidentiality* refers to an individual's right to control how identifiable information the client has divulged, or data about that individual, is handled, managed, and disseminated. Through confidentiality, individuals can retain control over the circumstances, timing, and extent to which personally sensitive information is shared with others. *Privacy* does not relate to information or data, but rather to the person themselves. Thus, privacy involves control over the circumstances, timing, and extent to which one wishes to share oneself physically, intellectually, and/or behaviorally with others. It is practiced by interviews in closed areas (not for information or data reasons, but for allowing expressions of emotion, sharing of thought processes, etc.), proper changing areas, and excusing others (including family, at times) from sharing experiences, etc. Confidentiality and privacy may be compromised for serious safety concerns, for the client or others.

116. C: Consult with your supervisor or legal counsel to ensure a proper response to the situation. It is significant to note that the NASW Code of Ethics (2008), Standard 1.09, bans all sexual involvement with both current and former clients and offers no time or circumstances limitation. Violation of this standard will thus result in prompt termination of any NASW membership. It is also important to note, however, that state licensing statutes vary on the topic (e.g., some states do not prohibit former client relationships at all, or may cite a 1 to 2 year prohibition only, after which such relationships are possible) and confidentiality requirements in such situations may also be complex; indeed, reporting may circumvent confidentiality in many ways. Therefore, it is important to know your individual state's laws, and to seek competent consultation from a skilled supervisor or legal advisor.

117. D: Allow only a partial review, withholding portions deemed too sensitive. Clients have the right to reasonable access to records kept about them personally. However, therapists also have an obligation to prevent a client from reading case notes deemed potentially harmful to the client, or that could breach confidentiality of others (e.g., a party reporting suspected abuse). In situations where appropriate explanations would suffice to mitigate any concern of harm, the therapist has the right to review the case record with the client to offer explanatory insights and understandings. Where harm cannot be otherwise avoided, the therapist must restrict the client from viewing any harmful portion. For such portions, summary notes can be produced for the client, if desired. Regardless, it should be noted in the file the date and time of the client's review, and the rationale for any restrictions on review should be fully explained and documented in the case record.

118. A: Refer the child to a counselor with experience in pediatric sleep disorders. Obtaining licensure is only a first step in establishing a competent clinical practice. Remaining in areas of clear clinical expertise is ethically important, and not leading families to believe you possess skills that you have not yet developed is essential. Where a new issue arises that is very closely related to your primary scope of practice, it is reasonable to broaden your skills through collateral research and consultation. However, if a treatment area (e.g., pediatric sleep disorders) is entirely beyond the scope of your practice, it would be inappropriate to try to produce requisite skills through brief reading or consultation, when the skills actually require extended training and experience to develop. In such situations it is essential that the client be referred to another clinician for proper evaluation of the presenting problem.

119. D: All of the above. The NASW Code of Ethics prohibits sexual harassment of colleagues or subordinates in any way. From the information available it seems clear that no harassment was intended or presumed. However, the gesture is fraught with potential overtures that would not be respectful or appropriate. Some individuals could feel that they were being the object of an unwanted advance, and feel disturbed or even threatened by the event. It is important for coworkers to understand boundaries of collegial respect, propriety, and professionalism. It is not possible to know the history, recent events, feelings, or state of mind of another individual, including another clinician. While some behaviors might seem benign, they may be deeply problematic for another. Or, conversely, they may be misinterpreted as an overture with more significance than intended, resulting in subsequent embarrassment for both parties. Consequently, circumspect behavior in such sensitive areas is required.

120. C: Set up a formal consultation appointment to discuss the issue(s) in the office. It is tempting to discuss client cases over a meal or after hours, as it saves work time and allows for more informal sharing. However, discussing clients in a public setting produces a substantial likelihood that client confidentiality will be breached with others seated or walking nearby. It may also seem easier to leave a client's file with a consultant for review, as the consultant can then thoroughly review the case and more closely examine all specifically relevant issues. However, it is unethical for a primary therapist to disclose more client information to a consultant than is essential for the consulting issue to be properly addressed. Leaving a client file with the consultant offers no confidentiality boundaries at all. Consequently, consultation in an office setting, during a formal appointment, and by direct confidentiality-focused dialogue is the proper way to obtain an ethically structured consultation.

121. C: Contact the colleague and discuss treatment options. As with any client, the most appropriate intervention is one that occurs voluntarily and openly, with adequate support and caring concern offered. If the colleague refuses to seek immediate help in this situation, then further steps are necessary, including reporting the problem to a supervisor who can the address the issue further in accordance with agency policy and guidelines. Certainly the safety and well-being of the colleague's clients must be preserved, and no delay in addressing the issue can be afforded. Similar guidelines apply to colleagues who unethically practice outside the scope of their area of competence, or who behave unethically with clients, coworkers, or other outside programs and staff.

122. B: Seek to bring the agency's policies and procedures into compliance. Simply quitting does nothing to resolve this underlying problem with ethics and standards of conduct. Neither does a blanket refusal to work with materials, resources, and conditions that are outside NASW Code of Ethics standards. Optimally, a social worker should utilize his or her professional skills to seek to bring about change. Explaining the applicable ethical standards, and pointing out the protections they afford both staff and clients, provides a compelling case for change. If no progress is subsequently made, it may become necessary for the social worker to resign and leave the work setting, and/or to report the ethical issues to any proper oversight entity. In this way, ethical standards can be provided to all clients in any agency setting.

123. C: A doctor with a doctoral degree. When providing social work services, it is generally considered unethical to utilize the title of a higher education credential in an unrelated field. The concern is that it may mislead the public to think that the professional with whom they

are working has greater knowledge and/or skills than they actually possess. In general, the title of Social Worker is used when an individual has at least a bachelor's degree in social work (BSW), and Master Social Worker is used only when the holder has a master's degree in social work (MSW). The term "doctor" is used in professional practice and services only if the degree is social work specific (DSW or PhD in social work) or in a closely related field (e.g., psychology). The NASW Code of Ethics specifically addresses issues of credentials, misrepresentation, and deception (see 4.04 and 4.06), and social workers should always ensure their professional practice remains within those standards.

124. D: All of the above. Informed consent requires not only information, but an understanding of that information. Relevant information includes potential risks along with expected benefits, and the anticipated likelihood of each. It also requires the sharing of risks to the extent that a "reasonable person" would want to know in order to make a decision. Thus, risks that are astronomically unlikely need not be belabored, but very likely risks with substantial burdens absolutely must be discussed. Other important aspects of recruiting participants include clearance with an Institutional Review Board (IRB) and a Human Subjects Research Committee if applicable; voluntary and written informed consent from each participant or an appropriate surrogate/proxy; clear communication of the right to withdraw at any time; ensuring foreseeably needed resources are available; protecting participants from undue distress, harm, or deprivation; use of data only for the purposes declared; maintaining confidentiality and privacy; reporting accurate findings and correcting any errors later revealed; and avoiding dual relationships with participants and/or conflicts of interest.

125. B: Empathy. Compassion involves concern for the misfortunes and welfare of another. Condolence involves expressions of compassion and sympathy. Sympathy literally means to feel with, or have a resonate feeling for another. Feelings of compassion and sympathy are expressed in carefully chosen words of condolence. *Empathy*, however, is deeper. It literally means to "feel into" the heart and mind of another, projecting oneself into their situation, feelings, and experiences. The term originated in psychology, drawn as a translation from a German term. It is an important tool in creating a therapeutic bond, as it involves a shared emotional state most fully realized when one has "been there," whereas sympathy is the natural state when one has not. Other important components of a strong therapeutic relationship include: 1) *warmth* (a show of genuine care and acceptance); 2) *authenticity/genuineness* (open and natural sharing in a meaningful way); and 3) *trust* (which involves a certainty of safety and predictability, and is maintained by practices such as confidentiality and privacy).

126. D: All of the above. It can become easy to use short-hand descriptors to refer to one's caseload. However, doing so can subtly but powerfully alter the way a case manager feels and even interacts with clients. Far better to describe a caseload as "numerous people with schizophrenia, several people with bipolar disorder, and some other clients struggling with borderline personality disorder." The use of the words *people* and *clients* lets them retain their humanity. Everyone needs to be seen as an individual with unique qualities and contributions. Casually categorizing and stereotyping clients can lead to losing sight of their humanity, individuality, and uniqueness. Casework is and must remain client-focused, respectful, and understanding of clients' unique circumstances, needs, and potential. Using care in the verbiage chosen to speak about clients can help social work case managers avoid the biases, prejudices, and cultural insensitivities that can otherwise enter the case management process.

127. A: Allowing judgment of how acceptable or not the feelings are. Feelings should not be appraised judgmentally. Rather, they should be evaluated for how they are affecting the client and how functional they are in the processes of living and interacting with others. Expressions of feelings offer an important window into understanding how a client perceives his or her life situation, as well as their sense of hopefulness, security, and safety. If feelings and emotions become too negative and burdensome, it may become important to incorporate the management of the client's feelings into the ongoing evaluation and treatment plan. Finally, if received and handled well, the sharing of deep feelings in a long-term case management or treatment processes further strengthens the therapeutic bond, which in turn enhances the effectiveness of the case manager/social worker in addressing the client's challenges and problems.

128. D: Seek to understand his feelings while soothing/deescalating them. Acknowledging and being sensitive to his feelings, even while reassuring, soothing, and comforting the client would produce the best result. This would allow him to feel heard, and yet not advance his expression of negative emotions. Confronting a client with a diagnosis of paranoid schizophrenia could easily cause an overreaction and escalation of emotion. Further, feelings of heightened anxiety and/or paranoia could easily grow to the extent that greater intervention could be required. Joining him in his anger could have a similar escalating result. Unless intense anger is coupled with threats, there would be no immediate need to evaluate the client for issues of homicidality or to involve law enforcement.

129. B: Limit the expression of intense or deep feelings. It should be noted that a client revealing highly personal or sensitive feelings too early on in the therapeutic process can produce a wedge of embarrassment and/or guilt, which can inhibit the therapeutic process and reduce the ability to provide needed services. This can be particularly problematic when: 1) the services are already of a very short-term nature; and 2) where the services provided are very narrow and do not allow for extensive emotional support. Further, if a client precipitously discharges considerable emotion, it can have the effect of over-burdening the social worker/case manager. Thus, the expression of feelings in the therapeutic relationship should: 1) be metered and managed to not outstrip the bonds and ties of the growing relationship; and 2) should be maintained within the scope and mission of the services being provided so as to not leave the client feeling abandoned when services are necessarily terminated.

130. A: Offering analysis and critique. Individuals do not disclose feelings in the hope of receiving an analytical and/or critical response. Rather they are seeking: 1) sensitivity: thoughtful reception demonstrated by verbal and nonverbal acceptance, and culturally competent insights; 2) understanding: accurate perceptions of what the client is communicating, in harmony with the client's individual personality, nature, and individual qualities, and confirmed by reflection and feedback; 3) a meaningful response: to include genuine empathy, and thoughtful and purposeful replies; and 4) unconditional positive regard (acceptance): no matter what the client's deficits, overall acceptance of the client as a valued and meaningful individual is essential. If information the client reveals cannot be received while maintaining this sense of acceptance, the clinician should seek supervisory help or request the client be transferred to a clinician who can offer such acceptance. Without respect and positive regard, a therapeutic bond cannot be established and maintained.

131. C: Ensure a nonjudgmental attitude, regardless of the client's past. Typically, clients are aware of longstanding societal mores, standards, expectations, and morality. While not always fully aware of the entire scope of the legal ramifications of their choices, most clients know when they are participating in illicit activities. Where an understanding of the consequences of their choices was lacking, by the time they have sought help (or have been mandated to seek it), they are typically well aware of many of the consequences involved. Thus, clients will usually feel averse to the social worker offering a roster of such things in response to their disclosures. Rather, clients are looking to be understood and accepted. Where their behavior is obviously unacceptable, the person should nevertheless be accepted and understood for the pain they are experiencing. Thus, blame, judgment, critique, and other such responses should be withheld and a nonjudgmental attitude should prevail. Where this is not forthcoming, the client will typically sense it, even if not verbalized, and it will hamper the development of a therapeutic bond and the ability to work together positively.

132. C: Meet with administration to address the use of the form. The release of information, particularly information about substance abuse, mental health, and HIV status, is governed by both federal and state laws. Federal HIPAA regulations always apply, and these regulations are not dependent upon an individual's legal standing (incarcerated, on parole or probation, etc.). Minimum standards for a release of information are: 1) the individual's identifying information; 2) identifying information for the recipient of information; 3) the purpose of the release; 4) the specific information to be released (with the client having the right to review the release of specific mental health information prior to authorizing it); and 5) the duration of validity of the signed release (ie, an expiration date). Other regulations apply in circumstances of imminent danger to the client or others, thus removing the need to circumvent an appropriate form. Both ethics and confidentiality laws are relevant in any release of information.

133. B: When a law enforcement official formally requests information. Law enforcement personnel are not entitled to confidential client information without a court order, unless there are imminent circumstances of life-threatening danger to the client or others. Valid exclusions to confidentiality include: 1) situations of actively expressed suicidal ideation by the client; 2) when a client leads a therapist to genuinely suspect a client may harm to others (if homicidality is suspected, Tarasoff regulations apply); 3) if a client discloses abuse (physical injury or gross neglect, sexual abuse, etc.) to a minor or a dependent adult; and 4) in situations of grave disability, where a client lacks the mental capacity to secure (or direct others to secure) essential food, clothing, shelter, essential medical care, etc. In all exceptions, the information to be released should be limited to that requisite to resolve the immediate circumstance involved.

134. D: All of the above. Confidentiality cannot be entirely assured in a group counseling setting; it is no longer just the therapist who is privy to confidential information. Even so, group participants can and should be put under commitment to keep confidential all information shared in group. This should extend to not discussing information about other participants outside group in any way, even among themselves. Further emphasis on confidentiality can be provided by including a confidentiality clause in written treatment consent paperwork. In spite of this, some participants may not manage confidentiality well and all group participants should be apprised of this when entering the group counseling agreement. In this way, participants can be particularly careful about sharing unnecessarily personal information in an open group setting.

135. C: Request the court withdraw the order, or limit its scope. When possible, psychologically damaging information should be protected from an open court setting. While a therapist may be compelled to testify in certain situations, it is always appropriate to petition the court to withdraw the order by providing a rationale for the concerns involved. Failing this, it remains appropriate to petition the court to limit the scope of the testimony being sought to information that would not be psychologically damaging to the client. While a prosecutor or plaintiff's attorney may attempt to exact as much testimony as possible to press the case more readily to a favorable conclusion, the judge will have no such bias and may agree to withdraw or revise a subpoena if given adequate rationale and insight. The client's mental health should always remain the therapist's first priority, along with honest efforts to maintain agreed upon confidentiality.

136. A: Remain in full force and effect. Confidentiality agreements are entered into between a client and his or her therapist. They remain legally binding for the two parties involved, even in the event of demise or incapacity. They also remain ethically binding for any new therapist who receives the records of a previous client, and upon the original therapist should his or her client die. To ensure continuity of confidentiality, it is important for social workers to make provisions for their records in the event they die or become cognitively incapacitated. This may involve reciprocal agreements with trusted colleagues or an attorney, or some other appropriate means. Regardless of the provisions made, they should adequately protect a client's confidential information and privacy as fully as possible. Failing to make such provisions constitutes a failure to look after the welfare and well-being of the therapist's clients, and legal action can be taken against a social worker's estate if this is neglected.

137. C: Seek supervision and/or consultation. Referring the client to another therapist is a profound disservice to the client. He will be difficult for anyone to work with, and reestablishing with another therapist will be time-consuming and costly. Sharing your feelings with the client will damage the relationship, and will certainly escalate the problem behaviors that have been so troublesome in the first place. Ignoring the problem will not improve it in any way. Clearly these behaviors are very entrenched in the client's interactive repertoire, and thus will continue unless properly addressed and redirected. Engaging in supervision and/or consultation is therefore essential, both for the client's well-being and to produce a therapeutic engagement plan that can be successful. Ongoing consultation and revision of any plan produced will almost certainly be required over time.

138. A: Explore the meaning of the gift with the family. Small tokens of appreciation can be graciously accepted, but gifts suffused with deeper meaning (assuming bonding, or symbolizing something that obligates the client to the clinician) should be avoided. When accepting even a small token gift, a clinician should cite ethical standards for the client's future reference. An open and gracious expression of appreciation should always be the response to a small gift. Adding information about ethical standards, however, is important to set the idea of boundaries. It is best, however, to preempt the issue during an intake session, explaining that professional standards prohibit receiving or exchanging gifts. In this way the family becomes aware of guidelines, without encountering a subsequent rejection of a modest gift. If cash or a check in a modest amount is received in the mail from a client or family of ample means, it may be donated to a cause important to the family and in their name (typically a notice of recognition and appreciation is then sent to the family by the

organization). Always document any gift situation and resolution in the clinical record so that the outcome is clear.

139. D: Decline the offer, citing professional ethics. At issue is the creation of a dual relationship, one that extends beyond the clinical setting into other areas of work and life. The social work *Code of Ethics* specifically addresses exploitive relationships, where the therapist holds an undue power advantage. Such relationships should be avoided. For non-exploitive exchanges, there are two views on the matter: the deontological (categorical), calling for total avoidance, and the utilitarian (situational), suggesting a reasoning process. With past clients, the following questions may help: 1) is it exploitive; 2) how much time has passed; 3) the nature (length and intensity) of the relationship; 4) events at termination; 5) the client's vulnerability; 6) the likelihood of a negative impact on the client. A boundary crossing occurs when one bends the code situationally, and boundary violations involve breaking the code. A crossing becomes a clear violation when the dual relationship has negative consequences for the client.

140. A: Take any cue the client offers as to how to respond. In a situation such as this, it is important to follow the client's lead. The client may feel uncomfortable and not wish to encounter this part of the past. Or, he may be in company of someone who could ask about how they know one another, putting him in the situation of unwanted disclosure or deceit. Any attempt by the social worker to script the encounter (quiet nodding, smiling, coming up to shake hands, etc.) could be unwanted and thus should ideally be avoided. If, however, the client smiles and nods, or voices a greeting, or comes forward to shake hands, then the situation becomes clear and responses in like manner would be appropriate.

141. C: Attend the funeral, but decline the luncheon invitation. In this situation it is entirely appropriate to accept an invitation to the funeral, demonstrating a show of care and respect for the deceased client and family. For many, it offers an important sense of closure to a loss that the social worker has also experienced. However, the family-only luncheon serves to place the social worker in a more intimate family-like relationship. It can also be a difficult situation for all involved, as gauging appropriate comments and conversation may be challenging among extended family members—a great many of whom will have no relationship with the social worker. Exploring the meaning of the invitation with the family at the time it is extended will allow the social worker to better reassure them and help them understand the important ethical issues involved in stepping out of a preexisting formal role of a counseling nature.

142. D: *Paraphrasing*. To be most effective, the restatements should focus primarily on the client's message, instead of the feelings involved. *Furthering Responses* involve techniques to encourage and promote conversation (e.g., and?, but?, or?), along with head nodding and attending posture to demonstrate high engagement. *Seeking Concreteness* includes techniques to help clients become more specific and clear, such as requesting their rationale, feelings, and detailed thoughts, along with drawing conclusions and using personalizing expressions with "I" and "me" in their communications. *Summarizing* involves condensing or overviewing segments of interactions to better organize and verify content, as well as sifting out irrelevant and distracting material.

143. A: *Leading Questions*. An example of a leading question would be, "You really do want to go back to school, don't you?" In this way, the client is prompted to agree to something important. However, caution must be used with such questions, as it does not allow for a

client's true feelings to necessarily find expression. *Stacked questions* are produced by asking questions in rapid succession, leaving no time for a response and thus shaping the course of the conversation. *Open-ended questions* are constructed to as to elude a "yes" or "no" response, and elicit greater meaning and interpretation (e.g., "How did that make you feel?"). *Close-ended questions* are intended to elicit short and specific answers (e.g., "When were you born?").

144. C: Confrontation. Empathic Responding refers to accurate perception of a client's feelings followed by accurate restating and sharing. While empathic responding can lead to better therapeutic outcomes, it is not the first-choice technique when a client persists in deluding herself into thinking violating behaviors were simple mistakes or happenings that were sought out by a victim with clear understanding. Reflective (Active) Listening is a useful tool for establishing mutual understandings between individuals. However, it is not designed to identify illicit behavior and directly prompt change. Confrontation can prompt change, though in a rather emotionally traumatic way. Because of this, confrontation must be: 1) carefully timed, usually immediately after the problematic expression or event; 2) with enough time remaining in session to reground the relationship; 3) specific to the issue being addressed; 4) client-focused (as opposed to allowing the therapist to vent at the client's expense); and 5) culturally centered: recognizing how the client will receive the experience, and using an interpreter of there is a language barrier.

145. B: An emotional reaction toward another, drawn from prior experiences with someone else. For example, feeling resentment toward an employer who seems to treat you in ways reminiscent of how your father treated you. Transference is typically something one remains unaware of without careful thought. It can be a substantial barrier to a therapeutic relationship unless it is addressed and resolved. When a therapist has reactions toward a client based upon the therapist's own background, it is called counter-transference. Other client-based communication barriers include the use of problem minimization or outright denial; reluctance to be honest about something for fear of rejection; limits on open sharing due a fear of losing emotional control; and limits on sharing due to mistrust. Therapist barriers to communication include excessive passivity, leaving the client feeling unsupported; over-aggression, causing the client to feel threatened and unsafe; premature assurance, limiting full disclosure; too much self-disclosure, focusing away from the client; as well as, sarcasm, guilt, judgment, interrupting, and inappropriate humor.

146. D: Privileged communication. *Privacy* refers to control over how one chooses to share oneself physically or intellectually. *Confidentiality* refers to control over how personal information is shared. *Informed consent* refers to becoming fully informed before giving consent. *Privileged communication* addresses confidential information in legal proceedings. Four conditions create a privileged communication: 1) a mutual understanding the exchange was confidential; 2) confidentiality is deemed important in the relationship; 3) that importance is widely recognized in the community; and 4) the harm of disclosure outweighs the benefits. For social workers, the US Supreme Court case of *Jaffe v. Redmond* (1996) recognized privileged communication in federal courts. Other exceptions (beyond #4, above) include: 1) if a lawsuit centers on emotional damages substantiated by counseling; 2) if the social worker must defend against a client's lawsuit; 3) if the client already disclosed to others; 4) if suicide or direct harm to others is involved; and 5) where minors are in a custody dispute, in criminal behavior, or were abused or neglected.

147. C: Journal notes. This term is never used to refer to a social worker's case notes in any way. The *primary client record* is sometimes referred to as the clinical or medical record. The second kind of case notes are referred to as *psychotherapy notes*. In this record the therapist records private notes for subsequent clinical analysis of therapist-client communications. All therapist notes may be more readily subject to subpoena or court-ordered disclosure if they are kept together. However, if kept separately, the private therapy notes are much more difficult to obtain. The primary client record includes information such as assessment, clinical tests, diagnosis, medical information, the treatment plan and treatment modalities used, progress notes, collateral information, billing records, dates and times of sessions, etc. If a subpoena is received requesting the "complete medical record," it need not include the separate psychotherapy notes without further legal stipulation.

148. C: Seek supervision and/or consultation to explore the issue further. The diagnosis problem cannot be ignored for two important reasons: 1) it leaves the underlying condition untreated, as the client currently receives medications for bipolar disorder and no treatment for the depression and grief issues; and 2) billing under a known erroneous diagnosis can constitute fraud, if it continues. Correcting a diagnosis made by a psychiatrist, however, would not typically be undertaken independently by a social work case manager. Instead, supervision and/or consultation should be obtained to ensure that any attempted corrective steps are not inappropriate, and to ensure that essential services for the client are not terminated without alternative support in place in advance.

149. D: Retained in accordance with state medical record statutes. Not all states have statutes governing the retention period for social work clinical notes. Of those states that do have statutes, the minimum retention period was 3 years and the maximum as much as 10 years. Other standards may apply for clients under the age of majority, who may have further need of the records during their minor years. Where no statutes exist, it has been advised that clinicians retain records in accordance with statutes governing the management of medical records. Regardless, clinicians should be sensitive to the fact that clients may return for further services at a future date, whereupon a prior record could be of considerable assistance in exploring, understanding, and resolving any subsequent problems.

150. A: Help the family explore their feelings about the defects, their family circumstances, and the meaning of available options. It is essential that the family be permitted to find their own answers in a way that meets their own values and allows them all their rights under the law. Merely offering a dispassionate review of options does not assist the family in discerning their personal and unique feelings about the circumstances. Providing a review of the sanctity of life serves to pressure them into a life-prolonging decision, and emphasizing the reasonable nature of raising a child with even mild defects again pressures them to bear a child in an absence of information that could help them fully understand the meaning and significance of raising that child. If the social worker does not feel able to assist them in fully and personally coming to a decision based on their own values and beliefs, then she should defer to a colleague to provide these important services.

FREE Study Skills DVD Offer

Dear Customer,

Thank you for your purchase from Mometrix! We consider it an honor and privilege that you have purchased our product and want to ensure your satisfaction.

As a way of showing our appreciation and to help us better serve you, we have developed a Study Skills DVD that we would like to give you for <u>FREE</u>. **This DVD covers our "best practices" for studying for your exam, from how to use our study materials to how to prepare for the day of the test.**

All that we ask is that you email us your feedback that would describe your experience so far with our product that we can post on our website in order to help other customers make a sound buying decision. Good, bad or indifferent, we want to know what you think!

To get your **FREE Study Skills DVD**, email <u>freedvd@mometrix.com</u> with "FREE STUDY SKILLS DVD" in the subject line and the following information in the body of the email:

   a. The name of the product you purchased.

   b. Your feedback. It can be long, short, or anything in-between, just your impressions and experience so far with our product. A good testimonial will include how our study material met your needs and will highlight features of the product that you found helpful.

   c. Your name as you would like for it to be displayed with the testimonial.

   d. Your full name and shipping address where you would like us to send your free DVD, along with your email address and phone number (for shipping purposes only).

If you have any questions or concerns, please don't hesitate to contact me directly.

Thanks again!

Sincerely,

Jay Willis
Vice President
<u>jay.willis@mometrix.com</u>
1-800-673-8175

Secret Key #1 - Time is Your Greatest Enemy

Pace Yourself

Wear a watch. At the beginning of the test, check the time (or start a chronometer on your watch to count the minutes), and check the time after every few questions to make sure you are "on schedule."

If you are forced to speed up, do it efficiently. Usually one or more answer choices can be eliminated without too much difficulty. Above all, don't panic. Don't speed up and just begin guessing at random choices. By pacing yourself, and continually monitoring your progress against your watch, you will always know exactly how far ahead or behind you are with your available time. If you find that you are one minute behind on the test, don't skip one question without spending any time on it, just to catch back up. Take 15 fewer seconds on the next four questions, and after four questions you'll have caught back up. Once you catch back up, you can continue working each problem at your normal pace.

Furthermore, don't dwell on the problems that you were rushed on. If a problem was taking up too much time and you made a hurried guess, it must be difficult. The difficult questions are the ones you are most likely to miss anyway, so it isn't a big loss. It is better to end with more time than you need than to run out of time.

Lastly, sometimes it is beneficial to slow down if you are constantly getting ahead of time. You are always more likely to catch a careless mistake by working more slowly than quickly, and among very high-scoring test takers (those who are likely to have lots of time left over), careless errors affect the score more than mastery of material.

Secret Key #2 - Guessing is not Guesswork

You probably know that guessing is a good idea. Unlike other standardized tests, there is no penalty for getting a wrong answer. Even if you have no idea about a question, you still have a 20-25% chance of getting it right.

Most test takers do not understand the impact that proper guessing can have on their score. Unless you score extremely high, guessing will significantly contribute to your final score.

Monkeys Take the Test

What most test takers don't realize is that to insure that 20-25% chance, you have to guess randomly. If you put 20 monkeys in a room to take this test, assuming they answered once per question and behaved themselves, on average they would get 20-25% of the questions correct. Put 20 test takers in the room, and the average will be much lower among guessed questions. Why?

1. The test writers intentionally write deceptive answer choices that "look" right. A test taker has no idea about a question, so he picks the "best looking" answer, which is often wrong. The monkey has no idea what looks good and what doesn't, so it will consistently be right about 20-25% of the time.
2. Test takers will eliminate answer choices from the guessing pool based on a hunch or intuition. Simple but correct answers often get excluded, leaving a 0% chance of being correct. The monkey has no clue, and often gets lucky with the best choice.

This is why the process of elimination endorsed by most test courses is flawed and detrimental to your performance. Test takers don't guess; they make an ignorant stab in the dark that is usually worse than random.

$5 Challenge

Let me introduce one of the most valuable ideas of this course—the $5 challenge:

You only mark your "best guess" if you are willing to bet $5 on it.
You only eliminate choices from guessing if you are willing to bet $5 on it.

Why $5? Five dollars is an amount of money that is small yet not insignificant, and can really add up fast (20 questions could cost you $100). Likewise, each answer choice on one question of the test will have a small impact on your overall score, but it can really add up to a lot of points in the end.

The process of elimination IS valuable. The following shows your chance of guessing it right:

If you eliminate wrong answer choices until only this many remain:	Chance of getting it correct:
1	100%
2	50%
3	33%

However, if you accidentally eliminate the right answer or go on a hunch for an incorrect answer, your chances drop dramatically—to 0%. By guessing among all the answer choices, you are GUARANTEED to have a shot at the right answer.

That's why the $5 test is so valuable. If you give up the advantage and safety of a pure guess, it had better be worth the risk.

What we still haven't covered is how to be sure that whatever guess you make is truly random. Here's the easiest way:

Always pick the first answer choice among those remaining.

Such a technique means that you have decided, **before you see a single test question**, exactly how you are going to guess, and since the order of choices tells you nothing about which one is correct, this guessing technique is perfectly random.

This section is not meant to scare you away from making educated guesses or eliminating choices; you just need to define when a choice is worth eliminating. The $5 test, along with a pre-defined random guessing strategy, is the best way to make sure you reap all of the benefits of guessing.

Secret Key #3 - Practice Smarter, Not Harder

Many test takers delay the test preparation process because they dread the awful amounts of practice time they think necessary to succeed on the test. We have refined an effective method that will take you only a fraction of the time.

There are a number of "obstacles" in the path to success. Among these are answering questions, finishing in time, and mastering test-taking strategies. All must be executed on the day of the test at peak performance, or your score will suffer. The test is a mental marathon that has a large impact on your future.

Just like a marathon runner, it is important to work your way up to the full challenge. So first you just worry about questions, and then time, and finally strategy:

Success Strategy

1. Find a good source for practice tests.
2. If you are willing to make a larger time investment, consider using more than one study guide. Often the different approaches of multiple authors will help you "get" difficult concepts.
3. Take a practice test with no time constraints, with all study helps, "open book." Take your time with questions and focus on applying strategies.
4. Take a practice test with time constraints, with all guides, "open book."
5. Take a final practice test without open material and with time limits.

If you have time to take more practice tests, just repeat step 5. By gradually exposing yourself to the full rigors of the test environment, you will condition your mind to the stress of test day and maximize your success.

Secret Key #4 - Prepare, Don't Procrastinate

Let me state an obvious fact: if you take the test three times, you will probably get three different scores. This is due to the way you feel on test day, the level of preparedness you have, and the version of the test you see. Despite the test writers' claims to the contrary, some versions of the test WILL be easier for you than others.

Since your future depends so much on your score, you should maximize your chances of success. In order to maximize the likelihood of success, you've got to prepare in advance. This means taking practice tests and spending time learning the information and test taking strategies you will need to succeed.

Never go take the actual test as a "practice" test, expecting that you can just take it again if you need to. Take all the practice tests you can on your own, but when you go to take the official test, be prepared, be focused, and do your best the first time!

Secret Key #5 - Test Yourself

Everyone knows that time is money. There is no need to spend too much of your time or too little of your time preparing for the test. You should only spend as much of your precious time preparing as is necessary for you to get the score you need.

Once you have taken a practice test under real conditions of time constraints, then you will know if you are ready for the test or not.

If you have scored extremely high the first time that you take the practice test, then there is not much point in spending countless hours studying. You are already there.

Benchmark your abilities by retaking practice tests and seeing how much you have improved. Once you consistently score high enough to guarantee success, then you are ready.

If you have scored well below where you need, then knuckle down and begin studying in earnest. Check your improvement regularly through the use of practice tests under real conditions. Above all, don't worry, panic, or give up. The key is perseverance!

Then, when you go to take the test, remain confident and remember how well you did on the practice tests. If you can score high enough on a practice test, then you can do the same on the real thing.

General Strategies

The most important thing you can do is to ignore your fears and jump into the test immediately. Do not be overwhelmed by any strange-sounding terms. You have to jump into the test like jumping into a pool—all at once is the easiest way.

Make Predictions

As you read and understand the question, try to guess what the answer will be. Remember that several of the answer choices are wrong, and once you begin reading them, your mind will immediately become cluttered with answer choices designed to throw you off. Your mind is typically the most focused immediately after you have read the question and digested its contents. If you can, try to predict what the correct answer will be. You may be surprised at what you can predict.

Quickly scan the choices and see if your prediction is in the listed answer choices. If it is, then you can be quite confident that you have the right answer. It still won't hurt to check the other answer choices, but most of the time, you've got it!

Answer the Question

It may seem obvious to only pick answer choices that answer the question, but the test writers can create some excellent answer choices that are wrong. Don't pick an answer just because it sounds right, or you believe it to be true. It MUST answer the question. Once you've made your selection, always go back and check it against the question and make sure that you didn't misread the question and that the answer choice does answer the question posed.

Benchmark

After you read the first answer choice, decide if you think it sounds correct or not. If it doesn't, move on to the next answer choice. If it does, mentally mark that answer choice. This doesn't mean that you've definitely selected it as your answer choice, it just means that it's the best you've seen thus far. Go ahead and read the next choice. If the next choice is worse than the one you've already selected, keep going to the next answer choice. If the next choice is better than the choice you've already selected, mentally mark the new answer choice as your best guess.

The first answer choice that you select becomes your standard. Every other answer choice must be benchmarked against that standard. That choice is correct until proven otherwise by another answer choice beating it out. Once you've decided that no other answer choice seems as good, do one final check to ensure that your answer choice answers the question posed.

Valid Information

Don't discount any of the information provided in the question. Every piece of information may be necessary to determine the correct answer. None of the information in the question is there to throw you off (while the answer choices will certainly have information to throw you off). If two seemingly unrelated topics are discussed, don't ignore either. You can be confident there is a relationship, or it wouldn't be included in the question, and you are probably going to have to determine what is that relationship to find the answer.

Avoid "Fact Traps"

Don't get distracted by a choice that is factually true. Your search is for the answer that answers the question. Stay focused and don't fall for an answer that is true but irrelevant. Always go back to the question and make sure you're choosing an answer that actually answers the question and is not just a true statement. An answer can be factually correct, but it MUST answer the question asked. Additionally, two answers can both be seemingly correct, so be sure to read all of the answer choices, and make sure that you get the one that BEST answers the question.

Milk the Question

Some of the questions may throw you completely off. They might deal with a subject you have not been exposed to, or one that you haven't reviewed in years. While your lack of knowledge about the subject will be a hindrance, the question itself can give you many clues that will help you find the correct answer. Read the question carefully and look for clues. Watch particularly for adjectives and nouns describing difficult terms or words that you don't recognize. Regardless of whether you completely understand a word or not, replacing it with a synonym, either provided or one you more familiar with, may help you to understand what the questions are asking. Rather than wracking your mind about specific detailed information concerning a difficult term or word, try to use mental substitutes that are easier to understand.

The Trap of Familiarity

Don't just choose a word because you recognize it. On difficult questions, you may not recognize a number of words in the answer choices. The test writers don't put "make-believe" words on the test, so don't think that just because you only recognize all the words in one answer choice that that answer choice must be correct. If you only recognize words in one answer choice, then focus on that one. Is it correct? Try your best to determine if it is correct. If it is, that's great. If not, eliminate it. Each word and answer choice you eliminate increases your chances of getting the question correct, even if you then have to guess among the unfamiliar choices.

Eliminate Answers

Eliminate choices as soon as you realize they are wrong. But be careful! Make sure you consider all of the possible answer choices. Just because one appears right, doesn't mean that the next one won't be even better! The test writers will usually put more than one good answer choice for every question, so read all of them. Don't worry if you are stuck between two that seem right. By getting down to just two remaining possible choices, your odds are now 50/50. Rather than wasting too much time, play the odds. You are guessing, but guessing wisely because you've been able to knock out some of the answer choices that you know are wrong. If you are eliminating choices and realize that the last answer choice you are left with is also obviously wrong, don't panic. Start over and consider each choice again. There may easily be something that you missed the first time and will realize on the second pass.

Tough Questions

If you are stumped on a problem or it appears too hard or too difficult, don't waste time. Move on! Remember though, if you can quickly check for obviously incorrect answer choices, your chances of guessing correctly are greatly improved. Before you completely give up, at least try to knock out a couple of possible answers. Eliminate what you can and then guess at the remaining answer choices before moving on.

Brainstorm

If you get stuck on a difficult question, spend a few seconds quickly brainstorming. Run through the complete list of possible answer choices. Look at each choice and ask yourself, "Could this answer the question satisfactorily?" Go through each answer choice and consider it independently of the others. By systematically going through all possibilities, you may find something that you would otherwise overlook. Remember though that when you get stuck, it's important to try to keep moving.

Read Carefully

Understand the problem. Read the question and answer choices carefully. Don't miss the question because you misread the terms. You have plenty of time to read each question thoroughly and make sure you understand what is being asked. Yet a happy medium must be attained, so don't waste too much time. You must read carefully, but efficiently.

Face Value

When in doubt, use common sense. Always accept the situation in the problem at face value. Don't read too much into it. These problems will not require you to make huge leaps of logic. The test writers aren't trying to throw you off with a cheap trick. If you have to go beyond creativity and make a leap of logic in order to have an answer choice answer the question, then you should look at the other answer choices. Don't overcomplicate the problem by creating theoretical relationships or explanations that will warp time or space. These are normal problems rooted in reality. It's just that the applicable relationship or explanation may not be readily apparent and you have to figure things out. Use your common sense to interpret anything that isn't clear.

Prefixes

If you're having trouble with a word in the question or answer choices, try dissecting it. Take advantage of every clue that the word might include. Prefixes and suffixes can be a huge help. Usually they allow you to determine a basic meaning. Pre- means before, post- means after, pro - is positive, de- is negative. From these prefixes and suffixes, you can get an idea of the general meaning of the word and try to put it into context. Beware though of any traps. Just because con- is the opposite of pro-, doesn't necessarily mean congress is the opposite of progress!

Hedge Phrases

Watch out for critical hedge phrases, led off with words such as "likely," "may," "can," "sometimes," "often," "almost," "mostly," "usually," "generally," "rarely," and "sometimes." Question writers insert these hedge phrases to cover every possibility. Often an answer choice will be wrong simply because it leaves no room for exception. Unless the situation calls for them, avoid answer choices that have definitive words like "exactly," and "always."

Switchback Words

Stay alert for "switchbacks." These are the words and phrases frequently used to alert you to shifts in thought. The most common switchback word is "but." Others include "although," "however," "nevertheless," "on the other hand," "even though," "while," "in spite of," "despite," and "regardless of."

New Information

Correct answer choices will rarely have completely new information included. Answer choices typically are straightforward reflections of the material asked about and will directly relate to the question. If a new piece of information is included in an answer choice that doesn't even seem to relate to the topic being asked about, then that answer choice is likely incorrect. All of the information needed to answer the question is usually provided for you in the question. You should not have to make guesses that are unsupported or choose answer choices that require unknown information that cannot be reasoned from what is given.

Time Management

On technical questions, don't get lost on the technical terms. Don't spend too much time on any one question. If you don't know what a term means, then odds are you aren't going to get much further since you don't have a dictionary. You should be able to immediately recognize whether or not you know a term. If you don't, work with the other clues that you have—the other answer choices and terms provided—but don't waste too much time trying to figure out a difficult term that you don't know.

Contextual Clues

Look for contextual clues. An answer can be right but not the correct answer. The contextual clues will help you find the answer that is most right and is correct. Understand the context in which a phrase or statement is made. This will help you make important distinctions.

Don't Panic

Panicking will not answer any questions for you; therefore, it isn't helpful. When you first see the question, if your mind goes blank, take a deep breath. Force yourself to mechanically go through the steps of solving the problem using the strategies you've learned.

Pace Yourself

Don't get clock fever. It's easy to be overwhelmed when you're looking at a page full of questions, your mind is full of random thoughts and feeling confused, and the clock is ticking down faster than you would like. Calm down and maintain the pace that you have set for yourself. As long as you are on track by monitoring your pace, you are guaranteed to have enough time for yourself. When you get to the last few minutes of the test, it may seem like you won't have enough time left, but if you only have as many questions as you should have left at that point, then you're right on track!

Answer Selection

The best way to pick an answer choice is to eliminate all of those that are wrong, until only one is left and confirm that is the correct answer. Sometimes though, an answer choice may immediately look right. Be careful! Take a second to make sure that the other choices are not equally obvious. Don't make a hasty mistake. There are only two times that you should stop before checking other answers. First is when you are positive that the answer choice you have selected is correct. Second is when time is almost out and you have to make a quick guess!

Check Your Work

Since you will probably not know every term listed and the answer to every question, it is important that you get credit for the ones that you do know. Don't miss any questions through careless mistakes. If at all possible, try to take a second to look back over your answer selection and make sure you've selected the correct answer choice and haven't made a costly careless mistake (such as marking an answer choice that you didn't mean to mark). The time it takes for this quick double check should more than pay for itself in caught mistakes.

Beware of Directly Quoted Answers

Sometimes an answer choice will repeat word for word a portion of the question or reference section. However, beware of such exact duplication. It may be a trap! More than likely, the correct choice will paraphrase or summarize a point, rather than being exactly the same wording.

Slang

Scientific sounding answers are better than slang ones. An answer choice that begins "To compare the outcomes..." is much more likely to be correct than one that begins "Because some people insisted..."

Extreme Statements

Avoid wild answers that throw out highly controversial ideas that are proclaimed as established fact. An answer choice that states the "process should used in certain situations, if..." is much more likely to be correct than one that states the "process should be discontinued completely." The first is a calm rational statement and doesn't even make a definitive, uncompromising stance, using a hedge word "if" to provide wiggle room, whereas the second choice is a radical idea and far more extreme.

Answer Choice Families

When you have two or more answer choices that are direct opposites or parallels, one of them is usually the correct answer. For instance, if one answer choice states "x increases" and another answer choice states "x decreases" or "y increases," then those two or three answer choices are very similar in construction and fall into the same family of answer choices. A family of answer choices consists of two or three answer choices, very similar in construction, but often with directly opposite meanings. Usually the correct answer choice will be in that family of answer choices. The "odd man out" or answer choice that doesn't seem to fit the parallel construction of the other answer choices is more likely to be incorrect.